GAME OF THRONES

PSYCHOLOGY

THE MIND IS DARK AND FULL OF TERRORS

edited by
TRAVIS LANGLEY, PhD

#GoTpsych
www.sterlingpublishing.com

STERLING
New York

STERLING
New York

An Imprint of Sterling Publishing Co., Inc.
1166 Avenue of the Americas
New York, NY 10036

ISBN 978-1-4549-1840-0

Distributed in Canada by Sterling Publishing Co., Inc.
c/o Canadian Manda Group, 664 Annette Street
Toronto, Ontario, Canada M6S 2C8
Distributed in the United Kingdom by GMC Distribution Services
Castle Place, 166 High Street, Lewes, East Sussex, England BN7 1XU

For information about custom editions, special sales, and premium and corporate purchases,
please contact Sterling Special Sales at 800-805-5489 or specialsales@sterlingpublishing.com.

Manufactured in Canada

2 4 6 8 10 9 7 5 3

www.sterlingpublishing.com

IMAGE CREDITS

Courtesy of Dover: 7, 9, 19, 47, 49, 61, 71, 85, 103, 117 (x4), 131, 141, 171, 181, 195
Depositphotos: © lhfgraphics: 227
Getty Images: Culture Club: 211
iStock: © ilbusca: 76 (bell); © KeithBishop: 161; © keko-ka: 76 (bowl);
   © kolb_art: 76 (dog)
National Gallery of Art: 157
Rijksmuseum: 101
Shutterstock: © KUCO: 251; © RRA79: 31; © sharpner: 239; ©truhelen: 213;
   throughout: © KateVogel (flourishes); © Lukiyanova Natalia/frenta (scrolls);
   © Seamartini Graphics (banners); © yaviki (parchments)

Dedication
To Connie,
who got us here.

Special Thanks
to Tolkien and Martin.

Contents

Acknowledgments:
Copious Details

Though the game of books spills less blood than does the game of thrones, the publication process presents challenges and hazards aplenty throughout the winding journey from inception to reception. The number of people writing, illustrating, editing, discussing, promoting, paying the bills, and supporting in other ways could rival the cast of characters listed in one of George R. R. Martin's 50-page appendices. While we'll not go that far, we need to honor a few.

House Sterling

As our work on *The Walking Dead Psychology* wound down and *Star Wars Psychology* started rolling, I was wondering whether to go ahead and suggest *Game of Thrones Psychology* as book three when my editor, Connie Santisteban, asked if we would consider covering *Game of Thrones*. We'd each separately known what the next topic needed to be. Working with Connie is a joy. She plans battles, wrestles wights, solves riddles, and knows the importance of hot tea. The fine folks at Sterling support our work in ways that make some of my friends who publish elsewhere turn green with envy. I must thank Toula Ballas, Michael Cea, Diana Drew, Lisa Geller, Marilyn Kretzer, Sari Lampert, Eric Lowenkron, Josh Mrvos, Rodman Neumann, Blanca Oliviery, Lauren Tambini, Theresa Thompson, and too many other Sterling folks to list in every book.

House Con

Such an ambitious series would never be possible without our chapter authors. Different conventions create opportunities for us psych geeks to get to know each other and to share ideas not only with each other but with audiences as well: the Comics Arts Conference (Peter Coogan, Randy Duncan, Kate McClancy), San Diego Comic-Con International (Eddie Ibrahim, Sue Lord, Adam Neese, Gary Sassaman), New York Comic Con (Lance Festerman), Southwestern Psychological Association (Jennifer Bonds-Raacke), many Wizard World cons (Christopher Jansen, Peter Katz, Donna Chin, Danny Fingeroth, Tony Kim, Mo Lightning, Madeleine McManus, Jerry Milani, Alex Rae, Aaron Sagers, Brittany Walloch), and more. The best part of any convention is making new friends and visiting with friends I don't normally see elsewhere, like many of our writers and my editorial assistants on this volume: Alan "Sizzler" Kistler and Legion of Leia founder Jenna Busch.

House Gygax

Those of us writing about *Game of Thrones* and those of you reading about it reached this point by many routes. Some of us owe Gary Gygax and company for creating a game. Mike Southerland introduced me to *Dungeons & Dragons*, and D&D introduced me to a lot of fantasy literature. Our roster of D&D warriors is lengthy, from those who played it with us way back at the beginning (Tim Cogburn, Dennis Cunningham, Misti Borders, Kevin Green) and those who came soon after (Darrell Barton, Melissa Langley Biegert, Craig Brown, Richard Castor, Wingo Johnson, Missy Johnston, Kevin Robbins, Scott Stewart, Ross Taylor) to pros who analyze the game with me on convention panels today (Genese Davis, Larry Elmore, Jon Peterson, Gygax biographer Michael Witwer) and over a hundred in between. If D&D players David Bush and Lisa Sunderman Kelly or *The Lord of the Rings* lover Lisa Crutchfield were still in our world, they might have some stimulating thoughts to share about George R. R. Martin's fictional world, and I want to remember them here.

House Henderson

Today's warriors, who also LARP, card-battle, and adventure online, include my university's Comic Arts Club and the Legion of Nerds, a lively campus organization which Ashley Bles, Dillon Hall, Coley Henson, and Bobby Rutledge founded and which leaders like Olivia Bean, Steven Jacobs, and John McManus keep going. Alumni formed the Comic Arts Council (Tommy Cash, Erica Ash Lemons, Greg Lemons, Robert O'Nale, Justin Poole) because nerdiness never has to expire. Teaching at Henderson State University, I have been fortunate to enjoy the support of administrators who value creative ways of teaching: President Glendell Jones, Provost Steve Adkison, Dean John Hardee. Librarians like Lea Ann Alexander keep our library full of fantastic resources. David Bateman, Lecia Franklin, Carolyn Hatley, Ermatine Johnston, and Linda Mooney help me and my students travel. Millie Bowden, Denise Cordova, Renee Davis, Sandra D. Johnson, and many other staff members make sure other essentials get done. Our faculty writers group (Angela Boswell, Matthew Bowman, Vernon Miles, Davis Sesser, Suzanne Tartamella, Michael Taylor, and Melanie Wilson) reviewed portions of this manuscript. My fellow psychology faculty members offer endless encouragement and insights of their own: Chair Aneeq Ahmad, Rafael Bejarano, Emilie Beltzer, Rebecca Langley, Paul Williamson.

House Langley

My sons Alex and Nicholas, who grew up loving fantasy novels and games galore, expanded our unofficial family by bringing other players into House Langley: Carly Cate, Renee Couey, Michael Dorman, Sarah Fuller, Marko Head, Katrina Hill, Stephen Huckabee, Ryne Johnston, Cordell Moss, Austin Phillips, Jimmy and Nicole Smith, Tim Yarbrough. Sister-in-law Sharon Manning takes care of so many things and needs to know how very much we value her. My parents, Lynda and Travis Sr., let me be me. My wife Rebecca gets the greatest credit as my sounding board, proofreader, best friend, and person who keeps up with all kinds of things when I must immerse myself in exploring these fantasy worlds.

House Web

Facebook friends and a Twitter army help us brainstorm, find facts, and have fun. While wikis are tricky because any fool may "fix" them and any varlet might vandalize, I must praise A Wiki of Ice and Fire (awoiaf.westeros.org) for providing an extensive resource regarding George R. R. Martin's books and the Game of Thrones Wiki (gameofthrones.wikia.com), an encyclopedic guide to the television series. While we always check the original sources, these online oracles sometimes point the way. The folks at OuterPlaces.com (Kieran Dickson, Louis Monoyudis, Janey Tracey) join us in our adventures, and everybody at NerdSpan (Dan Yun, Ian Carter, Ashley Darling, Keith Hendricks, Aaron Pruner, Garret Steele, and dozens more) also deserves a round of applause.

Rogues

My literary agent, Evan Gregory of the Ethan Ellenberg Literary Agency, suggested this book's subtitle and tends to more details than most readers want me to explain. Blaine Bellamy, Ron Currie, Jeffrey Henderson, Marcello Kilani, Jim and Kate Lloyd, Joshua Masson, Dustin McGinnis, and many others served as our series contributors' inspirations, founts of knowledge, reservoirs of patience, devil's advocates, partners in crime, or emotional support of many kinds. Kyle Maddock contributed an insightful foreword to this volume and is both fun and funny to hang out with during a con. We thank folks like FirstGlance's Bill Ostroff for all our author photos. Ed O'Neal, Lawrence Brenner, Kathleen Dalton-Woodbury, John Fugelsang, Karen Hancock, Diana Wynne Jones, Chris Murrin, Marc Nadel, Kaja Perina, Terry Pratchett, Fred Saberhagen, Matthew Smith, and many others deserve recognition for reasons diverse and occasionally bizarre.

Legends

We owe an ongoing debt to author George R. R. Martin, who gave us this elaborate fictional world with its rich cast of characters. Martin has often spoken of how J. R. R. Tolkien inspired him, and he includes Tad Williams, Robert Heinlein, Andre Alice Norton, and Stan Lee among his influences. We, the fans and scholars, owe them all.

Foreword:
Do You Still Believe in
Happy Endings?

KYLE MADDOCK

I talk about *A Song of Ice and Fire* and *Game of Thrones* all the time. I endlessly podcast about them and host a YouTube show on the topic, but this book is a different sort of beast. I'm used to scratching the surface of the story with discussions about favorite scenes and whether you think Jon Snow is really dead. This book delves much deeper than that. Why are we so fascinated by this seemingly horrific tale where the good guys never seem to win? What keeps us coming back week after week?

Game of Thrones was never supposed to be made. George R. R. Martin wrote *A Song of Ice and Fire* to be "unfilmable."[1] He was sick and tired of the limitations and difficulties of writing for television. Yet for a show that was never supposed to be, it sure is successful. In fact, it's the most successful HBO show ever made, trumping the ratings of the former champ *The Sopranos.*[2] So how does a show that was too big to be filmed do so well? There are too many characters, too many locations, too many plots. These hurdles were part of the reason I enjoyed it. In our high-speed, information-overloaded lives, we are confronted with countless stories that are often boiled down to a headline. Content providers seem to be afraid that we don't have the patience to enjoy something complex. It is an elaborate story spanning continents populated by morally gray characters that speak multiple languages, live in varied societies, and worship numerous faiths. I love this. I feel challenged by it and rewarded when the pieces fit together. There is a sense of satisfaction when you watch these characters spin their tangled webs and you can figure out their endgame. And when you can't, there's a delight in the reveal. Too many shows shy away from this sort of complexity. They shouldn't be afraid of it.

Now don't get me wrong. There is a need for *some* popcorn shows that make us smile and laugh and cheer and forget the woes of our day. *Game of Thrones* is not that show and that is a good thing.

Things seemed a lot simpler back when the story began.[3] For one, everyone was together. The Starks were still a family—a family welcoming the king and queen and their entourage into their home. On television, almost every "main" character was onscreen at the same time. The first episode wasn't jumping from location to location in a dizzying frenzy trying to touch on every story. It was set up in such a way that nothing seemed abnormal—a typical start to a fantasy adventure. The reluctant hero is forced into a position to help the king after a mysterious murder. It isn't until the final scene of the pilot that we the viewers realize this may not be typical fantasy fare. Bran climbs a tower, witnesses something he should not have seen, and is thrown from the tower to silence him. Is that the scene that made you take notice? Perhaps it was the next episode when Ned must kill his daughter's direwolf.[4] When Ned later dies,[5] any lingering thoughts I had of this being just another story were gone. The hero had lost. Why did this intrigue me? Why is this the moment that so many people point to when discussing the series? The mind really is dark and full of terrors if we're mesmerized by the death of the hero. Or is it more that in a sea of happily-ever-afters we're fascinated when that literary convention is turned on its head?

From there, the story—like the Stark family—scatters. We follow so many characters with so many various adventures. We bump into every walk of life that Westeros has to offer, from the commoners to the nobles, from the nice to the sadistic and everything in between. And on these adventures through the eyes of these characters, we see situations and circumstances that most of us have never faced and hopefully never will. We experience and relate to each one in a unique way that reflects our own beliefs and personal history. *Game of Thrones* is not painted in black and white. There are few characters that are truly good or evil. It is that gray that draws us into their stories. It is that moral ambiguity that lets us relate and connect to the choices and actions they make. If it was more clear-cut we could say, "That's bad" or "That's good," and move on. But it's not. The hard choices these characters make force viewers to discuss and debate what is right and what is wrong. That's a big reason I find these characters so intriguing. I root for the redemption of Theon Greyjoy while everyone around me hopes for his death. Why do we have such varying opinions? The scenes I watch on my TV aren't any different from those on yours.

We follow fan favorite Arya Stark as she's dragged away from her father's death. She's thrust onto the road and into a kill-or-be-killed world. It's easy to see why Arya is so beloved. She doesn't play the victim. Much like Brienne, these women stand up for themselves. They fight back. They're badass. They react in a way that many of us hope we would in those circumstances. But they're also well-rounded characters. You can see the wounds they carry. You can see the trials they've been through and how they don't let those trials dictate their actions. They're a joy to watch.

There are so many characters in *Game of Thrones* that we can relate to. Tyrion, the outcast who's forced to use brains over brawn; Daenerys, the orphan who's trying to find her way in the world while longing for home; and Jon Snow, the bastard who wants to make his father proud. But amid all these characters, there are some that are a lot harder for most of us to understand. Joffrey Baratheon, Gregor Clegane, and Ramsay Snow delight in the pain and suffering of others. Why is this? What makes them do what they do? Why do we watch? Can we separate ourselves from these sadistic scenes because it's a fictional story? It's certainly hard to watch. In fact, there are people who have stopped watching because of these characters. There are others who are fascinated by it. The mind is complex and for everyone out there that's filled with sunshine and rainbows there is another full of darker things.

In the end, we enjoy this story because it reflects our own human nature. It reflects our own struggle to survive in a difficult world. It is full of hope and fear, love and hate, good and evil. It is full of choices. We relate to these characters because we can see bits of ourselves in them and the decisions they make. We can, to one degree or another, understand what they are going through and because of this we care what happens to them.

Game of Thrones, arguably more than any other show on television, puts its characters through the most intense, arduous, and difficult challenges. After five seasons, they are still being beaten down. Yet we continue to watch. Are we gluttons for punishment and heartache or do we truly believe in happy endings? Is there a light at the end of the tunnel? Are we hoping that through it all the good guys will win?

Kyle Maddock is a host of "A Podcast of Ice and Fire," the Geekie Award–winning and longest-running podcast dedicated to George R. R. Martin's *A Song of Ice and Fire*. He hosts the *Game of Thrones* aftershow at AfterBuzzTV and is a frequent guest on other YouTube shows, podcasts, and panels. Outside of his passionate geek life, Kyle is an actor who can be seen in shows such as *How I Met Your Mother* and *Happy Endings*. Follow him on Twitter (@kylemaddock).

References

Itzkoff, D. (2011, April 8). *A heroic fantasy for skeptics*. New York Times: http://www. nytimes.com/2011/04/10/arts/television/game-of-thrones-on-hbo-from-george-r-r-martin-novels.html?_r=1.

Martin, G. R. R. (1996). *A game of thrones*. London, UK: Voyager.

West, K. (n.d.). *Game of Thrones beats The Sopranos as HBO's most popular series ever*. Cinema Blend: http://www.cinemablend.com/television/Game-Thrones-Beats-Sopranos-HBO-Most-Popular-Series-Ever-64500.html.

Notes

1. Itzkoff (2011).
2. West (n.d.).
3. Martin (1996); episode 1–1, "Winter Is Coming" (April 17, 2011).
4. Episode 1–2, "The Kingsroad" (April 24, 2011).
5. Episode 1–9, "Baelor" (June 12, 2011).

Introduction: But Insight Burns Them All Away

TRAVIS LANGLEY

"The night is dark and full of terrors, but the fire burns them all away."
—Melisandre, the Red Woman[1]

> *"In the deeps are the violence and terror of which psychology has warned us."*
> —author Annie Dillard[2]

What are they thinking? Why would they do that? Can't they see the harm they're inflicting on themselves?

We ask these questions all the time. Asking them about fictional characters differs a bit from asking them about living beings because we know the characters differently than we know those around us—better in some ways, more poorly in others. While we can read descriptions of Sansa's dreams and Cersei's frustrations or watch scenes that depict how Tyrion acts when he is all alone, we can only guess as to the thoughts, feelings, intentions, beliefs, and private actions of our relatives, friends, acquaintances, and strangers all around or take their word for it when they describe those things themselves. We can interact with people on this planet, though. We can ask them questions and provoke reactions that we will never elicit from characters in a fantasy world, but that can be tricky, even dangerous. Contemplating character motivation feels safer; sometimes it lets us look more objectively than when we consider the motivation of real people. It can also let us delve into darker subjects than we might otherwise dare to. Paradoxical as it might sound, fiction can help us see real people more accurately. Asking such questions about the person whose reality we each know best, though, can sometimes be hardest of all. People throughout recorded history have found it easier to scrutinize someone else's shortcomings than to face their own.[3]

Therapists from numerous schools of psychology have based their methods on the assumption that people need to understand themselves and their lives better in order to cope and grow. Insight-oriented approaches involve a lot of conversations and may take a great deal of time. Often called *insight therapy* or *talk therapy*, Freudian psychoanalysis can go on for years as the psychoanalyst guides the client into discovering and understanding unconscious conflicts and motivations.[4] *Client-centered therapy* (now more popularly known as *person-centered therapy*) lets the client guide the process while still pursuing a more realistic understanding of self and surroundings. The more philosophically oriented *existential therapy*[5] and *Gestalt psychology*[6] work toward objective understanding of one's existence and place in the world. *Rational-emotive behavior therapy* focuses on getting the client to think and more feel more rationally.[7] The list goes on and on.

No therapeutic method is suitable for every mental need, any more than aspirin should be dispensed for every physical malady. One criticism of insight-oriented approaches is that they work best for clients who already have the capacity for insight and the motivation to gain more. Not everyone wants to look into the mirror. People with *personality disorders*, whose personalities include enduring traits that broadly interfere with functioning in many areas of life, frequently lack both the motivation to change who they are and the insight that might help them do so.[8] No matter how much Cersei might benefit by seeing that her own petty motivations and her failures to foresee repercussions cause her plans to backfire and hurt her—as when she empowers a church that will later torment her—she does not want to see herself in that mirror. That does not mean she cannot see, but to do so would require change she might be unwilling to make. She is Cersei. She revels in being who she is. Just as her shortsightedness in certain areas endangers the throne, players in the game of thrones endanger their whole world by playing the game when a greater menace grows, a menace that most don't know about while some who see evidence of the world's danger simply refuse to believe. Because they do not want an army of the undead to destroy them all, they choose to live in a personal reality where no such army exists.

Facing dangers can be hard. Acknowledging truths can be difficult, even depressing. Blinding ourselves to hard truths can provide short-term relief but at the risk of escalating long-term jeopardy. We keep reading George R. R. Martin's stories and watching their onscreen depictions because we hope and believe enough of the characters will gain enough insight into their own natures and enough understanding of what really matters in time to save their world. Letting ourselves hope and believe in them helps us practice hoping and believing in ourselves and in the future before us all. We've done this all our lives, from when we learned during childhood by mimicking adults, by playing. Our fictions gave us insight.

Sometimes, to ready ourselves for life, we first must play a game.

> *"If you know the enemy and know yourself, you*
> *need not fear the result of a hundred battles."*
> —military strategist Sun Tzu, 6th century BCE[9]

References

American Psychiatric Association (2013). *Diagnostic and statistical manual of mental disorders (DSM-5)*. Washington, DC: American Psychiatric Association.

Dillard, A. (1982). *Teaching a stone to talk: Expeditions and encounters*. New York, NY: Harper & Row.

Ellis, A. (1957). Rational psychotherapy and individual psychology. *Journal of Individual Psychology, 13*(1), 38–44.

Ellis, A. (2004). *Rational Emotive Behavior Therapy: It works for me—it can work for you*. Amherst, NY: Prometheus.

May, R. (1994). *The discovery of being: Writings in existential psychology*. New York, NY: Norton.

Oltmanns, T. F., & Powers, A. D. (2012). Knowing our pathology. In S. Vazire & T. D. Wilson (Eds.), *Handbook of self-knowledge* (pp. 258–273). New York, NY: Guilford.

Oltmanns, T. F., & Turkheimer, E. (2009). Person perception and personality pathology. *Current Directions in Psychological Science, 18*(1), 32–36.

Perls, F. (1969). *Gestalt therapy verbatim*. Moab, UT: Real People.

Scaturo, D. (2002). Fundamental dilemmas in contemporary psychodynamic and insight-oriented psychotherapy. *Journal of Contemporary Psychotherapy, 32*(2), 145–165.

Sun Tzu (trans., 1910). *The art of war*. London, UK: Luzac.

Notes

1. Episode 2–1, "The North Remembers" (April 1, 2012).
2. Dillard (1982).
3. *Matthew* 7:3–5.
4. Scaturo (2002).
5. May (1994).
6. Perls (1969).
7. Ellis (1957, 2004).
8. American Psychiatric Association (2013); Oltmanns & Powers (2012); Oltmanns & Turkheimer (2009).
9. Sun Tzu (trans. 1910), p. 52.

A Song of Ice and Fire

book series by author George R. R. Martin

A Game of Thrones
(1996)

A Clash of Kings
(1998, Voyager; 1999, Bantam Spectra).

A Storm of Swords
(2000)

A Feast for Crows
(2005)

A Dance with Dragons
(2011)

The Winds of Winter

A Dream of Spring

Original publisher: Voyager Books. London, UK.
North American publisher: Bantam Spectra. New York, NY, USA.

Game of Thrones

Television Credits

Series creators/showrunners: David Benoiff and D. B. Weiss.

Executive producers: Frank Doelger, Bernadette Caulfield, Carolyn Strauss, George R. R. Martin, and the showrunners.

Original network: HBO.

Production companies: HBO Entertainment, Television 360, Startling Television, Bighead Littlehead.

Part One
Feasts

Many hungers drive the living—appetites for food, sex, comfort, warmth. Why do some indulge to excess while others scrape to survive? Why does one person with needs met crave even more while another can think in the long term about more complicated priorities? Why does anyone revel at the party when dangers are at hand? Who satisfies appetites in ways that also help others and who gets satisfaction by hurting others instead?

"Why?" It's the most basic question at the heart of psychology, a question we ask about both others and ourselves. Why do we do the things we do? What motivates anyone's behavior, whether selfish, selfless, or even self-destructive?

CHAPTER ONE

Need and Greed: Wherein Lies the Motive?

TRAVIS LANGLEY

" . . . prey to pride, ambition, lust, love, anger, jealousy, greed for gold, hunger for power, and all the other failings that afflicted lesser mortals."
—Ser Barristan Selmy regarding the Kingsguard.[1]

"Greed is a bottomless pit which exhausts the person in an endless effort to satisfy the need without ever reaching satisfaction."
—psychologist Erich Fromm[2]

Need and greed motivate many people in the actions they take—with their most self-serving deeds, arguably more so. Physical, emotional, and social insufficiencies prompt people to try to fill gaps in what they have. Some who feel satisfied do not grapple for more. Others, though, feel there is never enough and keep pursuing, keep amassing, keep trying to fill holes inside themselves that never can be filled. Why? What makes a person value one deficit or desire above another? Many motives may drive any action, and many causes can create each motive.

Hierarchies

When her future daughter-in-law Margaery plans to give a grand feast's leftovers to the poor, why does Cersei undermine her by ordering that the food go to the dogs instead?[3] What purpose does that serve? When we ask why Cersei goes behind Margaery's back, we are asking about her *motivation*, the processes that fuel her behavior and give it direction. We wonder what drives both her *overt behavior*—the actions we can observe—and her *covert behavior*—all the things she does that we cannot witness directly (mental activities such as her thoughts, feelings, attitudes, and beliefs). Why did she give that order, and where did the thought or feeling that she should give it come from?

Blood Before . . . ?

Motives are *hierarchical*, meaning that some are strong enough to rank persistently at the top of a hierarchy and take priority over others. Self-preservation is a powerful motive that is necessary to push each person to survive, as Martin's characters demonstrate in so many chapters in the books and on every episode on television. Some people value self-preservation above all other motives. Many do not. Motivation to protect loved ones, for example, is frequently even more powerful. Although Ned Stark values honor and truth above his own life, he relinquishes both—and consequently his life—for a chance to keep his family safe.[4] Theorists offer many suggestions about why people would ever risk their own well-being to help anyone, especially blood kin. Ethologists, sociobiologists, and others who take an evolutionary perspective explain much behavior—particularly selfishness and altruism—in terms of how every action affects the odds that the performer's genes will be passed down through future generations.[5] Behaviorists explain altruism in terms of gaining other rewards or discounting the personal risks.[6] Scientists and philosophers propose many additional reasons, some of which can be difficult to put to any test. Most likely, many factors figure in.

Not everyone puts family first, though. Even Stannis Baratheon, who cherishes his daughter so much that he searches the world at great effort and cost until he acquires the cure for her otherwise fatal disease, places his avarice for power above her. When he thinks the sacrifice to a fire god will grant him victory and eventually the Iron Throne, he burns his only child alive.[7] In his motive hierarchy, his crown outranks his heir.

Climbing the Pyramid

Psychologist Abraham Maslow proposed that our inborn needs naturally prioritize themselves because people must satisfy the most basic biological needs at least partially before they feel the urge to fulfill more psychologically oriented needs (see the diagram in Game File One: Primal Urges). Maslow saw the most primitive needs, the primal urges, as being inherently strong enough to overpower more advanced needs if they are not met. Tyrion can say, "The mind needs books like a sword needs a whetstone,"[8] more easily than a starving street orphan might. When given a choice between books and bread, the orphan will go for the bread. When teetering on the edge of death, with his nose bleeding and his vision blurring from the poison that courses through his veins, Sellsword Bronn stops acting too proud to compliment the woman who holds the antidote.[9] The Stark children, who grow up with supplies, shelter, support, and family love aplenty, find it easier than many might to work on self-esteem needs.

Despite his theory's popularity, evidence regarding its universality is mixed. Maslow's research was neither rigorous nor methodically controlled. "By ordinary standards of laboratory research," Maslow said of his own work, "this was simply not research at all."[10] He considered his studies of human nature to be exploratory pilot studies that would be confirmed by others.[11] Although a number of studies[12] indicate that people tend to progress through these needs in the order Maslow posited and that those whose needs are met feel greater satisfaction in life, a tendency is not a one-size-fits-all pattern. Not everyone fits Maslow's mold. People can prioritize motives in ways consistent with his views, but the exceptions may pose a problem for the theory. There are, for example, some starving people who nevertheless develop healthy self-esteem. Also, research does not consistently confirm his expectation that need deprivation will produce pathology.[13]

Maslow's hierarchy of needs remains a well-known model for contemplating the ways people prioritize their motives, though. Something about it resonates with how people understand motivation. What, then, do we really know about its different levels? The "Game File" features that appear at the end of every section in this book explore each level of that pyramid in greater depth.

Where, When, Why

Where do those motives come from, and when do they come out? Understanding why people prioritize them as they do may require greater understanding of the motives themselves.

Intrinsic vs. Extrinsic

When Robb Stark has sex with Talisa Maegyr, he does so because that is what he wants to do, not for any ulterior purpose.[14] The first time Daenerys has sex with her new husband, though, she submits for the same reason she marries him: to support a military alliance.[15] Robb's motivation is *intrinsic* in that he beds Talisa because it is what he wants to do, whereas Daenerys's motivation on television is *extrinsic* in that she initially accepts her expected duty only to serve some other goal.

Without knowing terms such as *intrinsic* and *extrinsic motivation*, people wonder about them all the time. Shae appears to stay with Tyrion out of progressively growing attachment, rejecting a bag of diamonds rather than leave him.[16] Ultimately, though, Shae betrays Tyrion[17] and he soon discovers she has been working for his father—an extrinsically motivated betrayal if it is motivated by payment from his father but intrinsically motivated if it is driven by feelings of spite, or maybe it is both.[18] People with trusting natures more readily accept others at face value and assume, for example, that those who do kind things are acting out of intrinsic kindness. Distrustful individuals, in contrast, suspect that people perform even the kindest acts for self-serving reasons, to get something from others. Either view can be wrong or right in different circumstances.

Extrinsic motives can drown the intrinsic. A person who likes to paint for its own sake may start to perceive it as a chore after people begin paying that individual to paint. Actor Jack Gleeson, who played Joffrey Baratheon, lost some of his interest in acting for just such a reason. "I just stopped enjoying it as much as I used to," he said. "It was always something I did for recreation with my friends, or in the summer for some fun. I enjoyed it. When you make a living from something, it changes your relationship with it."[19] When external rewards provide excessive justification for performing a task, enjoyment or drive to perform the task may diminish—a phenomenon known as the *overjustfication effect.*[20]

The Power of Here and Now

Politicians bicker over how to fight existing crime or terrorism and pass fewer laws aimed at improving the conditions that cultivate them in the first place. Long-term preparation, no matter how severely it is needed, does not readily produce victories about which lawmakers may boast before the next election. The more complicated or abstract an issue is and the wider its array of causal factors may be, the more those who need to solve a problem will have trouble rallying support for their efforts. An army of the undead White Walkers may not be as complicated as worldwide crime or terrorism, but to those who have not yet witnessed it, it is not a visible threat. Neither vivid nor immediate, it is not present in the here and now.

Even members of the Night's Watch, those who guard the Wall that keeps the undead from invading the living, bicker and fight their own in-house squabbles instead of preparing. Information presented to us vividly makes a stronger impact (the *vividness effect*).[21] Even those inclined to believe that Jon Snow and Sam Tarly saw White Walkers feel less motivated than they do to prepare. Because their fellow brothers and in-house squabbles are right there in front of them, they will attack one another immediately while the danger not yet in view keeps growing.

Urgency adds energy to a motive. The immediate need will

be more powerful than the long-term need; this is another reason Rangers fight wildlings or even one another, wasting time, energy, and resources that could save the world. Dangers and desires at hand command attention and can shove long-term needs to the back burner. This may be one reason Maslow's hierarchy of needs makes sense to many people. The needs at the bottom of the pyramid (e.g., hunger, lust) feel immediate, whereas the needs at the next level up (e.g., shelter, supplies) are more long-term in nature. Fulfilling an immediate purpose rewards the performer sooner. Both reward (*reinforcement*) and punishment are more effective at changing behavior when they are delivered right away,[22] although humans are better at learning from delays than are nonhuman animals. Learning *impulse control* is an important part of growing up and is considered a sign of maturity.[23] Youngsters experienced at postponing gratification tend to become more socially competent,[24] unlike the pampered Robin Arryn, who never learns patience, self-control, or how to get along with others.

Big Picture

The title *Game of Thrones* stresses that the conflict over who should rule whom is merely a game compared with more important things such as the undead army rapidly growing in the frozen north. Tyrion chides his sister Cersei several times for shortsightedness. Varys, the spymaster who sees far and wide, knows the world has greater needs than political games, yet he also finds a way to use the game to his advantage as if maneuvering kings and queens themselves might help him bring order to their world. Need and greed drive characters in their world and living people in our world to make decisions and take actions for purposes both bad and good, foolish and wise. The greatest threat to any civilization's continued existence may not be the White Walkers, global warming, alien invasion, or any other concrete peril. Instead, it may be whatever game misplaces their priorities regardless of whether winter or summer is coming.

References

Burt, A., & Trivers, R. (2008). *Genes in conflict: The biology of selfish genetic elements.* London, UK: Belknap.

Fehr, E., & Fischbacher, U. (2003). The nature of human altruism. *Nature, 425*(6960), 785–791.

Frey, K. P., & Eagly, A. H. (1993). Vividness can undermine the persuasiveness of messages. *Journal of Personality and Social Psychology, 65*(1), 32–44.

Fromm, E. (1969). *Escape from freedom.* New York, NY: Holt.

Gonzales, M. H.., Aronson, E., & Constanzo, M. (1988). Increasing the effectiveness of energy auditors: A field experiment. *Journal of Applied Social Psychology, 18*(12), 1049–1066.

Graham, W., & Balloun, J. (1973). An empirical test of Maslow's need hierarchy theory. *Journal of Humanistic Psychology, 13*(1), 97–108.

Hagerty, M. R. (1999). Testing Maslow's hierarchy of needs: National quality-of-life across time. *Social Indicators Research, 46*(3), 249–271.

Hibberd, J. (2014, April 13). *"Game of Thrones": Jack Gleeson talks royal wedding shocker.* Entertainment Weekly: http://www.ew.com/article/2014/04/13/jack-gleeson-joffrey-death.

Lepper, M., & Greene, D. (1978). *The hidden cost of reward.* New York, NY: Lawrence Erlbaum.

Lester, D. (2013). Measuring Maslow's hierarchy of needs. *Psychological Reports, 113*(1), 15–17.

Logue, A. W. (1998). Self-control. In W. T. O'Donohue (Ed.), *Learning and behavior therapy.* New York, NY: Academic Press.

Martin, G. R. R. (1996). *A game of thrones.* London, UK: Voyager.

Martin, G. R. R. (2011). *A dance with dragons.* New York, NY: Bantam.

Maslow, A. H. (1971). *The farther reaches of human nature.* New York, NY: Viking.

Maslow, A. H. (1979). *The journals of A. H. Maslow.* R. J. Lordy (Ed.). Pacific Grove, CA: Brooks/Cole.

Mischel, W., Shoda, Y., & Rodriguez, M. L. (1989). Delay of gratification in children. *Science, 244,* 933–938.

Rachlin, H., & Locey, M. (2011). A behavioral analysis of altruism. *Behavioural Processes, 87*(1), 25–33.

Renner, K. E. (1964). Delay of reinforcement: A historical review. *Psychological Bulletin, 61*(5), 341–361.

Taormina, R. J., & Gao, J. H. (2013). Maslow and the motivation hierarchy: Measuring satisfaction of the needs. *American Journal of Psychology, 126*(2), 155–177.

that90'skid (2015, April 4). *Social psychology is everywhere.* The Misfits Closet: https://themisfitscloset.wordpress.com/tag/jack-gleeson/.

Webster, G. D., Cottrell, C. A., Schember, T. O., Crysel, L. C., Crosier, B. S., Gesselman, A. N., & Le, B. M. (2012). Two sides of the same coin? Viewing altruism and aggression through the adaptive lens of kinship. *Social and Personality Psychology Compass, 6*(8), 575–588.

Notes

1. Martin (2011), p. 804.
2. Fromm (1969), chap. 4.
3. Episode 4–2, "The Lion and the Rose" (April 13, 2014).
4. Martin (1996); episode 1–9, "Baelor" (June 12, 2011).
5. Burt & Trivers (2008); Fehr & Fischbacher (2003); Webster et al. (2012).
6. Rachlin & Locey (2011).
7. Episode 5–9, "The Dance of Dragons" (June 7, 2015).
8. Episode 1–2, "The Kingsroad" (April 24, 2011).
9. Episode 5–7, "The Gift" (May 24, 2015).
10. Maslow (1971), p. 41.
11. Maslow (1979).
12. Graham & Balloun (1973); Hagerty (1999); Taormina & Gao (2013).
13. Lester (2013).
14. Episode 2–8, "The Prince of Winterfell" (May 20, 2012).
15. Episode 1–1, "Winter Is Coming" (April 17, 2011).
16. Episode 3–10, "Mhysa" (June 9, 2013).
17. Episode 4–6, "The Laws of Gods and Men" (May 11, 2014).
18. Episode 4–10, "The Children" (June 15, 2014).
19. Hibberd (2014).
20. Lepper & Greene (1978); that90'skid (2015).
21. Frey & Eagly (1993); Gonzales et al. (1988).
22. Renner (1964).
23. Logue (1998).
24. Mischel et al. (1989).

If the struggle to meet basic needs helps people become more mature, what becomes of those who never know that struggle? One spoiled child may outgrow infantile selfishness while another does not. At what point can we distinguish immaturity from true evil?

CHAPTER TWO

The Problem of
Young Psychopaths

DAVE VERHAAGEN

"Everyone is mine to torment!"
—King Joffrey Baratheon[1]

> *"Guilt? It's this mechanism we use to*
> *control people. It's an illusion. . . . I feel*
> *sorry for people who feel guilt."*
> —serial killer Ted Bundy[2]

How early does evil begin? Considering that children start out in life short on empathy and needing to learn moral values, at what point can a person be considered psychopathic? Joffrey Baratheon, one of the most heartless kings of Westeros, may be vicious and sadistic, even monstrous, but is he a psychopath? After all, he's only a child. Determining whether any child is a true psychopath is a surprisingly tricky and complicated proposition.

Evil, Thy Name Is King

For reasons of both nature and nurture, Joffrey has always been a cruel kid, one whose early incidents of cruelty include gutting a pregnant kitten to see its insides[3] before he becomes king. Throughout the world, early cruelty to animals has been linked to the perpetuation of violence later in life,[4] possibly because of the kind of callousness and hostility involved in committing such acts in the first place.[5] The earlier such cruelty begins, the greater the likelihood is that the person will manifest a lifelong pattern of antisocial behavior.[6] People do not turn into monsters overnight.

Joffrey's viciousness leads to his murdering a prostitute with his crossbow,[7] beheading his father's trusted advisor,[8] ordering a man's tongue cut out for singing a song[9]—the list goes on. Not just abusing one's position of power but actively taking joy in tormenting, torturing, and killing indicates a degree of *sadism*: taking delight in inflicting pain and harm on others. Not all psychopaths are sadistic,[10] to be sure, but adding sadism to some individuals' psychopathy makes for a dangerous combination. Joffrey has all the features of a psychopath, including emotional callousness, lack of remorse, manipulation, and rage, and all this is compounded by his sadism.[11] True psychopathy likely continues across the lifespan with little to no burnout.

How to Build a Psychopath
It has been estimated that 1 in every 100 people we encounter in daily life may be psychopaths.[12] This means that the folks at the DMV or behind the counter at the food court run into a handful of them every day. Few of these psychopaths in the general population will ever kill or torture anyone, but that's mostly because it doesn't suit their purposes.[13] Among high-ranking corporate professions, the rate may be as much as

four times higher, and upward of 25 percent of all prisoners are genuine psychopaths.[14]

Believe it or not, psychopathy is not a diagnosis that is listed in modern diagnostic manuals.[15] It's better thought of as a constellation of negative interpersonal, behavioral, and emotional traits that include narcissism, manipulation, and sometimes superficial charm. Psychopathic actions include antisocial and criminal behavior, extreme impulsivity, and pathological lying, and the emotional traits include lack of remorse and empathy, callousness, and shallow affect. A true psychopath does not have to have all these traits but is likely to have most of them to a much greater degree than do most people.[16] Most psychopaths are completely grounded in reality even though they may have very odd ways of relating to the world around them.

Psychopaths are both born and made. When we study psychopathic persons, we find that they typically have a differently wired brain, negative early experiences in life, or both.[17] To create a psychopath, you often begin with neuro-psychological deficits. It is possible that Joffrey had a brain that was different from the brains of other kids. One theory[18] suggests that problems in the brain's *ventromedial cortex* lead to a person's inability to determine whether an experience is good or bad. Consequently, these people do not avoid negative situations and tend to repeat negative behaviors. In other words, they don't learn the way most people do. Consider this: If a typical child pushes a younger brother down and loses his favorite toy as *punishment*, that child is less likely to do it again because the developing brain learns that this behavior leads to an aversive outcome. However, in complete contrast, a psychopath's brain may not care about the punishment, and consequently, would be more likely to keep knocking the poor brother down when it serves the psychopath's purposes or simply seems amusing providing *positive reinforcement* that strengthens the behavior and makes it more likely to happen again in the future.[19]

A number of other theories[20] see a tiny area deep in the temporal lobes of the brain called the amygdala as the key to understanding the psychopathic brain. The amygdala is a hidden but essential part of the brain that is responsible for processing emotion rapidly. When the amygdala does not recognize fear, as it may not in the psychopathic brain,[21] the person loses the ability to get lit up physiologically and put the brakes on behavior that normally is regarded as reckless or hurtful.

Could being the product of incest have done a number on Joffrey genetically, affecting some aspects of his brain development and causing him to be highly bold and disinhibited? Maybe. It's equally fair to guess that his early experience played a significant role in his later villainy. In many ways, his early childhood is a nearly perfect breeding ground for psychopathy: spoiled and indulged by those around him yet despised by his father, King Robert. His father at one point hits him so hard after learning that Joffrey cut open the pregnant cat that he knocks out two of the boy's baby teeth.[22] Thus, we now have the key ingredients for a psychopathic stew: overindulgence mixed with parental rejection sprinkled with harsh and abusive treatment of an already neurologically weird child. This may be how you create a psychopath.

Psychologist Christopher Patrick has proposed that psychopathy consists of three components, each of which is linked to a person's nature or nurture:[23]

- *Boldness*—low fear and high confidence with a lot of tolerance for danger. This probably is associated with differences in the amygdala and other neurological systems related to fearfulness.

- *Disinhibition*—low behavioral constraints and high need for immediate gratification. This may be connected to problems in areas of the frontal lobe that control planning, foresight, and self-control.
- *Meanness*—low empathy and positive attachments and high cruelty and exploitativeness. The meanness seems likely to be the product of one of the other two components coupled with a negative early environment.

For example, a highly fearless child (boldness) will not respond well to consequences and punishments but ordinarily may not develop a psychopathic personality if he has healthy attachments, positive feedback, and rewards. Similarly, a highly impulsive child (disinhibition) may wear everyone out, but being berated, rejected, or smacked around may tip that child into high meanness and thus psychopathy.

Patrick's proposal also may explain why psychopathy is relatively rare (about 1 percent of the population). There are plenty of fearless, disinhibited kids with nurturing families who do not become psychopaths, and there are plenty of kids with crappy families and early mistreatment who have intact wiring and don't tip over into the realm of psychopathy. Both factors undoubtedly must be present, as was the case for Joffrey, or one of the factors must be present to a ridiculous extreme.

Obviously, some kids have brains that are incredibly normal but were so tortured and mistreated that they become little Joffreys. That's fairly easy to understand because it lines up with our notions of how the world works: Child maltreatment often leads to bad outcomes, sometimes very bad outcomes.

These are also the kids with brains so prone to being impulsive, punishment-resistant, and risk taking that even with the most normal childhoods they grow up to be career felons. The *New York Times* featured a beautifully written article titled

"Can You Call a 9-Year-Old a Psychopath?" that spotlighted a child named Michael who had all the markers of psychopathy at an early age yet seemed to be raised in a normal intact family with skilled parents.[24] It seems to be a mystery because everything appears so normal on the outside. Because of this, his parents and many other parents of similar kids get the brunt of the blame. *Surely there are dark secrets lurking in that family! Surely this child was horribly mistreated by someone!* It's hard to accept that a psychopath could have been born in a normal family with normal parents, yet sometimes these children are. However, in Joffrey's case, there is no question about any of this. He definitely checks the horrible parent box and, thanks to the incest, possibly the lousy genetics box as well.

The Problem of Childhood Psychopathy

Psychopaths can fascinate us. We read books about them and watch television shows and movies about them. We are captivated by news stories about them. It has been this way for centuries. Real-life psychopaths throughout history include Hitler and Josef Mengele, Henry VIII, Jeffrey Dahmer, and Vlad the Impaler. Obviously, we should add evil King Joffrey to the list, right? Joffrey is vicious, depraved, and all-around horrible, but is he a true psychopath?

As obvious as it seems that the kid is a psychopath, the ability to determine psychopathy in children and teens is surprisingly tricky. Why? Because many of the traits—impulsivity, low empathy, lack of remorse, aggression—are not that stable and can't always be measured reliably when a person is young. For example, in one study,[25] among teenagers who ranked in the top 5 percent of psychopathy scores when they were Joffrey's age, only 29 percent were classified as psychopathic a decade later. In other words, among the teenagers in the 95th percentile or higher for psychopathy scores, more than 7 of 10 did not ring the bell for psychopathy when they were young adults. This is no small issue if we accept the notion that psychopathy is supposed to be a lifelong condition that continues through-out the life span with little or no burnout.

A misdiagnosis here can be a disaster, setting a kid on a course that could be ruinous to that child. It is hard to imagine a child designated a psychopath being given a break or a second chance in school or in society at large. It is impossible to think that the label, as emotionally charged as it is, could do anything other than produce fear in parents, teachers, and other concerned adults.

The truth is that many grade schoolchildren seem to lack empathy and remorse but grow up to be fine upstanding adults. Many middle schoolers are incredibly impulsive but are far from being psychopaths when they get older. Many high . school students engage in criminal, antisocial, and even violent behavior, but few of them keep it up past their early twenties. Thus, when you have a kid who is getting into fights, breaking the law, lying, doing drugs, and making a lot of other stupid decisions with seemingly no remorse and no regard for others, you really don't know what that child will be like as an adult. True, he could be a little psychopath who will continue on as a lifelong hardened criminal, but the smart money, statistically speaking, is that he will simply mature out of these behaviors.

Researchers have identified two types of teenagers who get in major trouble: the Life-Course Persistent (LCP) and the Adolescence Limited (AL).[26] LCP kids have gotten in trouble at every developmental stage. They were biting and fighting in preschool, and it did not let up through elementary, middle, and high school. By the time they become teenagers, they have committed three or more violent offenses a year for at least five years. This group contains the best candidates for lifetime psychopathy, but they account for less than 10 percent of all violent juvenile offenders.

AL teens don't begin their shenanigans until they are adolescents, but their behavior is indistinguishable from that of LCP kids in terms of the variety and frequency of their criminal and violent acts. However, unlike LCP offenders, who usually go on to a life of adult crime, more than three-quarters of AL kids simply stop breaking the law and hurting people by early adulthood.

Children and teens are not little adults, and so their trajectories are not the same. A 30-year-old man who is repeatedly breaking the law, conning people, stealing from them, and hurting them is not that likely to let up when he is 40, but a 13-year-old who is doing these kinds of things probably won't be doing them a few years later. Most simply stop. Pinning down real childhood psychopathy isn't nearly as easy as it seems.

Is the Boy King a Psychopath?

Is it possible that Joffrey would be like the 90 percent of teens who act out in nasty ways but end up being decent human beings as adults? Yes, it is possible, but it is extremely unlikely even with what we know about most kids who act out in nasty ways. Joffrey is exceedingly callous and extraordinarily cruel and delights in hurting others. *Premeditation*—planning actions ahead of time—is the difference between reactive and proactive aggression. *Reactive aggression* is an angry retaliatory response to a perceived provocation, usually an impulsive, unthinking response. By contrast, *proactive aggression* is unprovoked in the moment and there is no underlying anger driving it. Instead, it is driven by the belief that the violence will produce a favored outcome, whether humiliation, capitulation, or just pain. Proactive aggression indicates the deepest form of psychopathy, in which the violence and cruelty are not just the product

Rating Joffrey's Psychopathy with a Modern Instrument

The Hare Psychopathy Checklist: Youth Version (PCL: YV) is one of the most widely used scales for measuring these traits in teenagers. It consists of 20 items, each of which is rated on a 0–2 scale (0 denoting no resemblance to the trait and 2 denoting a high resemblance to the trait) on the basis of information gathered from interviews, observation, the historical record, and other sources. If Joffrey were rated on the PCL: YV,[27] even with our modern language and constructs, he still would score high. Here's how he probably would do:

- Impression management (trying to make yourself look good even when you might be doing terrible things)–0
- Grandiose sense of self-worth–2
- Stimulation seeking–2
- Pathological lying–1
- Manipulation for personal gain–1
- Lack of remorse–2
- Shallow affect–2
- Callous/lack of empathy–2
- Parasitic orientation–0
- Poor anger control–2
- Impersonal sexual behavior–0
- Early behavior problems–2
- Lacks goals–0
- Impulsivity–2
- Irresponsibility–2
- Failure to accept responsibility–2
- Unstable interpersonal relationships–2
- Serious criminal behavior–2
- Serious violations of conditional release–0
- Criminal versatility–2

His total score would place him at the 86th percentile for contemporary teenage boys who are currently on probation for breaking the law. Scores above the 85th percentile would be considered elevated, and so even if we use a modern-day instrument to assess psychopathy, Joffrey still rates high. Imagine if the instrument focused more on cruelty and violence. He'd be off the chart!

of being impulsive or reckless but come from sheer meanness, from a deeper evil within. It is the kind that allows a person to delight in torture, murder, and humiliation.

Yes, Joffrey Baratheon—His Grace, Joffrey of Houses Baratheon and Lannister, First of His Name, King of the Andals and the First Men, Lord of the Seven Kingdoms, and Protector of the Realm—is a psychopath. There is no question about it. He is one of the worst people in the history of literature and television—and as a result one of the best psychopaths ever.

References

American Psychiatric Association (2013). *Diagnostic and statistical manual of mental disorders* (DSM-5). Washington, DC: American Psychiatric Association.

Babiak, P., & Hare, R. D. (2007). *Snakes in suits: When psychopaths go to work*. New York, NY: HarperBusiness.

Blair, R. J. R (2008). The amygdala and ventromedial prefrontal cortex: Functional contributions and dysfunction in psychopathy. *Philosophical Transactions of the Royal Society B: Biological Sciences, 363*(1503), 2557–2565.

Borum, R., & Verhaagen, D. (2006). *Assessing and managing violence risk in juveniles*. New York, NY: Guilford.

Cima, M, Tonnaer, F., & Hauser. M. D. (2010). Psychopaths know right from wrong but don't care. *Social Cognitive and Affective Neuroscience, 5*(1), 59–67.

Dutton, K. (2013). The wisdom of psychopaths: What saints, spies, and serial killers can teach us about success. New York, NY: Farrar, Straus & Giroux.

Fallon, J. (2014). *The psychopath inside: A neuroscientist's personal journey into the dark side of the brain*. New York, NY: Current.

Forth, A., Kosson, D., & Hare, R. (2003). *Hare Psychopathy Checklist: Youth Version*. New York, NY: Multi-Health Systems.

Guerra, N. G. (2012). Can we make violent behavior less adaptive for youth? *Human Development, 55*(3), 105–106.

Haden, S. C., & Scarpa, A. (2005). Childhood animal cruelty: A review of research, assessment, and therapeutic issues. *Forensic Examiner, 14*(2), 23–32.

Kahn, J. (2012, May 11). Can you call a 9-year-old a psychopath? *New York Times*, p. MM32.

Larson, C. L., Baskin-Sommers, A. R., Stout, D. M., Balderston, N. L., Curtin, J. J., Schultz, D. H., Kiehl, K. A., & Newman, J. P. (2013). The interplay of attention and emotion: Top-down attention modulates amygdala activation in psychopathy. *Cognitive, Affective, and Behavioral Neuroscience, 13*(4), 757–770.

Lilienfeld, S. O., & Arkowitz, H. (2007). What "psychopath" means. *Scientific American, 18*, 90–91.

Martin, G. R. R. (1996). *A game of thrones*. London, UK: Voyager.

Martin, G. R. R. (2000). *A storm of swords*. London, UK: Voyager.

Mellor, D., Yeow, J., Hapidzal, N. F. M., Yamamoto, T., Yokoyama, A., & Nobuzane, Y. (2009). Cruelty to animals: A tri-national study. *Child Psychiatry and Human Development, 40*(4), 527–541.

Meloy, J. R. (1997). The psychology of wickedness: Psychopathy and sadism. *Psychiatric Annals, 27*(9), 630–633.

Michaud, S. G., & Aynesworth, H. (2000). *Ted Bundy: Conversations with a killer.* Irving, TX: Authorslink.

Murphy, C., & Vess, J. (2003). Subtypes of psychopathy: Proposed differences between narcissism, borderline, sadistic, and antisocial psychopaths. *Psychiatric Quarterly, 74*(1), 11–29.

Patrick, C., Fowles, D. C., & Krueger, R. F. (2009). Triarchic conceptualization of psychopathy: Developmental origins of disinhibition, boldness, and meanness. *Development and Psychopathology, 21*(3), 913–938.

Skeem, J. L., Polaschek, D. L. L., Patrick, C. J., & Lilienfeld, S. O. (2011). Psychopathic personality: Bridging the gap between scientific evidence and public policy. *Psychological Science in the Public Interest, 12*(3), 95–162.

Tallichet, S. E., & Hensley, C. (2004). Exploring the link between recurrent acts of childhood and adolescent animal cruelty and subsequent crime. *Criminal Justice Review, 29*(2), 304-316.

Walters, G. D. (2014). Testing the direct, indirect, and moderated effects of childhood animal cruelty on future aggressive and non-aggressive offending. *Aggressive Behavior, 40*(3), 238–249.

Notes

1. Episode 3–10, "Mhysa" (June 9, 2013).
2. Michaud & Aynesworth (2000), p. 281.
3. Martin (2000).
4. Haden & Scarpa (2005); Mellor et al. (2009); Tallichet & Hensley (2004).
5. Walters (2014).
6. American Psychiatric Association (2013).
7. Episode 3–6, "The Climb" (May 5, 2013).
8. Martin (1996); episode 1–9, "Baelor" (June 12, 2011).
9. Episode 1–10, "Fire and Blood" (June 19, 2011).
10. Meloy (1997); Murphy & Vess (2003).
11. Lilienfeld & Arkowitz (2007).
12. Babiak & Hare (2007).
13. Dutton (2013).
14. Lilienfeld & Arkowitz (2007).
15. e.g., American Psychiatric Association (2013).
16. Skeem e al. (2011).
17. Fallon (2014).
18. Cima et al. (2010).
19. Guerra (2012).
20. Blair (2008).
21. Larson et al. (2013).
22. Martin (2000).
23. Patrick et al. (2009).
24. Kahn (2012).
25. Skeem et al (2011).
26. Borum & Verhaagen (2006).
27. Forth et al. (2003).

Appetites drive many base behaviors. They motivate us to meet whatever needs we might feel. Hunger can become habit. Some who discover hunger that they've never known before can stay hungry and maybe fight for the power to make sure no one else will deprive them of meals, power, or control of their own lives ever again.

CHAPTER THREE

The Moon Rises with the Sun: Overcoming Abuse

JAY SCARLET

"[Viserys] was a pitiful thing. He had always been a pitiful thing. Why had she never seen that before? There was a hollow place inside her where her fear had been."
—author George R. R. Martin[1]

"I had a childhood that was really lousy. . . . There was no emotional support, no physical support, there was really nothing and I somehow crawled up out of it and made a life for myself."
—anonymous child abuse survivor[2]

Daenerys Stormborn grows up living in fear of unleashing her brother Viserys's temper, or "waking the dragon" as he calls it.[3] As a result of his physical and emotional abuse, Dany appears to be a meek, nervous young woman.[4] In this suffering, she is not alone: A million children or more in the United States are maltreated in one way or another every year.[5] Although many abused children are able to overcome a history of abuse and lead happy lives, many others have great difficulty throughout their lives as a result of the maltreatment they experienced as children.

Child abuse, which may include physical, emotional, or sexual abuse or neglect, has been linked with a wide variety of consequences, including physical conditions (e.g., cancer, stroke, and diabetes[6]); neurological changes and alterations in brain chemistry and structure, potentially resulting in a reduced capacity for attention, memory, or impulse control;[7] and psychological issues (e.g., risky sexual behavior, poor judgment, anxiety, depression, and suicidality).[8] The fact that Daenerys seems to fall into the category of those who are able to overcome a history of abuse despite her early trajectory is due at least in part to discovering her resilience and taking advantage of opportunities to develop self-efficacy. Through this process, Dany experiences posttraumatic growth, which enables her to become a realistic contender for the Iron Throne.

Resilience

Resilience (the ability to overcome a significant risk factor such as a history of abuse during childhood) is not a binary characteristic that one either has or does not have but rather is something that can be manifested to varying degrees depending on the time and environment.[9] Dany is a perfect example of this, as she appears to become generally more resilient throughout the course of her story; however, this is clearly not a linear process, as she pushes Viserys away one moment but the next reverts to feeling helpless and afraid before the threat of his anger. There are a number of ways in which resilience can be developed, including interactions with others and internal experiences.[10]

Some researchers have described major life changes as *turning-point* or *second chance opportunities*, speculating that events such as military service, college, and marriage may serve as a catalyst that results in increased resilience.[11] In a study of adults who transcended their abusive childhoods, nearly half claimed to have been aided greatly in this process by a spouse.[12] In the case of Daenerys, much of her growth seems to have stemmed from how she asserts herself in her marriage.

On their wedding night (in the books), Drogo attempts to make Dany feel comfortable and safe by asking permission to touch her and providing her with some degree of control over what happens; this is quite possibly the first time she has ever felt control. This sense of safety and of being able to influence one's environment is an important factor in building resilience.[13] Research suggests that a feeling of having control over one's environment may be associated with better long-term health outcomes, both physical, such as reduced cancer risk, and psychological, especially among women.[14]

In addition, Drogo's actions allow Dany to feel emotionally supported. Even when her growing self-confidence and strong moral compass lead her to take actions that run counter to Dothraki tradition, for example, when she attempts to save as many women as possible from being raped during a raid on the Lamb Men, Drogo supports her and even shows pride in her increasing strength of character: "See how fierce she grows!"[15] This sort of unconditional support is one of the chief characteristics of helpful spouses described by people who have transcended their history of abuse.[16]

Being open to receiving this kind of support may be difficult for child abuse survivors initially, as they very often struggle with experiencing emotions, perhaps because they feel certain

Loving-Kindness Meditation

Positive emotions have been shown to have a wide variety of benefits to health, both physical and psychological, as well as other desirable outcomes, such as increased marital satisfaction and a higher income.[17] Whereas Dany's first experience of unadulterated joy is a result of connecting with her horse, another way of increasing positive emotion is through the practice of *loving-kindness meditation* (LKM). This type of meditation is designed to increase feelings of compassion and warmth toward oneself and others. Psychologists have used LKM to treat a range of conditions, including posttraumatic stress disorder,[18] depression,[19] and schizophrenia.[20]

The positive emotions produced by LKM can initiate a feedback loop in which the participant feels a greater sense of social connection with others. Because people have evolved to be social, research has found that social connection is linked to a number of health-related outcomes, including reduced risk of cardiovascular disease and cancer and a longer life. Feeling more connected to others and healthier thus leads to more positive emotions.[21] The perception of social connection can be created through even a very brief LKM intervention.[22] Over time, feeling positive emotions repeatedly can lead one to become more open to experiences and closer to people, as Dany becomes, thus providing personal resources and potentially building resilience.[23]

emotions, especially fear, much more strongly than do their nonabused peers, leading to difficulty in regulating those emotions. However, a recent study found that with guidance, although their brains used different processes, teens with histories of abuse were able to achieve emotional responses similar to those of teens with no history of maltreatment.[24] Alternatively, some trauma survivors seek to control their emotions by numbing them. Unfortunately, emotional numbing can make an individual's symptoms worse and make it more likely that he or she will develop or continue to have *posttraumatic stress disorder* (PTSD).[25] In contrast, the ability to connect with one's emotions, positive or negative, can provide for a meaningful healing experience.[26] For Dany, who is initially scared and avoidant of Drogo, it is allowing herself to connect with the horse he gives her that allows her to forget "to be afraid . . . for the first time ever."[27] Furthermore, the horse causes Dany to feel positive emotions such as excitement and joy, which have been shown to buffer the effects of stress.[28]

Self-Efficacy

Ultimately, Dany and Drogo's relationship helps increase her sense of *self-efficacy*, the feeling of having control over herself and events around her. This is a feeling that is often lacking in people who were abused as children and would have been especially difficult for Dany to develop earlier because of the lack of stability in her life before her marriage, as Viserys moves himself and his sister from city to city and Dany is never able to form lasting friendships. Self-efficacy has been linked to both physical and psychological health in survivors of abuse and also is considered to be one of the assets that can foster resilience.[29] Indeed, some theorists believe that self-efficacy is one of the primary factors in recovery from traumatic experiences such as abuse.[30]

One way Daenerys discovers a sense of self-efficacy is by taking advantage of opportunities to act independently. Drogo rarely spends time with Dany during the day, leaving her in charge of a small troop of servants and warriors. This gives her the experience of making decisions and giving commands. Ser Jorah observes this, commenting, "You are learning to talk like a queen."[31] Though being a queen is not a career path that is available to most people, school or workplace success (including promotions and taking on leadership roles) can be part of the healing process for many survivors of abuse[32] as well as being an important part of normal adolescent development.[33]

Posttraumatic Growth

Despite her history as a survivor of abuse, Dany comes to feel capable at decision making, more in control of her environment, loved and supported, and safe and secure. Research indicates that after all these positive experiences she would be likely to be able to enter a sort of positive feedback loop. In this type of situation, she would use the resources gained through her relationship with her partner to engage in more positive interactions with others, thus gaining more support from more sources. This would lead to greater social connection and further self-development.[34] This is exactly the arc that Daenerys undergoes. As she develops initially through her relationship with Drogo, her growth allows her to attract and retain the loyalty and support of a number of other individuals with whom she goes on to truly become a queen.

Perhaps the most notable feature of Daenerys's reign is her desire to end slavery and protect those she has freed. It is possible that the compassion and desire to help others that Daenerys exhibits are signs of *posttraumatic growth*. This construct acknowledges that in addition to the very real potential for problems caused by traumatic experiences, in certain circumstances some people may undergo positive changes as a result of the trauma. Many people who experience posttraumatic growth report changes in the ways they relate to others, including feeling more compassion and a stronger urge to be helpful.[35]

Becoming a Queen

The social support Dany gains throughout her healing process, along with her newfound sense of self-efficacy, serves her especially well when her resilience is put to the ultimate test and Drogo, her beloved sun and stars, dies. Rather than giving in to despair, Daenerys is able to begin anew, rededicated to the purpose of taking back the Iron Throne. On her journey to grow and recover from her trauma, Dany has found a new meaning for her life: to become the queen and help others. Research suggests that people who are able to make meaning from their traumatic experiences are more likely to overcome the negative effects of trauma,[36] and that is exactly what Daenerys does.

Although the cards initially seem to be stacked against her, Daenerys is able to gain not only a sense of self-efficacy but a new sense of purpose. Her relationship with Khal Drogo might have been the impetus for this, but after his death it was Daenerys's newly found resilience that allowed her to recover from her loss and begin her journey to becoming the Unburnt, Queen of Meereen, Queen of the Andals and the Rhoynar and the First Men, Khaleesi of the Great Grass Sea, Breaker of Chains, and Mother of Dragons.[37]

References

Benight, C. C., & Bandura, A. (2004). Social cognitive theory of posttraumatic recovery: The role of perceived self-efficacy. *Behaviour Research and Therapy, 42*(10), 1129–1148.

Feuer, C. A., Nishith, P., & Resick, P. (2005). Prediction of numbing and effortful avoidance in female rape survivors with chronic PTSD. *Journal of Traumatic Stress, 18*(2), 165–170.

Fredrickson, B. L., Cohn, M. A., Coffey, K. A., Pek, J., & Finkel, S. M. (2008). Open hearts build lives: Positive emotions, induced through loving-kindness meditation, build consequential personal resources. *Journal of Personality and Social Psychology, 95*(5), 1045–1062.

Glad, K. A., Jensen, T. K., Holt, T., & Ormhaug, S. M. (2013). Exploring self-perceived growth in a clinical sample of severely traumatized youth. *Child Abuse and Neglect, 37*(5), 331–342.

Hall, J. M., Roman, M. W., Thomas, S. P., et al. (2009). Thriving as becoming resolute in narratives of women surviving childhood maltreatment. *American Journal of Orthopsychiatry, 79*(3), 375–386.

Hart, H., & Rubia, K. (2012). Neuroimaging of child abuse: A critical review. *Frontiers in Human Neuroscience, 6*(52). http://http://journal.frontiersin.org/article/10.3389/fnhum.2012.00052/.

Hofmann, S. G., Petrocchi, N., Steinberg, J., et al. (2015). Loving-kindness meditation to target affect in mood disorders: A proof-of-concept study. *Evidence-Based Complementary and Alternative Medicine, 2015*, 1–11.

Hutcherson, C. A., Seppala, E. M., & Gross, J. J. (2008). Loving-kindness meditation increases social connectedness. *Emotion, 8*(5), 720–724.

Irving, S. M., & Ferraro, K. F. (2006). Reports of abusive experiences during childhood and adult health ratings: Personal control as a pathway? *Journal of Aging and Health, 18*(3), 458–485.

Johnson, D. P., Penn, D. L., Fredrickson, B. L., et al. (2009). Loving-kindness meditation to enhance recovery from negative symptoms of schizophrenia. *Journal of Clinical Psychology, 65*(5), 499–509.

Kearney, D. J., Malte, C. A., McManus, C., et al. (2013). Loving-kindness meditation for posttraumatic stress disorder: A pilot study. *Journal of Traumatic Stress, 26*(4), 426–434.

Kendall-Tackett, K. (2002). The health effects of childhood abuse: Four pathways by which abuse can influence health. *Child Abuse and Neglect, 26*(6–7), 715–729.

Kok, B. E., Coffey, K. A., Cohn, M. A., et al. (2013). How positive emotions build physical health: Perceived positive social connections account for the upward spiral between positive emotions and vagal tone. *Psychological Science, 24*(7), 1123–1132.

Maples, L. A., Park, S. S., Nolen, J. P., & Rosén, L. A. (2014). Resilience to childhood abuse and neglect in college students. *Journal of Aggression, Maltreatment and Trauma, 23*(10), 1001–1019.

Martin, G. R. R. (1997). *A game of thrones.* New York, NY: Bantam Spectra.

Martin, G. R. R. (2011). *A dance with dragons.* London, UK: Voyager.

Masten, A. S., Obradović, J., & Burt, K. B. (2006). Resilience in emerging adulthood: Developmental perspectives on continuity and transformation. In J. J. Arnett & J. L. Tanner (Eds.), *Emerging adults in America: Coming of age in the 21st century* (pp. 173–190). Washington, DC: American Psychological Association.

McLaughlin, K. A., Peverill, M., Gold, A. L., Alves, S., & Sheridan, M. A. (2015). Child maltreatment and neural systems underlying emotion regulation. *Journal of the American Academy of Child and Adolescent Psychiatry, 54*(9), 753–762.

Monfort, S. S., Stroup, H. E., & Waugh, C. E. (2015). The impact of anticipating positive events on responses to stress. *Journal of Experimental Social Psychology, 58*(1), 11–22.

Orbke, S., & Smith, H. L. (2013). A developmental framework for enhancing resiliency in adult survivors of childhood abuse. *International Journal for the Advancement of Counselling, 35*(1), 46–56.

Orsillo, S. M., & Batten, S. V. (2005). Acceptance and commitment therapy in the treatment of posttraumatic stress disorder. *Behavior Modification, 29*(1), 95–129.

Park, C. L., & Ai, A. L. (2006). Meaning making and growth: New directions for research on survivors of trauma. *Journal of Loss and Trauma, 11*(5), 389–407.

Penza, K. M., Heim, C., & Nemeroff, C. B. (2003). Neurobiological effects of childhood abuse: Implications for the pathophysiology of depression and anxiety. *Archives of Women's Mental Health, 6*(1), 15–22.

Sachs-Ericsson, N., Medley, A. N., Kendall-Tackett, K., & Taylor, J. (2011). Childhood abuse and current health problems among older adults: The mediating role of self-efficacy. *Psychology of Violence, 1*(2), 106–120.

Skogrand, L., Woodbury, D., DeFrain, J., DeFrain, N., & Jones, J. E. (2005). Traumatic childhood and marriage. *Marriage and Family Review, 37*(3), 5–26.

Theokas, C., Almerigi, J. B., Lerner, R. M., et al. (2005). Conceptualizing and modeling individual and ecological asset components of thriving in early adolescence. *Journal of Early Adolescence, 25*(1), 113–143.

Notes

1. Martin (1997), p. 231.
2. Reported in Hall et al. (2009).
3. Martin (1997).
4. Martin (1997).
5. Hall et al. (2009).
6. Kendall-Tackett (2002).
7. Hart & Rubia (2012).
8. Penza et al. (2003).
9. Maples et al. (2014).
10. Orbke & Smith (2013).
11. Masten et al. (2006).
12. Skogrand et al. (2005).
13. Orbke & Smith (2013).
14. Irving & Ferraro (2006).
15. Martin (1997), p. 670.
16. Skogrand et al. (2005).
17. Fredrickson et al. (2008).
18. Kearney et al. (2013).
19. Hofmann et al. (2015).
20. Johnson et al. (2009).
21. Kok et al. (2013).
22. Hutcherson et al. (2008).
23. Fredrickson et al. (2008).
24. McLaughlin et al. (2015).
25. Feuer et al. (2005).
26. Orsillo & Batten (2005).
27. Martin (1997), p. 106.

28. Monfort et al. (2015).
29. Sachs-Ericsson et al. (2011).
30. Benight & Bandura (2004).
31. Martin (1997), p. 227.
32. Hall et al. (2009).
33. Theokas et al. (2005).
34. Orbke & Smith (2013).
35. Glad et al. (2013).
36. Park & Ai (2006).
37. Martin (1997; 2011).

Primal Urges

TRAVIS LANGLEY

"Hunger turns men into beasts."
—Margaery Tyrell[1]

> *"I was often humiliated to see men disputing for a piece of bread, just as animals might have done. My feelings on this subject have altered very much since I have been personally exposed to the tortures of hunger. I have discovered, in fact, that a man . . . is governed, under certain conditions, much more by his stomach than by his intelligence and heart."*
> —19th-century scientist François Arago[2]

Basic primal instincts can be powerful, even overpowering when they get in the way of other needs or desires. Starving people can riot and try to kill their pampered boy-king.[3] Thirst can drive a wealthy king's mother to drink from a dirty floor.[4] Attraction, sex, and love can pull an honorable man away from a carefully arranged betrothal that ensures a needed ally's support.[5] The list of ways in which ancient, animal drives can motivate behavior may go on without end.

Psychologist Abraham Maslow described what he saw as natural priorities, the *hierarchy of needs* that guide human behavior

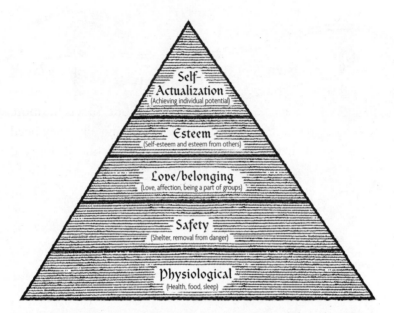

Hierarchy of needs: Stronger needs—those most immediate and physical in origin—form the pyramid's base. Maslow felt they must be met before individuals can work on long-term and mental needs.[6]

and psychological growth.[7] Once the lowest needs in the hierarchy are met, starting with the most immediate and primitive, we naturally feel the higher-level needs. Evidence in support of his view is mixed.[8] People might, for example, starve themselves to make political statements. King Tommen, however, simply seems moody when he refuses to eat while his wife and mother are imprisoned.[9] The cases in which some such protestors eventually give in to hunger before their strikes succeed support Maslow's view, but not everyone gives in. Maslow discussed such exceptions without fully explaining them. The model remains popular nonetheless because of all the instances in which it does fit observed actions and intuitive understanding of how people make choices. Some motives clearly compel us before others.[10] Maslow diagrammed the sequence of priorities as levels in a pyramid (see diagram), which varied a bit at different points in his career.

On the hierarchy's bottom level, the foundation upon which all the others are built, are the most basic physiological needs—appetites of assorted kinds. They're about survival, more survival, and sex. People need food, water, and air. They need to get out of the sun before they overheat or out of the cold before they freeze to death. How different might the choices made by Night's Watch Rangers be if they did not have to devote so much time and effort to keeping themselves from freezing? How different might the lives of many people and characters be, even among those sworn to chastity, if they did not surrender other needs to sexual desire?

Between the most ancient brain structures and the most advanced lies the *limbic system*, a set of neural structures that regulate motivation, affect emotion, and produce primitive pleasure. In the limbic system, the *amygdala* can stimulate aggression and fear. The *hypothalamus* (actually a cluster of limbic-system structures, even though we usually talk about it as if it were all one part) is often called the "center of motivation" because of its importance in regulating the so-called "4 Fs" (which really should be known as the 5 Fs to include freezing/temperature regulation): fighting, fleeing, feeding, and—so to speak—fornicating.[11] In other words, it regulates much of the behavior at the bottom of Maslow's pyramid, even though he himself did not experiment on brain parts. A dragon would be more heavily and immediately influenced by the limbic system than would most mammals. Its reptilian brain might make it more impulsive and give it less capacity for developing self-control, making Daenerys's babies increasingly difficult to control as they grow.

The appetites in the pyramid's bottom level are also known as *primary drives* (as opposed to *secondary drives*, which are at least partly learned). *Drive-reduction theory* holds that physical need creates an aroused, motivated state (a *drive*) that pushes us to take action that will reduce that drive.[12] Hunger drives the person to eat, which then reduces hunger. Though undead wights are reanimated corpses, something drives them to attack the living even when no White Walker is around to direct them. Their nature is so enigmatic that it's even hard to say that they act on *instinct* (which is complex behavior inherited through a species[13]), although their behavior is certainly instinct-like. Wights could arguably be considered a species that reproduces by replacing another species. The undead impulse to kill serves the same ultimate function as the living desire to copulate— reproduction—and that may pose the greatest danger in the entire series.

All of these basic urges serve adaptive purposes for the survival of self and species. All can be maladaptive, too, when allowed to control behavior too often, in the wrong situations, or to the neglect of other needs. "When I see what desire does to people—what it's done to this country," spymaster Varys says of these primal urges, "I am very glad to have no part in it. Besides, the absence of desire leaves one free to pursue other things."[14]

References

Arago, F. (1859). *Biographies of distinguished scientific men*. Boston, MA: Ticknor & Fields.

Hull, C. (1943). *Principles of behavior*. New York, NY: Appleton-Century Crofts.

Maslow, A. H. (1970). *The farther reaches of human nature*. New York, NY: Viking.

Miner, J. B. (1984). The validity and usefulness of theories in an emerging organizational science. New York, NY: Human Sciences.

Pribram, K. H. (1958). Comparative neurology and the evolution of behavior. In A. Roe & G. G. Simpson, *Behavior and evolution* (pp. 140–164). London, UK: Yale University Press.

Pribram, K. H. (1960). A review of theory in physiological psychology. *Annual Review of Psychology, 60*(1), 1–40.

Tay, L., & Diener, E. (2011). Needs and subjective well-being around the world. *Journal of Personality and Social Psychology, 101*(2), 354–365.

Tinbergen, N. (1951). *The study of instinct*. Oxford, UK: Clarendon.

Notes

1. Episode 3–1, "Valar Dohaeris" (May 21, 2013).
2. Arago (1859), p. 55.
3. Episode 2–6, "The Old Gods and the New" (May 6, 2012).
4. Episode 5–8, "Hardhome" (May 31, 2015).
5. Episode 2–8, "The Prince of Winterfell" (May 20, 2012).
6. Maslow (1971; 1979).
7. Maslow (1970).
8. Miner (1984).
9. Episode 5–8, "Hardhome" (May 31, 2015).
10. Tay & Diener (2011).
11. Pribram (1958, 1960).
12. Hull (1943).
13. Tinbergen (1951).
14. Episode 4–6 "The Laws of Gods and Men" (May 11, 2014).

Part Two
Dances

One advances; another retreats. Forward and backward, side to side. Dancing, fencing, fighting, mating, maneuvering. In love and war and everyday life, people weave in and out of each other's power for reasons both malignant and benign.

Trauma will tear some people down, but not everyone—and even those who fall may manage to get back up. Not everyone has to "get over it." Some of those whose trauma cuts most deeply might make meaning out of that pain and find purpose in life ahead. Some will grow.

CHAPTER FOUR

The Stark Sisters: On Trauma and Posttraumatic Growth

JENNA BUSCH AND JANINA SCARLET

"There's no shame in fear, my father told me, what matters is how we face it."
—Jon Snow[1]

"Persons who have a strong sense of efficacy deploy their attention and effort to the demands of the situation and are spurred by obstacles to greater effort."
—psychologist Albert Bandura[2]

Life-shattering experiences would put many people at risk for developing posttraumatic stress disorder (PTSD), anxiety, depression, brief psychotic disorder, or other disorders. In

Game of Thrones, the Stark sisters, Sansa and Arya, endure a series of traumas, including deaths, kidnappings, and torture, that cut them off from their past lives and their entire family. Having neither family nor the familiarity of home, they lack the social support that normally would lessen these risks, and ongoing stressors such as domestic violence and combat further complicate their healing. On their precarious journey after the trauma of seeing their father executed, the sister who had dreamed of marrying a prince suffers from imprisonment and torture by him instead and the sister who had yearned to be like the boys must give up her identity and fight to survive on a harrowing journey. What happens to these girls emotionally after this incident, and what might the experiences they endure teach us about real trauma survival?

Trauma

Traumatic Loss and Bereavement

Arguably the first major traumatic event that the Stark sisters experience in the series is the violent death of their father.[3] Bereavement can be difficult to process at any age, but for young children the loss of a parent can be especially traumatic. Young children and adolescents may experience depression, anxiety, guilt, irritability, and social withdrawal after losing a family member.[4]

Children who lose their parents at an early age are likely to display psychological and academic difficulties for one to two years after the death. Specifically, bereaved children are more likely to experience anxiety and underperform in school than are children who have not lost a parent. In fact, as many as 20 percent of children who lose their parents may develop a psychiatric disorder in the year after the death.[5] This effect appears to be more pronounced in girls than in boys.[6] In fact, Sansa goes through a period of depression after her father is killed and she is forced to live with the perpetrators, who constantly torture and humiliate her. She struggles with eating, spends a lot of time sleeping, and cries in her room, shutting herself away from the world.[7] She is isolated in the absence of her mother, father, and siblings.

In addition, the people who are able to overcome tragic losses are often those who have had adequate social support. Specifically, social support in the form of allowing the bereaved person to share his or her feelings, as opposed to advice giving, has been shown to be most helpful in assisting people who are grieving in the recovery process.[8] Unlike Sansa, who is isolated and feels alone even in crowded castles, Arya has support from several people. A warrior loyal to her father protects her at his execution,[9] and during her journey she befriends many others who help her, including developing a bond of sorts with the Hound, an enemy who captures her but also protects and trains her; she is even able to find a loyal group of boys to travel with her for a while. She is never as alone or isolated as her sister is.

Torture

Unfortunately, Sansa does not have a proper support group at King's Landing, and she is also tortured by Joffrey and his men. *Torture* refers to the deliberate infliction of physical or emotional harm.[10] Not only does Joffrey hurt her himself, he has the men of the Kingsguard take turns beating and humiliating her as he insists, "Leave her face; I like her pretty."[11] Such continuous physical and psychological torture makes people more likely to develop PTSD and physical health problems such as chronic pain, hearing problems, and weight loss[12] as well as depression, sleep disorders, anxiety, and personality changes.[13]

The Development of PTSD

Research suggests that PTSD occurs because of the way people think, feel, and act. For example, many people may experience what is called a *fight-flight-or-freeze* response, in which a certain cue in their environment (e.g., a loud noise) may trigger physiological arousal similar to that of being in actual danger. If an individual escapes from the situation or avoids a situation in which these cues may occur, he or she is not likely to learn which situation is actually safe and which is dangerous and may experience "false alarms."[14]

In addition, after a traumatic experience many individuals may change the way they think about themselves or the world.[15] For example, Sansa initially believes that people, in particular knights, are overall good-natured and kind individuals. However, after being in an abusive relationship with Joffrey, she drastically changes her view.[16]

The beliefs that individuals form after a traumatic event sometimes may be at least somewhat exaggerated and may prevent these individuals from recovering from PTSD. Therapists who treat PTSD help trauma survivors challenge and reduce their maladaptive thoughts and reduce their unhelpful avoidance behaviors.[17]

An additional factor that may make an individual more vulnerable to developing PTSD or a related disorder after experiencing torture is related to the individual's identity. Individuals whose identities are changed as a result of trauma are more likely to experience physical and psychological effects of the trauma than are individuals who are able to maintain their own identity.[18] On the surface Sansa and Arya both appear to have lost their identity as each pretends to be someone she is not. Arya initially pretends to be a boy while traveling and changes her name repeatedly, depending on where she lands. Sansa continues to call her late father and her brothers traitors to keep herself safe from Joffrey and Cersei. At their core, though, the personalities of both sisters remain intact. Sansa frequently wishes that her brother Robb would kill Joffrey, and Arya tries to reunite with her family.[19] The ability to stay true to one's own identity as well as the ability to anticipate torture even in the face of the most horrendous circumstances potentially can protect someone against PTSD.[20]

Sexual Assault

Sexual assault, such as the repeated attacks Sansa experiences, can lead to a number of physical and psychological disorders, including PTSD, chronic pain, and sexual disorders.[21] In fact, people who respond passively to an attack, as Sansa is forced to do, and those who are attacked by an intimate partner are more likely to exhibit shame and develop PTSD than are people who were assaulted by a stranger.[22] Sansa experiences both types of trauma.

Additionally, some findings suggest that sexual trauma produces more PTSD symptoms than do other traumas, such as war-related traumas. For example, sexual assault survivors are more likely to experience higher avoidance and higher *hypervigilance* (high alert) symptoms than are the survivors of other traumas.[23] In the television version, we see this in Sansa after she has been sexually assaulted and held captive by her husband,

Ramsay Bolton. Hypervigilance especially can have a negative effect on an individual's health because of the way it affects the brain. Specifically, hypervigilance or chronic stress can activate a person's *hypothalamic-pituitary-adrenal (HPA) axis* (the stress response system in which the nervous system communicates with the endocrine, or hormone, system). When the HPA axis is chronically activated, as it often is after a traumatic experience, the individual may experience anxiety, irritability, sleep difficulties, and higher blood pressure as well as cell death in the brain, which can lead to other illnesses, such as Alzheimer's disease.[24]

Posttraumatic Growth

It is common to think that after a traumatic experience an individual will develop PTSD, but actually that is not usually the case. Most people who experience a traumatic event naturally recover over time, whereas approximately 10 to 20 percent develop PTSD.[25] To be diagnosed with PTSD, a person has to have directly experienced or witnessed a traumatic event, after which he or she has developed a number of symptoms of distress. These symptoms include intrusion symptoms (flashbacks, nightmares), mood changes (anger, guilt, feelings of detachment), hyperarousal and reactivity symptoms (hypervigilance, difficulty concentrating), and avoidance of any trauma-related activities. For a person to be diagnosed with PTSD, these symptoms need to last for at least one month.[26]

Surprisingly, neither Sansa nor Arya ever seems to meet the criteria for PTSD fully. In fact, in the later books in the series they often display the opposite pattern, one indicative of positive psychological changes: *posttraumatic growth* (PTG). Some studies suggest that as many as 30 to 90 percent of individuals who go through a traumatic event may experience PTG.[27] Other findings indicate that after a traumatic event, the survivors are more likely to report posttraumatic growth (74.4 percent) than posttraumatic stress (41.1 percent). However, some people, in particular younger adolescents, are likely to experience both.[28] Finally, some researchers go so far as to say that some trauma survivors, particularly women, are more likely to report positive life changes and satisfaction compared with people who did not undergo a traumatic event.[29]

What are some of the factors that make it more likely that an individual will experience PTG? Some of the most commonly reported *resiliency factors* (factors that prevent an individual from developing PTSD) that help a trauma survivor experience posttraumatic growth include optimism, extraversion, perceived personal control, and social support, to name just a few.[30] In addition, the age and sex of the trauma survivor also seem to play a role in whether that individual will experience PTG. Specifically, younger survivors tend to be more likely to undergo PTG than are older ones,[31] and female survivors are more likely to display PTG than males are.[32] For Sansa and Arya, it seems that this last factor might assist them in not developing PTSD and assist them in developing PTG.

Among all the factors allowing the survivor to develop a sense of posttraumatic growth, the most important one appears to be *meaning making.* Meaning making refers to a newly found sense of purpose that can develop after a traumatic experience.[33] An example of someone who clearly exhibits PTG and uses meaning making is Daenerys, whose tortured past inspire her to end slavery in Astapor, Meereen, and Yunkai.[34]

For both Sansa and Arya, the new sense of purpose includes revenge, and both sisters will learn to see the need for a greater purpose. Arya seeks to kill those who wronged her by making "a list of names"[35] and later killing Ser Meryn Trant.[36] Sansa's need for revenge is there, though it is expressed by her plan to leave King's Landing, her collusion with Petyr Balish, and her humiliation of Joffrey when he is afraid to fight alongside his men. The sisters' hunger for revenge is not uncommon among trauma survivors, in particular those who have lost family members to homicide or other forms of violence.[37] Although research typically suggests that revenge is more likely to intensify the symptoms of grief and PTSD,[38] the Stark sisters find strength and growth on their path to vengeance.

The Path to Recovery

As characters, both Arya and Sansa suffer tragic losses and, to some extent, a loss of identity. However, both young women are able to overcome those traumatic experiences and experience posttraumatic growth. Their age and gender may have been a protective factor against the development of PTSD. By connecting with a new sense of purpose, they are able to face additional challenges and survive, although they have taken vastly different paths to get there.

References

Abdelnoor, A., & Hollins, S. (2004). The effect of childhood bereavement on secondary school performance. *Educational Psychology in Practice, 20*(1), 43–54.

Abrahams, N., Jewkes, R., & Mathews, S. (2013). Depressive symptoms after a sexual assault among women: Understanding victim-perpetrator relationships and the role of social perceptions. *African Journal of Psychiatry, 16*(4), 288–293.

American Psychiatric Association (2013). *Diagnostic and statistical manual of mental disorders* (DSM-5) (5th ed.). Washington, DC: American Psychiatric Association.

Bandura, A. (1986). *Social foundations of thought and action: A social cognitive theory.* Englewood Cliffs, NJ: Prentice-Hall.

Black, K., & Lobo, M. (2008). A conceptual review of family resilience factors. *Journal of Family Nursing, 14*(1), 33–55.

Diehl, M., & Hay, E. L. (2010). Risk and resilience factors in coping with daily stress in adulthood: The role of age, self-concept incoherence, and personal control. *Developmental Psychology, 46*(5), 1132–1146.

Dowdney, L. (2000). Annotation: Childhood bereavement following parental death. *Journal of Child Psychology and Psychiatry, 41*(7), 819–830.

Hárdi, L., & Kroó, A. (2011). The trauma of torture and the rehabilitation of torture survivors. *Zeitschrift für Psychologie, 219*(3), 133–142.

Herringa, R. J., Phillips, M. L., Fournier, J. C., Kronhaus, D. M., & Germain, A. (2013). Childhood and adult trauma both correlate with dorsal anterior cingulate activation to threat in combat veterans. *Psychological Medicine, 43*(7), 1533–1542.

Johnson, H., & Thompson, A. (2008). The development and maintenance of post-traumatic stress disorder (PTSD) in civilian adult survivors of war trauma and torture: A review. *Clinical Psychology Review, 28*(1), 36–47.

Johnson, R. J., Canetti, D., Palmieri, P. A., Galea, S., Varley, J., & Hobfoll, S. E. (2009). A prospective study of risk and resilience factors associated with posttraumatic stress symptoms and depression symptoms among Jews and Arabs exposed to repeated acts of terrorism in Israel. *Psychological Trauma: Theory, Research, Practice, and Policy, 1*(4), 291–311

King, A. P., Abelson, J. L., Britton, J. C., Phan, K. L., Taylor, S. F., & Liberzon, I. (2009). Medial prefrontal cortex and right insula activity predict plasma ACTH response to trauma recall. *Neuroimage, 47*(3), 872–880.

Kuwert, P., Glaesmer, H., Eichhorn, S., Grundke, E., Pietrzak, R. H., Freyberger, H. J., & Klauer, T. (2014). Long-term effects of conflict-related sexual violence compared with non-sexual war trauma in female World War II survivors: A matched pairs study. *Archives of Sexual Behavior, 43*(6), 1059–1064.

Laufer, A., & Solomon, Z. (2006). Posttraumatic symptoms and posttraumatic growth among Israeli youth exposed to terror incidents. *Journal of Social and Clinical Psychology, 25*(4), 429–447.

Lehman, D. R., Ellard, J. H., & Wortman, C. B. (1986). Social support for the bereaved: Recipients' and providers' perspectives on what is helpful. *Journal of Consulting and Clinical Psychology, 54*(4), 438.

Lu, S., Gao, W., Wei, Z., et al. (2013a). Reduced cingulate gyrus volume associated with enhanced cortisol awakening response in young healthy adults reporting childhood trauma. *Plos ONE, 8*(7): http://journals.plos.org/plosone/article?id=10.1371/journal.pone.0069350.

Lu, S., Wei, Z., Gao, W., et al. (2013b). White matter integrity alterations in young healthy adults reporting childhood trauma: A diffusion tensor imaging study. *Australian and New Zealand Journal of Psychiatry, 47*(12), 1183–1190.

Martin, G. R. R. (1996). *A game of thrones.* London, UK: Voyager.

Martin, G. R. R. (1998). *A clash of kings.* New York, NY: Bantam Spectra.

Martin, G. R. R. (2000). *A storm of swords.* London, UK: Voyager.

National Center for PTSD (2014, November 10). *How common is PTSD?* U. S. Department of Veteran Affairs: http://www.ptsd.va.gov/public/PTSD-overview/basics/how-common-is-ptsd.asp.

Padgett, D. A., & Glaser, R. (2003). How stress influences the immune response. *Trends in Immunology, 24*(8), 444–448.

Park, C. L., & Ai, A. L. (2006). Meaning making and growth: New directions for research on survivors of trauma. *Journal of Loss and Trauma, 11*(5), 389–407.

Powell, S., Rosner, R., Butollo, W., Tedeschi, R. G., & Calhoun, L. G. (2003). Posttraumatic growth after war: A study with former refugees and displaced people in Sarajevo. *Journal of Clinical Psychology, 59*(1), 71–83.

Punamäki, R. L., Qouta, S. R., & El-Sarraj, E. (2001). Resiliency factors predicting psychological adjustment after political violence among Palestinian children. *International Journal of Behavioral Development, 25*(3), 256–267.

Punamäki, R. L., Qouta, S. R., & El-Sarraj, E. (2010). Nature of torture, PTSD, and somatic symptoms among political ex-prisoners. *Journal of Traumatic Stress, 23*(4), 532–536.

Resick, P. A., Monson, C. M., & Chard, K. M. (2008) *Cognitive processing therapy veteran/ military version: Therapist's manual.* Washington, D.C.: Department of Veterans Affairs.

Resick, P. A., & Schnicke, M. K. (1992). Cognitive processing therapy for sexual assault victims. *Journal of Consulting and Clinical Psychology, 60*(5), 748–756.

Tedeschi, R. G., & Calhoun, L. G. (1996). The Posttraumatic Growth Inventory: Measuring the positive legacy of trauma. *Journal of Traumatic Stress, 9*(3), 455–471.

Ulirsch, J. C., Ballina, L. E., Soward, A. C., et al. (2014). Pain and somatic symptoms are sequelae of sexual assault: Results of a prospective longitudinal study. *European Journal of Pain, 18*(4), 559–566.

Van Denderen, M., de Keijser, J., Gerlsma, C., Huisman, M., & Boelen, P. A. (2014). Revenge and psychological adjustment after homicidal loss. *Aggressive Behavior, 40*(6), 504–511.

Van Slyke, J. (n. d.). *Post-traumatic growth* (white paper). Naval Center Combat & Opera-tional Stress Control: http://www.med.navy.mil/sites/nmcsd/nccosc/item%28changed %29/post-traumatic-growth-white-paper/index.aspx.

Wheeler, I. (2001). Parental bereavement: The crisis of meaning. *Death Studies, 25*(1), 51–66.

World Medical Association (1975). *The World Medical Association declaration of Tokyo. Guidelines for physicians concerning torture and other cruel, inhuman or degrading treatment or punishment in relation to detention and imprisonment.* World Medical Association: http:// www.wma.net/en/30publications/10policies/c18/.

Notes

1. Martin (1998), p. 96.
2. Bandura (1986), p. 394.
3. Martin (1996).
4. Abdelnoor & Hollins (2004).
5. Dowdney (2000).
6. Abdelnoor & Hollins (2004).
7. Martin (1996).
8. Lehman et al. (1986); Wheeler (2001).
9. Martin (1996); episode 1–9, "Baelor" (June 12, 2011).
10. World Medical Association (1975).
11. Episode 2–4, "Garden of Bones" (April 21, 2012).
12. Punamäki et al. (2010).
13. Hárdi & Kroó (2011).
14. Resick & Schnicke (1992); Resick et al. (2008).
15. Resick & Schnicke (1992); Resick et al. (2008).
16. Episode 2–4, "Garden of Bones" (April 21, 2012).
17. Resick & Schnicke (1992); Resick et al. (2008).
18. Hárdi & Kroó (2011).
19. Episode 1–9, "Baelor" (June 12, 2011).
20. Johnson & Thompson (2008).
21. Kuwert et al. (2014); Ulirsch et al. (2014).
22. Abrahams et al. 2013; Punamäki et al. (2001).
23. Kuwert et al. (2014).

24. Herringa et al. (2013); King et al. (2009); Lu et al. (2013a); Lu et al. (2013b); Padgett & Glaser (2003).
25. National Center for PTSD (2014).
26. American Psychiatric Association (2013).
27. Van Slyke (n.d.).
28. Laufer & Solomon (2006).
29. Tedeschi & Calhoun (1996).
30. Black & Lobo (2008); Diehl & Hay (2010); Johnson et al. (2009); Tedeschi & Calhoun (1996).
31. Powell et al. (2003)
32. Laufer & Solomon (2006).
33. Park & Ai (2006); Wheeler (2001).
34. Martin (1998).
35. Episode 3–5, "Kissed by Fire" (April 28, 2013).
36. Episode 5–10, "Mother's Mercy" (June 14, 2015).
37. Van Denderen et al. (2014).
38. Van Denderen et al. (2014).

Depictions of sexual aggression can and should be unnerving, even controversial, because the topic itself should disturb. Maybe such depictions help us contemplate the nature of real sexual violence, or maybe they're just gratuitous. Forensic psychologist Martin Lloyd takes a look at rapist types, drawing examples from fiction to examine the nature of real sexual offenders.

CHAPTER FIVE

Sex as a Weapon: Rape in the Realms

MARTIN LLOYD

"You know what I saw? Butchery. Babies, children, old men. More women raped than you could count. There's a beast in every man and it stirs when you put a sword in his hand."
—Jorah Mormont[1]

"Rape is primarily used to hurt, defile, and degrade."
—media psychologist Joyce Brothers[2]

Statistics indicate that approximately one in five women will be sexually assaulted in their lifetimes,[3] though this is not to say as large a number of men will perpetrate sexual assaults. What, then, differentiates those who do? Various explanations for rape have been offered over time. Traditionally, rape was viewed as an act of sexual deviance;[4] that is, rapists were thought to be motivated by a desire for sex but differed from others in having uncontrollable urges or actually being aroused by the use of force. More recently, rape has been conceptualized as a means of achieving power and control, with sex being incidental.[5] The totality of the available research indicates that neither explanation, on its own, is entirely true. Different types of rapists exist and they differ in their motivations. The various depictions of actual and attempted sexual assault on *Game of Thrones* illustrate some of these differing motivations.

Dividing Rapists

Given the differing motives of those who rape, various systems have been developed to identify types of rapists, defined by their motives and behaviors. There is no universally agreed-upon system. Rather, various systems have been developed, each serving different purposes. The FBI developed its own.[6] In academic circles, one of the most widely known typologies is the Massachusetts Treatment Center: Revised Rapist Typology.[7] While various revisions have been proposed, this system is still used by professionals to classify rapists. This system identifies five main types based on motivations and offense behavior as noted in Table 5–1.

Rapist Subtype	Motivation
Opportunistic	Impulsivity, often during commission of another crime
Pervasively angry	Generalized anger
Vindictive	Anger toward women
Sexual (Nonsadistic)	Sexual gratification
Sexual (Sadistic)	Inflicting pain for sexual gratification

Power and Control

Sansa Stark is the victim of completed or attempted sexual assault on several occasions. In the first of these, she is dragged off and nearly raped by rioters angry over King Joffrey's policies.[8] Thus, the rape seems to be a pure expression of anger. The attackers do not appear to have any preconceived plans to seek sex, by force or otherwise. Rather, they are starving, angry, and frustrated about the callous policies that left them that way. They seek to lash out, to hurt someone as they had been hurt. In attempting sexual assault to express their anger, Sansa's attackers show characteristics of *pervasively angry* rapists.[9] Such individuals are motivated by anger generalized toward the world at large. Pervasively angry rapists tend not to premeditate sexual assaults; rather, their assaults are crimes of opportunity. Sansa's attackers could not have known that a riot would break out at that time; they simply use the opportunity to lash out. Pervasively angry rapists, ultimately, are not motivated by sex. By extension, Sansa's assailants are not motivated by sexual desire; they just want to hurt someone. In this instance, rape would have been a means of attaining the power they lacked in their own lives.

Many people, both in Westeros and the real world, are angry. Most, however, do not become rapists. What, then, is different about those angry people who turn to rape? One possibility is that pervasively angry rapists have higher levels of psychopathic traits than most other types of rapists.[10] Psychopathy is a cluster of personality traits primarily involving a lack of empathy for others. It breaks down into two broad factors involving emotional deficits and criminal lifestyle. Pervasively angry rapists tend to have high levels of each factor. Thus, they are generally more apt to engage in aggressive or criminal behavior (i.e., the second factor), and so tend to react violently to frustration as a matter of course. By lacking empathy (i.e., the first factor),

Cruelty with a Crown:
A Case of Sexual Sadism

When people derive sexual pleasure from hurting others, they fit a diagnostic category from the *Diagnostic and Statistical Manual of Mental Disorders*: sexual sadism.[11] This disorder is defined by both of the following:

1. Repeatedly becoming sexually aroused by inflicting physical or mental suffering on another.
2. Acting on the urge to hurt someone with someone who does not consent or being disturbed by having this urge, even if one does not act on it.

If any character is sexually aroused by others' suffering, it is Joffrey Baratheon. While there are numerous examples of Joffrey delighting in tormenting others, the sexual sadism is most obvious when he is offered the chance to have sex and chooses violence instead.[12] If anything, Joffrey seems uncomfortable with sex; violence is more natural to him. For him, the needs that sex fulfills for most people are met via torture.

they are free from the normal prohibitions against inflicting pain on others. They can bring themselves to do horrendous things, such as rape, because they genuinely do not care about the victim's experience, nor are they capable of caring. Sansa's attackers, then, are most likely the subset of the angry mob who lack the ability to connect emotionally to others.

A Culture of Rape

One of the best predictors of sexual assault is a trait called *hyper-masculinity*. This trait involves valuing fighting, viewing danger as exciting, and having callous or impersonal attitudes toward sex.[13] In other words, it describes the Dothraki (as depicted) pretty much exactly. As nomadic warriors, they seemingly live to conquer. Once they conquer a people, it is a matter of course for them to rape the women, though Daenerys does put a temporary stop to this practice.[14] Her efforts, however, are met with fierce resistance, as the Dothraki note it is their way to take women as spoils of war. Given the widespread accep-tance of rape in the Dothraki culture, it may not be feasible to conceptualize any individual Dothraki warrior as a subtype of rapist, as in the previous section. There are certain concepts, however, that may explain how a culture can come to embrace such a horrendous act.

Hypermasculinity is the product of socialization. That is, it results from men being taught to be aggressive and dominant and supporting one another in holding aggressive and adversar-ial attitudes toward sex.[15] In the real world, such socialization has been found to occur, among other places, in all-male groups on college campuses.[16] The Dothraki also clearly promote adversarial and aggressive sex, as is apparent in their wedding rituals.[17] These attitudes turn to sexual violence when hyper-masculine men begin to view women as both different and also deficient or even dangerous. This sets up a scenario where women are both desired and feared, leading to an expression of sexual power and control.[18] This is illustrated by the Dothraki's treatment of Mirri Maz Duur, who is raped while also being feared as a witch.[19] Hypermasculinity is a significant issue in any patriarchal society, of which the Dothraki are one. When males hold superior power, that leads to a sense of sexual enti-tlement,[20] which will be discussed in more detail in the next section, and sexual entitlement interacts with hypermasculinity to increase the likelihood of rape.[21] Thus, nearly every aspect of the hypermasculine Dothraki culture leads them to view rape as acceptable.

Rape has historically been a common part of warfare and the victors rape those they conquer. One of the reasons for this is that rape and war are driven by the same masculine values, and warriors are almost universally subject to the male socialization described above.[22] Additionally, many conquerors commit rapes primarily after the fighting has ended, not during combat, as sexual assault can be used as a means of relieving both stress and aggression.[23] The Dothraki are an example of how rape is used during warfare. By committing the rapes at the conclusion of battle, they view the act as exacting vengeance on those who fought against them and a form of dehumanization of the conquered, viewing them as less than human.[24] It is simply easier to mistreat people when they are not afforded the basic rights and dignities of human beings.

Acquaintance Rape

Rape by acquaintances, including within a romantic partnership, is actually more common than stranger rape. In fact, approximately 80 percent of women and girls who are sexually assaulted are assaulted by some form of acquaintance.[25] The factors that motivate such assaults within partnerships are many and varied. Several examples of spousal or partner rape from *Game of Thrones* illustrate some of these motivations, with the most controversial example between Jaime and his sister Cersei in front of their son's corpse (in the television version of the event).[26] While some may contend this was not a rape, any viewing of the scene would suggest otherwise.

In terms of motivation behind this act, Jaime shares many traits already discussed. As a knight, he likely received hypermasculine socialization, being trained to excel in competition and combat at any cost. As a child of privilege, he likely experiences some entitlement. As a father, he experiences grief over his son's murder and feels a sense of failure for not protecting him, all of which are exacerbated by Cersei's blame and rejection. Rape is often preceded by the perpetrator's negative emotions.[27] Additionally, many rapists experience feelings of inadequacy,[28] which Jaime may feel due to the loss of his hand and therefore the martial prowess that had defined him. Ultimately, a confluence of factors led to this assault.

Rape and Lack of Empathy

A subtype of rapists called sadistic rapists derive sexual pleasure from the act of harming or humiliating another.[29] Ramsey Bolton's rape of Sansa on their wedding night[30] exemplifies this type of rapist. While Ramsey clearly enjoys hurting others, seen in his delight at mutilating Theon,[31] it is unclear if he experiences specifically sexual pleasure from the harm, as Joffrey appears to. It is therefore difficult to classify Ramsey as a sadistic rapist. He may well have more in common with the pervasively angry rapists described earlier. He expresses his rage by lashing out at others. Nonetheless, his offenses show substantial evidence of premeditation, which is much more commonly seen in sadistic than pervasively angry rapists.[32] Although the extent of his sexual motivation is unclear, one thing is certain: Ramsey is clearly a psychopath who experiences no empathy for any living thing. The lack of a conscience frees a person to do whatever brings him or her pleasure.

Why Understand the Rapist?

Why take a clinical view of people who rape? Such a scientific or dispassionate analysis serves a specific purpose: It is impossible to solve a problem that is not properly understood. While this chapter does not address the effects on the victims, it is precisely for the victims that studies such as those described herein are conducted. In the real world, as in Westeros, an almost unfathomable number of women and also men are victims of rape. The fault for these acts lies entirely with the aggressors, but the factors that drive these aggressors must be understood if there is ever to be hope for change.

References

American Psychiatric Association (2013). *Diagnostic and statistical manual of mental disorders* (5th ed.). Arlington, VA: American Psychiatric Publishing.

Bergen, R. K. (1996). *Wife rape: Understanding the response of survivors and service providers*. London, UK: Sage.

Black, M. C., Basile, K. C., Breiding, M. J., Smith, S. G., Walters, M. L., Merrick, M. T., Chen, J., & Stevens, M. R. (2011). *The national intimate partner and sexual violence survey (NISVS): 2010 summary report*. Atlanta, GA: National Center for Injury Prevention and Control, Centers for Disease Control and Prevention.

Brothers, J. (1974, March 2). Separate myth from fact on rape. *Chicago Tribune*, 1–17.

Brown, S. L., & Forth, A. E. (1997). Psychopathy and sexual assault: Static risk factors, emotional precursors, and rapist subtypes. *Journal of Consulting and Clinical Psychology, 65*(5), 848–857.

Carr, J. L., & Van Deusen, K. M. (2004). Risk factors for male sexual aggression on college campuses. *Journal of Family Violence, 19*(5), 279–289.

Finkelhor, D., & Yllo, K. (1985). *License to rape: Sexual abuse of wives*. New York, NY: Free Press, Macmillan.

Hazelwood, R. R. (1987). Analyzing the rape and profiling the offender. In R. R. Hazelwood & A. W. Burgess (Eds.), *Practical aspects of rape investigation: A multidisciplinary approach* (pp. 169–199). New York, NY: Elsevier.

Hegeman, N., & Miekle, S. (1980). Motivations and attitudes of rapists. *Canadian Journal of Behavioural Science, 12*(4), 359–372.

Hill, M. S., & Fischer, A. R. (2001). Does entitlement mediate the link between masculinity and rape-related variables? *Journal of Counseling Psychology, 48*(1), 39–50.

Knight, R. A., & Prentky, R. A. (1990). Classifying sexual offenders: The development and corroboration of taxonomic models. In W. L. Marshal, D. R. Laws, & H. E. Barbaree (Eds.), *Handbook of sexual assault: Issues, theories, and treatment of the offender* (pp. 23–52). New York, NY: Plenum Press.

Locke, B. D., & Mahalik, J. R. (2005). Examining masculinity norms, problem drinking, and athletic involvement as predictors of sexual aggression in college men. *Journal of Counseling Psychology, 52*(3), 279–283.

Mosher, D. L., & Sirkin, M. (1984). Measuring a macho personality constellation. *Journal of Research in Personality, 18*(2), 150–163.

National Victim Center & Crime Victims Research and Treatment Center. (1992). *Rape in America: A report to the nation.* Arlington, VA: National Victim Center.

Pemberton, A. E., & Wakeling, H. C. (2009). Entitled to sex: Attitudes of sexual offenders. *Journal of Sexual Aggression, 15*(3), 289–303.

Peters, J., Nason, C., & Turner, W. M. (2007). Development and testing of a new version of the Hypermasculinity Index. *Social Work Research, 31*(3), 171–182.

Vikman, E. (2005). Modern combat: Sexual violence in warfare, part II. *Anthropology and Medicine, 12*(1), 33–46.

Zurbriggen, E. L. (2010). Rape, war, and the socialization of masculinity: Why our refusal to give up war ensures rape cannot be eradicated. *Psychology of Women Quarterly, 34*(4), 538–549.

Notes

1. Episode 3–3, "Walk of Punishment" (April 14, 2013).
2. Brothers (1974), p. 1–17.
3. Black et al. (2011).
4. Hegeman & Miekle (1980).
5. Hegeman & Miekle (1980).
6. Hazelwood (1987).
7. Knight & Prentky (1990).
8. Episode 2–6, "The Old Gods and the New" (May 6, 2012).
9. Knight & Prentky (1990).
10. Brown & Forth (1997).
11. American Psychiatric Association (2013).
12. Episode 2–4, "Garden of Bones" (April 22, 2012).
13. Mosher & Sirkin (1984).
14. Episode 1–8, "The Pointy End" (June 5, 2011).
15. Reviewed in Carr & Van Deusen (2004).
16. Carr & Van Deusen (2004); Locke & Mahalik (2005).
17. Episode 1–1, "Winter is Coming" (April 17, 2011).
18. Reviewed in Peters, Nason, & Turner (2007).
19. Episode 1–8, "The Pointy End" (June 5, 2011).
20. Reviewed in Carr & Van Deusen (2004).
21. Hill & Fischer (2001).
22. Zurbriggen (2010).
23. Vikman (2005).
24. Vikman (2005).
25. National Victim Center (1992).
26. Episode 4–3, "Breaker of Chains" (April 20, 2014).
27. Brown & Forth (1997).
28. Reviewed in Hegeman & Miekle (1980).
29. Knight & Prentky (1990).
30. Episode 5–6, "Unbowed, Unbent, Unbroken" (May 17, 2015).
31. Episode 3–7, "The Bear and the Maiden Fair" (May 12, 2013).
32. Brown & Forth (1997).

P ain, loss, irritation, and suffering of many kinds can feel like torture at the time. In cases of intentional torture, someone actively inflicts suffering upon another. But why? What inspires the torturer? How deeply does it wound the tortured and in what ways? Can the victim ever be the same?

CHAPTER SIX

The Breaking of a Man: Torture and Transformation

COLT J. BLUNT

"Power is in tearing human minds to pieces and putting them together again in new shapes of your own choosing."
—author George Orwell[1]

The world of *Game of Thrones* is a harsh environment filled with death and despair, but one character, Theon Greyjoy, receives a sentence that is arguably worse than death. The last surviving son of Balon Greyjoy, Lord of the Iron Islands, Theon is introduced as a proud, arrogant man trying to find his place in Westeros but becomes someone vastly different when he experiences torture at the hands of a madman. What purpose does Theon's torture serve? Is a victim of torture likely to reveal useful information in such circumstances? How might the long-term experience of torture affect someone's personality? Psychology has been on both sides of the torture game, providing research in opposition to the practice and being complicit in its practice.[2]

Torture at the Hands of a Madman

Torture, the infliction of physical or psychological pain to punish or coerce, is a practice that often is reviled and seen as barbaric in modern society. The United Nations (UN) has taken a staunch stance against the use of torture by its member nations. However, torture continues to exist in one form or another in contemporary society. Even the United States, a country with constitutional protections against cruel and unusual punishment, has a recent track record of engaging in forms of torture (e.g., waterboarding, sensory deprivation, and sleep deprivation) during interrogations. As mentioned above, even the field of psychology is not innocent of acts of torture in the United States. However, in the land of Westeros, where morality and law are at best dictated by the decrees of lords and monarchs, no protections are guaranteed.

In the simplest sense, torture can be said to have three goals: (1) extracting information, (2) forcing a confession to a crime, and (3) inflicting punishment. Methods of torture historically have varied widely among societies but often have showcased the darkest reaches of human ingenuity. The severity of torture typically varied significantly, with some methods designed to inflict no lasting harm (e.g., foot whipping) and others resulting in gross disfigurement, dismemberment, or even death (e.g., submerging the victim in a boiling liquid). The chosen methods varied by civilization and period but also depended on the social standing of the subject and the purpose of the torture (i.e., interrogation versus punishment). The more memorable forms of torture have included stretch-

Torture in British Legal Proceedings

The modern field of forensic psychology, including the concept of competency to stand trial, has ties to the practice of torture in the past. In the seventeenth and eighteenth centuries, English jurisprudence required the accused to enter a plea before the trial could proceed. If defendants failed to enter a plea, they were considered to be either "mute of malice" (voluntary) or "mute by visitation of God" (involuntary). The courts ultimately settled on the practice of pressing, which involves placing increasing weights of stones on the chest of the accused until they spoke or were crushed. Those who screamed out were considered to be mute of malice, and those who were silent until death were considered to be mute by visitation of God.[3]

In place of torture, modern forensic psychology utilizes a thorough interview, observation, a review of records, and consultation with collateral sources to determine whether a defendant is competent to stand trial. In cases in which the *etiology* (cause) of the defendant's behavior is in question, such as situations in which the defendant is believed to be faking a mental illness, forensic psychologists utilize specific tests to determine the veracity of the defendant's symptomatology.

ing (such as on the rack), whipping, burning, stoning, and thumbscrews; the iron maiden, perhaps the most stereotypical instrument of torture, is now believed to have been fictitious or the result of multiple artifacts being conflated erroneously. One of the most sinister torture devices was the brazen bull. This device, which was used in ancient Greece, was a life-size hollow bronze cast of a bull. Victims, often criminals, were placed inside the bull, which then was placed over a roaring fire, roasting them to death.[4] Similar to House Bolton, the Assyrians were believed to have skinned or flayed their prisoners alive.[5]

Theon's torture at the hands of Ramsay appears to have little purpose other than amusing Ramsay and satisfying his sociopathic tendencies. The information sought from Theon while he is being "questioned" is largely immaterial to the efforts of House Bolton. That is beneficial for House Bolton because, although it was believed historically that information obtained through torture was likely to be accurate,[6] more recent experts have expressed concern that torture is unlikely to result in useful information or accurate confession as its victims are likely to say whatever they feel may result in an end to the torture or to mislead torturers purposely.[7] In the case of Theon, it is equally difficult to argue that the torture is for the purpose of punishment, since Ramsay does not let Theon go or cease torturing him once House Bolton changes allegiance and targets House Stark. Thus, it appears most likely that Theon's torture is intrinsically rewarding to the sadistic Ramsay (see Chapter 14, "Ramsay: Portrait of a Serial Killer").

Theon experiences both physical and psychological torture at the hands of Ramsay. Physical torture is easier to identify. Theon is beaten while strapped to a rack, has his teeth broken, has screws placed in his feet, and has his fingernails

THE BREAKING OF A MAN

removed; in addition, his finger is flayed and parts of his body are amputated. All this serves to destroy Theon's self-identity and self-worth and ultimately lead to his becoming Reek. By its very nature, physical torture is likely to cause significant psychological distress as manifested by rapid heart rate, elevated blood pressure, and other hallmark indicators of stress and anxiety.[8] In the television series, some sessions of torture are preceded by Ramsay sounding a trumpet, which could result in a classically conditioned response. *Classical conditioning* occurs when a previously neutral stimulus (in this case the trumpet) is paired with a stimulus (torture) that causes a natural response (Theon's psychological distress). With time, Theon could come to experience such distress merely at the sound of a trumpet regardless of the presence of actual physical torture. However, Ramsay is not consistent in his methods; as a result, much of Theon's torture cannot be predicted, and thus he comes to accept that he could be tortured at any time and in any way. A person in such an environment eventually will exhibit signs of *learned helplessness*: the tendency among those subjected to repeated aversive stimuli to learn that they cannot control the situation and therefore take no action to avoid it. Theon's learned helplessness progresses to the point where he can be released from his restraints because Ramsay is confident that he will not try to escape.

In addition to physical torture, a captured person such as Theon often experiences severe psychological torture. He is kept alone in a dark cell for a significant period, resulting in sensory deprivation. *Sensory deprivation* (the removal of external sources of stimuli, such as being placed in a dark room without sound) alone can lead to mental health symptomatology, including anxiety, depression, and psychosis.[9] Food and water are withheld from him, including incidents in which they are

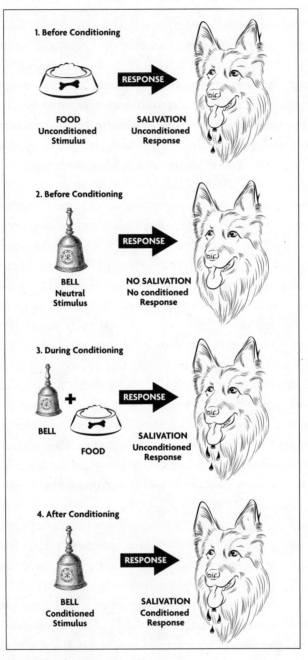

Classical Conditioning

dumped on the floor beyond his reach. Ramsay forces Theon to play a game in which incorrect answers result in the flaying of his finger. At one point, Ramsay allows Theon to escape and get a taste of freedom before recapturing him and making it clear that he will never be free of his torturer. Like any accomplished torturer, Ramsay is able to read his victim to determine Theon's fears, weaknesses, and breaking point. The most sinister example of Theon's torture is the amputation of his penis, destroying his identity and effectively ending the Greyjoy bloodline. Through physical torture combined with psychological torture, Ramsay breaks Theon, and Theon gives up and seems to accept that Ramsay is in control and always will be. At that point, Theon becomes Reek and his willingness to adopt that role allows him to *dissociate*, essentially distancing himself emotionally from the horrors he endured and continues to endure.

Physical and Psychological Effects of Torture

Torture has both immediate and long-term effects. The immediate effects are much easier to identify. Physically, subjects can experience broken bones, burns, lacerations, punctures, tears, bruises, damaged organs, concussions, and brain damage. Psychologically, subjects can experience extreme fear and anxiety.[10] The effects, both physical and mental, often do not cease when the torture ends. Physical injuries received during torture often are not given proper medical attention; thus, broken bones do not heal correctly; cuts are not disinfected or sutured, increasing the potential for scarring and infection; and more serious injuries, such as those to the organs or head, can result in system failures, cognitive deficits, epilepsy, dementia, or death.[11] Beyond ongoing medical issues, surviving the physical effects of torture can lead to significant psychological issues similar to those sustained by soldiers or survivors of disasters. Crippled or amputated limbs and internal injuries that require medical oversight or assistance can affect the quality of life significantly and lead to anxious and depressive symptoms, including hopelessness, social withdrawal, social anxiety, lack of motivation to engage in daily life, and suicidality.[12] Even superficial injuries such as scars and burns can serve as reminders of the torture, calling up bad memories whenever the survivor sees them in the mirror or is asked about them. This can lead to survivors being hypersensitive about their external injuries and believing they are always the focus of the people they encounter in their day-to-day lives. In the books, Theon's torture is shown to result in significant physical changes as he presents as emaciated and appears to have aged greatly, to the extent that he is virtually unrecognizable to those who knew him before his capture.[13]

A large percentage of torture survivors experience long-term psychological effects.[14] The most likely manifestation of this is *posttraumatic stress disorder* (PTSD), which involves reexperiencing traumatic events, avoidance of similar situations, psychological distress when involved in analogous situations, hypervigilance, changes in behavior, a feeling of detachment from reality, and dissociation. However, PTSD in its current formulation largely focuses on individuals who have experienced circumscribed trauma, such as those who have been involved in major accidents, natural disasters, or other near-death experiences. Researchers and clinicians have long described a distinct form of PTSD secondary to prolonged trauma that has been called *complex PTSD*. Trauma survivors with complex PTSD experience symptoms that are often more difficult to treat, display personality changes, and are vulnerable to future harm that can be self-inflicted or come at the hands of others.[15]

Complex PTSD may explain many of Theon's reactions and changes in response to his prolonged torture, most notably his extreme shift in personality structure and his changing concept of identity. Indeed, research with torture survivors in Turkey[16] suggests that the effects of torture are chronic and are unlikely to abate with time. The same researchers found increased depression among torture survivors who had insufficient social support. Complex PTSD has not been codified as a separate disorder in the *Diagnostic and Statistical Manual for Mental Disorders* (DSM)[17] but instead is considered a variation that some researchers and clinicians have observed.[18]

Survivors of torture are likely to generalize stimuli and associate them with their traumatic experiences. For instance, Theon may be frightened by the sound of trumpets years after his torture has ended. The sight of someone bearing even a slight resemblance to Ramsay may cause him to have intense flashbacks, cripple him with fear, or even activate his fight-or-flight response, causing him to either flee or lash out.

In the real world, PTSD often requires long-term treatment by qualified mental health professionals; even with treatment, many of the victims continue to experience symptoms. In a world in which psychological issues are dealt with by a trip to the maester for a draught of dreamwine, it is unlikely that Theon will ever receive any treatment that will free him from his trauma. Furthermore, Theon is a pariah in the eyes of his biological and adopted families, and so they are unlikely to provide the support necessary to heal him.

Stockholm Syndrome

Stockholm syndrome, named after a 1973 Swedish bank robbery[19] involving the taking of hostages, is the phenomenon in which captives are thought to develop a trust in and bond with their captors. However, this does not necessarily mean that the bond is meaningful or genuine. Contrary to the romanticized view of Stockholm syndrome (and I mean that literally as there are scores of romance novels with this premise), researchers[20] have hypothesized that it is an unconscious attempt by the hostage to avoid punishment by the captor rather than bona fide affection. Victims in captivity may actively refuse rescue or speak positively of their captors even in situations in which their actions are incongruent with their actual feelings. This appears all but assured in the case of Theon, who rejects his sister's aid in the television series, probably out of fear that the rescue attempt will fail, and frequently praises Ramsay both in his presence and in the presence of others. Perhaps the most salient example of this is Theon's willingness to betray the ironborn, the very people whose praise he was trying to gain by conquering Winterfell. It is ultimately fear and the avoidance of further torture rather than love that explains Theon's apparent loyalty to Ramsay. However, when pushed, Theon comes to the aid of Ramsay's abused bride (Sansa in the television series,[21] Jeyne Poole in the books[22]) and makes a hasty escape into the frozen north toward either salvation or further torment.

The Transformation

Ramsay, a master of human deconstruction, successfully tears apart everything that makes Theon who he is. After unrelenting physical and psychological torture, Theon enters a state of learned helplessness, realizing that further resistance would yield nothing but continued pain and torture. As was noted above, the personality and identity of a torture survivor experiencing complex PTSD such as Theon change and shift, especially when the victim gives up and no longer believes that freedom is possible. Theon, devoid of hope and spirit, believes he is no longer Theon but rather a blank canvas awaiting the brushstrokes of his master. He lets go, assuming the identity chosen by Ramsay. He emerges as Reek, his master's servant.

In contrast to Theon, Reek is meek and subservient. The Boltons must restrain Theon to keep him captive, but not Reek, who exists to please and serve his master, probably as a product of Stockholm syndrome. Reek holds no allegiance to those who knew Theon and dreads the times when his master orders him to pretend to be Theon; he has been conditioned to assume this new identity of Reek, and being Theon forces him to relive his torture, abuse, and destruction. Reek lives in fear and is reminded constantly of the cost of disobeying. Although a person eventually may escape from torture, it is safe to say that that person will be changed forever and severely and bear little resemblance to the person he or she was before being victimized.

References

American Psychiatric Association (2013). *Diagnostic and statistical manual of mental disorders* (5th ed.). Washington, DC: American Psychiatric Association.

Basoglu, M., Paker, M., Ozmen, E., Tasdemir, O., & Sahin, D. (1994). Factors related to long-term traumatic stress responses to survivors of torture in Turkey. *Journal of the American Medical Association, 272*(5), 357–363.

Black, E. G. (1927). Torture under English law. *University of Pennsylvania Law Review and American Law Register, 75*(4), 344–348.

Bradley, L., & Tawfiq, N. (2006). The physical and psychological effects of torture in Kurds seeking asylum in the United Kingdom. *Torture, 16*(1), 41–47.

Franklin, J. (2009). Evidence gained from torture: Wishful thinking, checkability, and extreme circumstances. *Cardozo Journal of International and Comparative Law, 17*(2), 281–290.

Grassian, S. (2006). Psychiatric effects of solitary confinement. *Washington University Journal of Law and Policy, 22*(1), 325–383.

Herman, J. L. (1992). Complex PTSD: A syndrome in survivors of prolonged and repeated trauma. *Journal of Traumatic Stress, 5*(3), 377–391.

Hoffman, D. H., Carter, D. H., Viglucci Lopez, C. R., Benzmiller, H. L., Guo, A. X., Latifi, S. Y., & Craig, D. C. (2015, July 2). *Report to the special committee of the board of directors of the American Psychological Association: Independent review relating to APA ethics guidelines, national security interrogations, and torture.* http://www.apa.org/independent -review/APA-FINAL-Report-7.2.15.pdf.

Janoff-Bulman, R. (2007). Erroneous assumptions: Popular belief in the effectiveness of torture interrogation. *Peace and Conflict: Journal of Peace Psychology, 13*(4), 429–435.

Jung, E. G. (2007). *Kleine Kulturgeschichte der Haut* [A brief cultural history of skin]. Darmstadt, Germany: Steinkopff Verlag.

Klein, C. (2013, August 23). *The birth of "Stockholm syndrome," 40 years ago.* http://www. history.com/news/stockholm-syndrome.

Martin, G. R. R. (2011). *A dance with dragons.* London, UK: Voyager.

Melusky, J. A. (2011). From burning at the stake to lethal injections: Evolving standards of decency and methods of execution. *National Social Science Proceedings, 46*(2), 152–162.

O'Mara, S. (2011). On the imposition of torture, an extreme stressor state, to extract information from memory. *Zeitschrift für Psychologie, 219*(3), 159–166.

Orwell, G. (1949/1977). *1984.* New York, NY: Penguin.

Quiroga, J., & Jaranson, M. (2005). Politically-motivated torture and its survivors: A desk study review of the literature. *Torture, 16*(2–3), 1–111.

Rasmussen, A., Rosenfeld, B., Reeves, K., & Keller, A. S. (2007). The effects of torture-related injuries on long-term psychological distress in a Punjabi Sikh temple. *Journal of Abnormal Psychology, 116*(4), 734–740.

Roth, S., Newman, E., Pelcovitz, D., Van Der Kolk, B., & Mandel, F. S. (1997). Complex PTSD in victims exposed to sexual and physical abuse: Results from the DSM-IV field trial for posttraumatic stress disorder. *Journal of Traumatic Stress, 10*(4), 539–555.

Strentz, T. (1980). Stockholm syndrome: Law enforcement policy and ego defenses of the hostage. *Annals of the New York Academy of Sciences, 347*, 137–150.

Notes

1. Orwell (1949/1977).
2. Hoffman et al. (2015).
3. Black (1927).
4. Melusky (2011).
5. Jung (2007).
6. Janoff-Bulman (2007).
7. Franklin (2009).
8. O'Mara (2011).
9. Grassian (2006).
10. O'Mara (2011).
11. Rasmussen et al. (2007).
12. Quiroga & Jaranson (2005).
13. Martin (2011).
14. Bradley & Tawfiq (2006).
15. Herman (1992).
16. Basoglu et al. (1994).

17. American Psychiatric Association (2013).
18. Roth et al. (1997).
19. Klein (2013).
20. Strentz (1980).
21. Episode 5–10, "Mother's Mercy" (June 14, 2015).
22. Martin (2011).

Liberty and security can conflict. Is it better to suffer the risks and dangers of unyielding freedom or bow knee before a liege who rules us? Do we oppose those whose walls protect us? Who relinquishes freedom to feel safe, and who would rather run free?

CHAPTER SEVEN

To Kneel or Not to Kneel: Choosing Between Freedom and Security

ERIN CURRIE

"It's dangerous being free, but most come to like the taste o' it."
—Ygritte[1]

> *"Man still is anxious and tempted to surrender his freedom to dictators of all kinds, or to lose it by transforming himself into a small cog in the machine, well fed, and well clothed, yet not a free man. . . ."*
> —psychologist Erich Fromm[2]

To kneel or not to kneel, that is the question. If the answer is yes, then to whom does one kneel? This is a matter of life or death in Westeros. Psychologist Erich Fromm pondered this question as he tried to explain why the people of Germany submitted to the fascist Nazi regime, allowing their individual identities to be overtaken by a larger cultural identity. He wanted to know why people give up personal freedom with seeming enthusiasm. In his book *Escape from Freedom*, Fromm theorizes about why, how, and in what circumstances people sacrifice freedom. The wide cast of characters makes *Game of Thrones* an excellent fictional laboratory in which one can see Fromm's theory in action as characters decide whether to pursue individual freedom or to "kneel" and sacrifice their freedom.

The Basic Human Dilemma: Fromm's Freedom Versus Security

According to Fromm, people innately desire *positive freedom*: the ability to grow into—and live as—one's true self. Free people are aware of their individual needs, values, strengths, and weaknesses. They take responsibility for their actions and the resulting consequences, whether good or bad. This allows them to create genuine connections and healthy relationships with other people.

The desire for positive freedom is expressed first through curiosity and exploration of the world.[3] Bran Stark explores all of Winterfell by climbing the castle's walls. On the rooftops he can see the workings of his whole world. He learns about the lives of the people who serve his family, something he might never have seen if he had stayed on the ground. As exploration continues and adventures range farther from the protection of family, exposure to the world's chaos is inevitable and awareness of one's relative powerlessness in the larger world develops.[4] For Bran, curiosity and his rooftop view of the world end up being his downfall when he discovers the queen's incestuous relationship. His experience of powerlessness begins when the queen's brother pushes him out of the window, and it continues with the loss of the use of his legs and his greater dependence on others.

According to Fromm, people also seek who they truly are—the *authentic self*. Unfortunately, their self-exploration is limited by parents who try to teach them the rules for acceptable behavior in their community.[5] Arya is fierce for a highborn girl. She is thrilled when she gets a sword from her brother and lessons in how to use it. All this has to be done in secret by her father because her authentic "unladylike" behavior is disapproved of in their community. The consequence of social disapproval often takes the form of being set apart from others.[6] Social isolation is psychologically harmful, and most people fear the resulting increase in vulnerability.[7] True to Fromm's theory, Arya's mother punishes her for her unladylike behaviors with separation from her family: She frequently is sent to her room and left there alone.

Through the experiences of vulnerability and isolation it is easy to come to fear the freedom one naturally desires. Feeling safe, feeling that life is certain and predictable, is a powerful natural desire.[8] During times of insecurity, when it is impossible to balance safety and freedom, each person must choose which one he or she will pursue and which one he or she will sacrifice. Characters who choose to strive for positive freedom must face their fears boldly and be true to themselves. The rest seek new sources of security; Fromm calls this *escape from freedom*.[9]

Choosing Security Over Freedom

"Is there not also . . . besides an innate desire for freedom,
an instinctive wish for submission?"
—psychologist Erich Fromm[10]

There are several roads people can choose to escape from freedom, and those roads are well traveled. They range from relatively benign to exceedingly violent. According to Fromm, the most common and benign road for avoiding being alone and feeling powerless is simple *conformity*. By actively taking on the physical and psychological characteristics and behaviors preferred by one's family and community (conforming), one is more likely to be accepted by that community and ultimately be protected by it. A prime example of conformity, Sansa is able to take on the characteristics and behaviors of a proper lady with ease and is rewarded for her conformity by her betrothal to the heir to the throne, thus gaining more access to power. Later, in the face of abuse by the royal family, she "hides behind courtesy as if it's a castle wall,"[11] trying to win her safety by being "the perfect Lady."

Unfortunately for some characters, their natural physical or psychological characteristics are too different from what is considered normal for them to be able to blend in; an example would be Tyrion's height (physical) and the sharp wit he uses to compensate for his physical appearance (psychological). As a result, he is denied his birthright, the lordship of Casterly Rock, and the power that comes with it.

Authoritarianism

A second road that people can choose to avoid the fear inherent in an authentic life is authoritarianism.[12] People who choose authoritarianism believe that those with less power must submit to those with more power.[13] In Westeros, power usually is inherited. Lords pass their title, property, and authority over the common folk to their oldest sons. Groups and institutions such as religion also can have power and inspire submission. Regardless of the details, Fromm describes authoritarianism as a symbiotic relationship between the dominant and the submissive.

Submission

Westeros is full of dangers, and greater awareness of one's mortality is associated with greater motivation to identify with a more powerful entity.[14] Therefore, the characters find another person, group, or higher power to which they can bind themselves in submission. They submit their will to the other entity, and then all their decisions are made for them. In theory, the entity then takes all the risks. In return, they feel powerful by association. This is the living definition of "bending the knee."

Brienne of Tarth chooses submission by pledging her sword and her service to others. Her early attempts to follow the path appropriate for a lady of a noble house lead to humiliation and rejection because of her inability to conform to Westerosi social ideals. Because she is unable to find a socially sanctioned role that is suitable to her, she pledges her life to those who see her as having worth.

In both submission and conformity, the characters must thwart the continued impulse toward freedom. To do this, they must separate themselves completely from their authentic thoughts, feelings, and desires. Eventually the characters who fully commit to kneeling lose their sense of self, the sense of "I am." To fill this void of identity, they fully take on the identity and values of the entity to whom they have submitted. For instance, they may say, "I am a Lannister," "I am a man of the Night's Watch," or "I am Renly's man/woman."

Domination

Only someone who needs others can feel the need to control others.[15] The dominant characters want someone to submit to them as much as the submissive characters want someone to dominate them. The dominant characters avoid the fear of isolation and powerlessness by means of dependence on others. They delude themselves that they are truly immune from the dangers of the world by surrounding themselves with those over whom they have power.

Many characters in *Game of Thrones* seek domination as a reaction against powerlessness. Petyr "Littlefinger" Baelish is an excellent example. As the son of a lesser lord, he is denied what he wants most in his formative years: Catelyn Stark. As an adult with a keen mind for manipulation and making money, Littlefinger increases his influence. By using that influence, he builds relationships in which people of power are obligated to give him what he wants whether they realize it or not.

Domination may seem like the best option for escaping from freedom and its difficulties. Who wouldn't want the power to get what he or she wants? It is not that easy, though. Fromm points out that staying on top requires a lot of work because there are always people trying to take one's place. Juggling personal favors, debts, and intrigues is a full-time job. Littlefinger is a slave to his own power whether *he* realizes it or not.

Sadomasochistic Extremes

Masochism and sadism are the extreme ends of the submission–domination dynamic. According to Fromm, physical pain and humiliation create an even stronger wall of separation from the self and a closer relationship between the sadist and the masochist. This dynamic plays out in Theon Greyjoy's worst hours as Reek. Ramsay Snow fully breaks him by using physical and psychological torture.[16] Overwhelming helplessness is created when neither action nor inaction guarantees safety or relief from pain.[17] Thus, Theon's safest immediate option is to disconnect from himself and become Reek, loyal to Ramsay to the point where he acts against his own best interests, including turning away those who have come to save him.[18]

Sadists create a dependent relationship that they can control, giving them a sense of security. As a lord's "bastard," Ramsay has a precarious place in the world, and he knows it. His sadism stems from the fear of this powerlessness. Feeling powerless, he uses his role as his lord father's designated torturer to break the will of Theon, a trueborn heir of a prideful house. Now he has a lordling doing his bidding and the approval of his powerful father.

Destructiveness

The third major road for escaping from isolation and powerlessness is destructiveness. Those who choose destruction are trying to eliminate any person or group they see as a potential threat, and they tend to enjoy doing it.[19] In Westeros, threats include actual physical danger and loss of wealth or position. Even threats to one's esteem, including suggestions of weakness or destruction of a family's honor, are taken seriously.[20] Joffrey Baratheon is one of the characters who use destructiveness in reaction against powerlessness. Woe to those who kneel to King Joffrey seeking security. They will not be receiving it. In fact, they may find themselves short a head.

Destruction is different from choosing violence as a way of dealing with real immediate threats. For a destructive person, violence is an ongoing tendency.[21] This appetite for violence does not necessarily require a real threat.[22] Compared with those characters whose acts of violence are clearly justified, Joffrey often uses violence for his personal amusement. When he uses destruction strategically, it is often to silence those who would dare question his authority.[23]

Destruction is also different from sadism. Although physical injury is part of the sadist's repertoire, the sadist's ultimate goal is to cement a relationship with the people he or she hurts. It is very difficult to have a relationship with someone who is dead. Joffrey's use of violence does not have the incredible intimacy of Ramsay's torture of Theon, and he has no problem putting people to death.

Choosing Freedom Over Security

Although it is difficult, some characters work toward positive freedom. These characters face their fears of isolation and powerlessness and their self-doubt and pursue a life characterized by loyalty to the whole authentic self. By doing this they are able to create real connections to other people and the larger world around them.

The *whole authentic self* includes connection with one's physical body, including using it to its fullest glorious potential. Going against the conventions of mainstream psychoanalysts in his time, Fromm recommended connecting with our basic instincts, including sex and procreation. The Sand Snakes in

Dorne and the wildlings each provide a glimpse into the lives of those who fully embrace sexuality.[24]

From a psychological perspective, the authentic self includes a person's natural personality traits, aptitudes, and innate tendency toward curiosity. Children may offer the best example of this authenticity. [25] They are spontaneously and truly themselves, seeking to understand their world by exploring and asking questions.[26] Jojen Reed and Bran Stark both embrace their psychic abilities and try to improve them. They make the dangerous journey north of the Wall knowing that their destinies involve using their special abilities. Without the "guidance" of adults, they are free to rely on their instincts, their cunning, and each other.

The best example of a community that chooses positive freedom may be the wildlings north of the Wall: the Free Folk. Individuality and freedom are highly valued among the Free Folk, and so they see the unquestioning obedience of the "kneelers" south of the Wall as a weakness. Positions of power are earned instead of inherited. The people who follow Mance Rayder choose to do so because he has proved his strength and intelligence in the face of a threat they know they cannot overcome alone.

As Fromm's theory predicts, interpersonal relationships north of the Wall tend to be authentic. People who are honest with themselves are better at being honest with one another. Ygritte makes it clear that women are free to love whomever they deem worthy. Although she tells Jon Snow that she is his because he stole her, she also tells him that if she didn't want him, she would be done with him even if she had to kill him. She later tries to make good on that threat when she puts an arrow through his leg as he escapes to the Wall.[27]

Freedom includes having an authentic relationship to one's environment. The Free Folk are connected to the land. They live from day to day, hunting and provisioning as needed. Each person is expected to be responsible for his or her own welfare. Yet they also work together, contributing their skills to their larger clan or community. They know that life is hard, and they don't hide from that truth.

The Struggle for Freedom

Choosing to kneel instead of taking the difficult path toward freedom is easy to understand when the ruler is honorable. Ned Stark values justice, protection, and honor and deals with his followers on the basis of those principles. The characters who choose to submit to people who torture and kill their followers are harder to understand. Even when one knows the struggles of the road to freedom, it is hard to imagine giving up one's freedom to monsters, whether fictional kings or historical fascists.

The people of Westeros are raised with the expectation that they will submit to authoritarian rule. For them it is the natural order. People tend to focus on information and experiences that support their beliefs while filtering out anything to the contrary.[28] The Westerosi protect themselves from the reality of being submissive to rulers who hurt them instead of protecting them by singing songs of long-dead noble kings and knights and kind beautiful queens. They disparage freedom by creating fantastic stories of depravity and violence about the Free Folk. However, Dalla of the Free Folk says it best:

> Free Folk and kneelers are more alike than not, Jon Snow. Men are men and women women, no matter which side of the wall we were born on. Good and bad, heroes and villains, men of honor, liars, cravens, brutes . . . we have plenty, as do you.[29]

The strength of the characters in *Game of Thrones* who are facing the fear of isolation, powerlessness, and violence to pursue their true selves is admirable. Jon Snow tries to follow his family's values of protecting the less powerful by trying to save the Free Folk from the Others. Samwell Tarly is finally on his way to becoming a maester. Daenerys Targaryen attempts to be a just leader of free people. Only time and the rest of the series will show us who ultimately will become fully free and authentic people. Perhaps Westeros one day will be a community of truly Free Folk.

References

Abramson, L. Y., Seligman, M. E. P., & Teasdale, J. D. (1978). Learned helplessness in humans: Critique and reformulation. *Journal of Abnormal Psychology, 87*(1), 49–74.

Cacciopo, J. T., & Cacciopo, S. (2014). Social relationships and health: The toxic effects of perceived social isolation. *Social and Personality Psychology Compass, 8*(2), 58–72.

Dunwoody, P. T., Plane, D. L., Trescher, S. A., & Rice, D. (2014). Authoritarianism, social dominance, and misperceptions of war. *Peace and Conflict: Journal of Peace Psychology, 20*(3), 256–266.

Elbert, T., Weierstall, R., & Schauer, M. (2010). Fascination violence: On mind and brain of man hunters. *European Archives of Psychiatry and Clinical Neuroscience, 260*(Supp. 2), S100–S105.

Fromm, E. (1969). *Escape from freedom.* New York, NY: Holt.

Greenberg, J., Schimel, J., Martens, A., Solomon, S. & Pyszczynski, T. (2001). Sympathy for the Devil: Evidence that reminding whites of their mortality promotes more favorable reactions to white racists. *Motivation and Emotion, 25*(2), 113–132.

Levitt, S. D., & Dubner, S. J. (2014). *Think like a freak.* New York, NY: HarperCollins Publishers.

Martin, G. R. R. (1996). *A game of thrones.* London, UK: Voyager.

Martin, G. R. R. (1999). *A clash of kings.* London, UK: Voyager.

Martin, G. R. R. (2000). *A storm of swords.* New York, NY: Bantam Spectra.

Martin, G. R. R. (2005). *A feast for crows.* London, UK: Voyager.

Martin, G. R. R. (2011). *A dance of dragons.* New York, NY: Bantam Spectra.

Maslow, A. H. (1943). A theory of human motivation. *Psychological Review, 50*(4), 370–396.

Nickerson, R. S. (1998). Confirmation bias: A ubiquitous phenomenon in many guises. *Review of General Psychology, 2*(2), 175–220.

Sandseter, E. B. H. (2012). Restrictive safety or unsafe freedom? Norwegian ECEC practitioners' perceptions and practices concerning children's risky play. *Child Care in Practice, 18*(1), 83–101.

Walker, J. S. & Bright, J. A. (2009). False inflated self-esteem and violence: A systematic review and cognitive model. *Journal of Forensic Psychiatry and Psychology, 20*(1), 1–32.

Notes

1. Martin (2000), p. 93.
2. Fromm (1969), p. xiii.
3. Sandseter (2012).
4. Fromm (1969).
5. Fromm (1969).
6. Fromm (1969).
7. Cacciopo & Cacciopo (2014).
8. Maslow (1943).
9. Fromm (1969).
10. Fromm (1969), p. 5.
11. Martin (2000), p. 393.
12. Fromm (1969).
13. Dunwoody et al. (2014).
14. Greenberg et al. (2001).
15. Fromm (1969).
16. Martin (2005).
17. Abramson et al. (1978).
18. Episode 4–6, "The Laws of Gods and Men" (May 11, 2014).
19. Fromm (1969).
20. Walker & Bright (2009).
21. Fromm (1969).
22. Elbert et al. (2010).
23. Martin (1999).
24. Martin (2011).
25. Levitt & Dubner (2014).
26. Sandseter (2012).
27. Martin (2000).
28. Nickerson (1998).
29. Martin (2011), p. 297.

Safety and Security

TRAVIS LANGLEY

"Safety? Where . . . ?"
—The Hound[1]

> *". . . one can choose to go back toward safety or forward*
> *toward growth. Growth must be chosen again and*
> *again; fear must be overcome again and again."*
> —psychologist Abraham Maslow[2]

Karen Horney, one of numerous early Freudians who broke away from Sigmund Freud as their views grew further apart, felt that the *need for safety* dominates childhood, when the growing child who feels a sense of security and freedom from fear will grow up with a more stable personality and greater mental health.[3] How parents treat their children determines how secure the child feels, according to Horney. Tyrion Lannister may have grown up with indulgences enjoyed as a child of a noble house, but his father never makes him feel secure in life. A rigid, callous parent like Tywin can undermine the child's security and foster hostility by ridiculing or humiliating the child, visibly preferring other siblings, failing to keep promises, isolating the child from peers, and punishing the child unfairly—all of which Tyrion experiences and, as a result, he eventually kills his heartless father with a crossbow bolt to the heart.

Heavily influenced by Horney, even though he rarely acknowledged the fact, Erich Fromm considered the conflict between freedom and security to be the most basic human dilemma.[4] People desire the liberty to do as they please, and yet they also want to feel safe and sound. Frightened people may give up many freedoms in order to feel safe. Others reach a different extreme and rebel, sacrificing safety in order to feel free. The Free Folk live in the frozen lands north of the Wall, beyond the Seven Kingdoms, rather than bow before any flag. Recognizing no authority but the leaders whom they choose to follow and can unfollow at any time, these people, known to others as "wildlings," relinquish the greater safety of warmer climate so that they might run free. As noted in Chapter Seven, they seek *positive freedom*, the ability to grow into and become their true selves. Fromm predicted, though, that greater freedom and independence would cause people to feel lonelier, more alienated, and less significant than when they feel that they're part of something greater than themselves. Those who feel the most isolated among the Free Folk might be more ready to seek security by surrendering their independence and giving up their freedoms. When White Walkers and their wights attack, killing thousands of Free Folk, survivors resign themselves to traveling south of the Wall, sacrificing unfettered freedom for greater safety.[5] They give up security to feel free, but eventually give up much of their freedom to feel secure.

Fromm described a number of mechanisms for regaining security when people do not feel safe. Once they relocate south of the Wall into the lands of people who aren't also Free Folk, the Free Folk likely feel a *symbiotic relatedness* to each other, their lives woven more tightly together with a heightened awareness of "us" (Free Folk) because of the everyday proximity of "them" (everyone else). Fromm said people can also make themselves feel more secure through *withdrawal-destructiveness*, passively withdrawing or actively destroying to gain a sense of control. To protect himself and the woman he loves, Samwell Tarley withdraws from other members of the Night's Watch.[6] To protect themselves from the whims of their chaotic "Mad King," Jaime Lannister and others band together to kill Aerys Targaryen II so that they may feel more secure through his destruction.[7]

Those who lack safety and security may find themselves the most vulnerable to life's dangers, the most threatened by its storms.

References

Fromm, E. H. (1941/1969). *Escape from freedom.* New York, NY: Holt.
Fromm, E. H. (1955). *The sane society.* New York, NY: Rinehart.
Horney, K. (1937). *The neurotic personality of our time.* New York, NY: Norton.
Maslow, A. H. (1966). *The psychology of science.* New York, NY: Harper & Row.
Martin, G. R. R. (1996). *A game of thrones.* New York, NY: Bantam.
Martin, G. R. R. (2005). *A feast for crows.* New York, NY: Bantam.
Martin, G. R. R. (2011). *A dance with dragons.* New York, NY: Bantam.

Notes

1. Episode 4–10, "The Children" (June 15, 2014).
2. Maslow (1966), p. 22.
3. Horney (1937).
4. Fromm (1941/1969; 1955).
5. Fromm (1941/1969).
6. Martin (2011).
7. First described by Martin (1996).

Part Three
Tempests

Storms rage. War wages between people and emotions churn within. Chaos throws the land into upheaval. Plans capsize. Souls are lost at sea. Storms end, and survivors mourn, mend what's broken, and carry on because not everything changes.

Making relationships work can be hard. One psychologist and marriage researcher proposed a popular set of principles for marital success or failure. What might someone applying his principles predict for relationships in a brutal fantasy world?

CHAPTER EIGHT

Can Love and Marriage Go Together in Westeros?

Jonathan Hetterly

"The things I do for love."
—Jaime Lannister[1]

> *"Contempt is the sulfuric acid for love."*
> —psychologist John Gottman[2]

The quality of a marriage relationship greatly impacts the partners' psychological well-being.[3] In Westeros, marriages can even instigate or interrupt civil war. *Game of Thrones* is a medieval soap opera, dealing with marriage, infidelity, and warring families. But what about "love"? Where does love fit into the characters' motivations and actions? And how does it factor into marriage, the most significant institution that governs land and power?

In *The Seven Principles for Making Marriage Work*, clinical psychologist and marriage researcher John Gottman reveals what he considers to be the features of a successful marriage relationship.[4] Gottman and his colleagues studied hundreds of couples, interviewed them, videotaped their interactions, and even monitored their heart rate, sweat flow, blood pressure, and immune function to measure their stress levels. In their "Love Lab," he and his team recorded hundreds of hours of different couples interacting and sometimes arguing with no therapist in the room, and this data helped Gottman identify factors that predicted marital failure or longevity.[5] In addition to identifying four negative factors that can predict divorce, Gottman identified seven positive principles that predict marital success. He and his researchers first claimed they could predict with 91 percent accuracy whether a couple will thrive or fail after watching and listening to them for just five minutes.[6]

Gottman's methods and results have their challengers. Some have criticized the small sample size and the lack of cross-validation. But the biggest critique has been whether or not his prediction for divorce is accurate.[7] One study showed the accuracy for divorce prediction to be much lower. The cost to follow up with an increased number of couples over the same amount of time as Gottman's original research was deemed too costly for the authors of the study, which means that these factors' long-term predictive ability needs greater confirmation.[8]

The relationship between Eddard and Catelyn Stark appears to be the warmest and brightest marriage in the *Game of Thrones* universe. Jaime and Cersei Lannister's incestuous relationship is one of the more dark and disturbing relationships. And the television version of Sansa Stark has experienced several different relationships and marriages during her young life. How do these relationships stack up against Gottman's seven principles?

1. Enhance Your Love Maps[9]

*"Your father didn't love me when we married. He hardly
knew me or I him. Love didn't just happen to us. We
built it slowly over the years, stone by stone, for you,
for your brothers and sisters, for all of us."*
—Catelyn Stark to her son Robb[10]

The more you are familiar with your partner, the more intimacy happens. This is what Gottman calls having a love map of your partner. This helps maintain intimacy, and better prepares one to deal with stressful events and conflict. Also known as *companionate love*, Gottman's love map encapsulates affection and tenderness that people feel for those with whom their lives are deeply connected. It is often described as friendship love and involves shared values, deep attachment, long-term commitment, and intimacy.[11] Ned and Catelyn grow to love each other over time. Their love is not an adolescent crush or driven by lustful passion. It is a love developed as they learn the deepest longings, hopes, and virtues of each other. They confide in each other and display a degree of vulnerability that is not often displayed with others.

Gottman encourages partners to explore "who am I" and identify past injuries and need for healing. Trust and respect are two elements missing in Joffrey's betrothal to Sansa. Her affection for Joffrey is more about loving the idea of being queen and the ideal of love than actually loving the future king. She did not know him, was not familiar with him, and without intimacy there can be no love map. Tyrion actually understands or attempts to understand Sansa's love map. He recognizes the injustice that Sansa has faced in her engagement to Joffrey as well as being forced to marry him. Despite their mutual unhappiness at the marriage, Tyrion and Sansa

Four Horsemen of the Apocalypse

*"You're a hateful woman, why have the gods
condemned me to love a hateful woman?"*
—Jaime Lannister[12]

Gottman and his researchers claim they can predict with 91
percent accuracy whether a couple will thrive or fail after
watching and listening to them for just five minutes. They
have been studying how couples argue and resolve conflict
and have followed hundreds of couples over time to see if their
marriages last. Using a scientific approach, they have found
four negative factors that can predict divorce and seven positive principles that predict marital success.

Gottman says he looks for certain kinds of negativity, which
he calls the "Four Horsemen of the Apocalypse," to predict a
relationship's failure:

- *Criticism*: Global negative statements about your
  partner's character or personality.
- *Contempt*: Sarcasm, cynicism, name-calling, eye-
  rolling, sneering, mockery, and hostile humor can
  be poisonous because they convey disgust.
- *Defensiveness*: This is a way of blaming your
  partner and can escalate the conflict.
- *Stonewalling*: A partner may disengage from the
  relationship, signaled by looking away without
  saying anything and acting as though he/she
  doesn't care about what the other is saying.

Gottman's Four Horsemen don't predict the absence of love
so much as it identifies what can sabotage love.

demonstrate an understanding of one another and the situation they have been put in.

2. Nurture Your Fondness and Admiration[13]

Gottman found that 94 percent of the time when couples put a positive spin on their marriage's history, they are likely to have a happy future.[14] This is one of the most critical elements in a rewarding and long-lasting marriage. It involves feeling that your partner is still worthy of honor and respect in spite of his or her flaws. Gottman claims that fondness and admiration are two of the most important elements in a satisfying and long-term relationship. *Fondness* and *admiration* help to prevent the "Four Horsemen" (see sidebar).

Without *fondness* and *admiration*, the relationship has little if any basis. Catelyn wasn't originally going to marry Ned Stark, but did so after Ned's brother and father died. Despite tragic origins for their relationship, the Starks not only have put a positive spin on their marriage but they also exhibit a high degree of honor and respect for following through with a marriage neither intended.

Tyrion and Sansa's marriage is a surprising example of fondness and admiration. After his forced marriage to her, Tyrion attempts to bond and comfort her and makes the best of their situation.[15] He promises he won't mistreat her. Sansa admits that there are worse Lannisters she could be wed to.

In direct contrast, the relationship that Cersei and Jaime have with one another becomes more and more corrupt and dysfunctional as their relationship progresses. When Jaime exhibits humility and thoughtfulness, Cersei scoffs at his changes and views them as weaknesses. She often lashes out at him when the two of them are alone together. Cersei tends to be spiteful. However, it is difficult to sympathize with Jaime. He also can be incredibly selfish and prone to fling ugly and hurtful words at Cersei. In rare moments when Cersei exhibits vulnerability, Jaime doesn't listen. He is stuck in his desire to have sex with her and is not in the mood for honest, vulnerable conversation. They may love one another, but Gottman's Four Horsemen would predict a doomed tenure.

3. Turn Toward Each Other Instead of Away[16]

Happily married couples do not have less conflict, but they are better able to repair their relationship before it gets out of hand and negative sentiments override the positive ones. Ned and Catelyn openly disagree, fight, or question each other. She is not happy that he accepts the position of Hand of the King over her objections. Despite their challenges, they make themselves available to one another, listening to each other's words, concerns, complaints, and hopes. Their positive sentiments toward each other greatly outweigh the negative.

Couples that turn toward each other have more in their "emotional bank account,"[17] a distinguishing characteristic in happy marriages. With more positivity and goodwill stored up, these couples have an emotional savings cushion that helps buffer them in times of conflict and stress.

When a partner makes a bid for your attention, affection, humor, or support, turning toward your partner is the basis of emotional connection. The real secret is to turn toward each other in little ways every day. Regardless of the conflict that they experience, it is clear that the positives in the Stark marriage greatly outweigh the conflicts and stressors.

In contrast to Ned and Catelyn's relationship, Cersei vacillates between drawing toward and withdrawing from her lover Jaime. Although he has been faithful to her, Cersei has had other sexual partners. Love appears to come and go for Cersei. Upon Jaime's return to King's Landing, Cersei rejects his attempts at intimacy, blaming him for being captured. Despite Jaime's declaration that he was driven to return to her, she coldly rebuffs him, stating "You took too long."[18]

The stored-up positivity and goodwill needed for a healthy relationship is not present here. Rather than adopting an "us versus the problem" approach when facing adversity, couples who turn away from each other exhibit a "you versus me" attitude where one of the partners is viewed as the problem.

4. Let Your Partner Influence You[19]

A happy couple is a team of two members who consider each other's perspective and feelings. They make decisions together and search out common ground. Letting your partner influence you isn't about having one person hold the reins; it's about honoring and respecting both people in the relationship. The happiest marriages are those where the husband is able to convey honor and respect for his wife and does not resist sharing power and decision making.

Gottman found women were more likely to let their husbands influence them when they felt their husbands took their opinions and feelings into account. Women tend to match or reduce negativity. Men tend to escalate it, usually with one of the *four horsemen* (criticism, contempt, defensiveness, or stonewalling). But when a partner feels listened to and emotionally validated, the choice made doesn't become the only way validation is expressed.

Ned and Catelyn argue, sometimes very bitterly. However, despite their sometimes bitter arguments, they still allow themselves to be influenced by each other. Maester Luwin and Catelyn disagree about Eddard's options, each respectfully advising him that he is Robert's best hope against any potential plot against him by the Lannisters. Despite his loyalty and allegiance to Robert and the throne, Eddard respects his wife's opinion and counsel to the point that he considers not only her words but also her recommendations.[20] Gottman highlights how arguments, harsh phrasing, and agendas make it harder to compromise. Gottman contends that learning to yield is an important lesson in life and one he equates to "emotional intelligence."[21] Although Ned's duty was to the throne, he understood that Catelyn's feelings were important and that listening to her was how he showed honor and respect.

5. Solve Your Solvable Problems[22]

Gottman divides marital problems into two separate categories: conflicts that can be resolved and perpetual problems that can't. Solvable problems are situational with no underlying conflict, while perpetual problems (69 percent of conflicts are perpetual) have underlying assumptions and issues that cannot be grounded and fixed. Gottman devised a five-step model for resolving solvable conflicts:

- Step 1. *Soften startup*: Start the conversation without criticism or contempt.
- Step 2. *Make and receive "repair attempts"*: Any action or statement that de-escalates tension.

- Step 3. *Soothe yourself and then your partner.* Take a break in a fight to calm down enough so you don't completely or permanently withdraw.
- Step 4. *Compromise*: When conflicts arise, consider what you agree on, what your common goals and feelings are, and how you can accomplish them.
- Step 5. *Show tolerance of each other's faults*: Compromise is impossible until you can accept your partner's flaws.

Ned and Catelyn exhibit quick tempers that sometimes get the better of them. Yet, their fondness and admiration for each other often kicks in and both are able to laugh at themselves and each other. Catelyn continues to resent Jon Snow and what he represents in her marriage and family. She makes her feelings known about him constantly, both to Eddard and to Jon himself, yet all three of them have learned to tolerate and live with the situation. Although it continues to sting and highlights the biggest blemish in their marriage, they continually compromise or allow for the hope of future compromise so their marriage or their relationship doesn't derail over issues from the past.

Gottman highlights the need for "soft startups" rather than harsh tones that put people on edge. Gottman calls out "blaming" as a toxic component, something that Cersei is guilty of, and not just in her relationship with Jaime. Cersei exhibits scapegoating and blaming among her primary defense mechanisms as she faces frustrating and disappointing events throughout her life.

6. Overcome Gridlock[23]

Resolving *major* marital conflicts is not the essential component to happy marriages. Gottman identified the majority of conflict in marriages as perpetual and revolving around issues that are present throughout the entirety of the marriage. Gottman says that the goal with perpetual problems is for couples to move from gridlock to dialogue. What usually underlies gridlock is unfulfilled dreams. Gridlock is a sign that you have dreams for your life that aren't being addressed or respected by each other.[24] Happy couples believe in the importance of helping one another realize their dreams. The first step in overcoming gridlock is to determine the dream or dreams that are causing your conflict. Successful couples know that the marriage is meant to benefit each partner's dreams. Hidden dreams are only likely to emerge after the marriage feels safe. After Jon Arryn is murdered and Robert Baratheon calls upon Ned to serve as the new Hand of the King, Ned struggles between his duty to his family and his duty to the realm. Catelyn suspects Ned will ultimately choose his duty to the realm, but her dialogue communicates her hopes and dreams for their future together.

"The goal is to 'declaw' the issue, to try to remove the hurt so the problem stops being a source of great pain," Gottman writes.[25] Ending gridlock doesn't mean solving the problem, but rather moving from gridlock to dialogue. In a world where duty and oaths are prioritized above marital satisfaction, Ned and Catelyn try their best to acknowledge the obstacles their marriage faces and try their best not to allow those obstacles to be a wedge between them.

7. Create Shared Meaning[26]

Marriage may have a spiritual dimension that has to do with creating an inner life together—an environment rich with rituals, and an appreciation for your roles and goals that link you, and that lead you to understand what it means to be a part of the family you have become.[27]

While Ned sits by the heart tree cleaning his sword, Catelyn comments that even after all the years of their marriage, she still feels like an outsider when she comes to this place of his northern Gods. He smiles at that, saying that she isn't an outsider, as she has bore five northern children.[28] Ned views his religion as inclusive of Catelyn. In Ned's mind, her devotion to him and the children she bore is seen as a spiritual act in and of itself. These spiritual acts deem her worthy of inclusion in his religion of the Old Gods, regardless of whether or not Catelyn believes in the Old Gods or the Faith of the Seven. It is clear that although the Stark marriage starts with duty, it ends with love.

If the Stark marriage is founded on friendship, loyalty, and duty, the relationship that Cersei and Jaime have is based on lust, betrayal, and secrecy. Their sexual misconduct has produced three children that they are passing off as King Robert's offspring. Their secrets could destroy their lives and the lives of their incestuous offspring. While admitting her struggles to control Joffrey, Cersei fears that Joffrey's madness may be a consequence of her incestuous relationship.[29] Finally, Cersei's duplicity results in Robert's murder.

Marriage: More Powerful Than War

Gottman's principles provide a science of healthy relationships based on systematic longitudinal and observational research. *Game of Thrones* has continued to build a reputation for pushing the boundaries beyond Westernized tastes for sex, violence, incest, and rape. Looking beyond the headline-grabbing sensationalism, however, *Game of Thrones* has created a multilayered, complex world where the institution of marriage is one of the most powerful institutions guiding all of Westeros. In the end, Gottman's principles do not heavily guide the marriages in these games.

References

Gottman, J. (1995). *Why marriages succeed or fail: And how you can make yours last*. New York, NY: Simon & Schuster.

Gottman, J., & Silver, N. (1999). *The seven principles for making marriage work*. New York, NY: Three Rivers.

Hatfield, E., & Rapson, R. L. (1993). *Love, sex, and intimacy: Their psychology, biology, and history*. New York, NY: HarperCollins.

Heyman, R., & Smith, A. (2001). The hazards of predicting divorce without crossvalidation. *Journal of Marriage and the Family, 63*(2), 473–479.

Madathil, J., & Benshoff, J. M. (2008). Importance of marital characteristics and marital satisfaction: A comparison of Asian Indians in arranged marriages and Americans in marriages of choice. *The Family Journal: Counseling and Therapy for Couples and Families, 16*(3), 222–230.

Martin, G. R. R. (1996). *A game of thrones*. New York, NY: Bantam.

Martin, G. R. R. (2000). *A storm of swords*. New York, NY: Bantam.

Stanley S. M., Bradbury, T. N., & Markman, H. J., (1998). Structural flaws in the bridge from basic research on marriage to interventions for couples. *Journal of Marriage and the Family, 62*(1), 256–264.

Notes

1. Episode 1–1, "Winter is Coming" (April 17, 2011).
2. Gottman & Silver (1999).
3. Madathil & Benshoff (2008).
4. Gottman & Silver (1999).
5. Gottmann & Silver (1999).
6. Gottman (1995).
7. Stanley et al. (1998).
8. Heyman & Smith (2001).

 9. Gottman & Silver (1999).
10. Martin (1996).
11. Hatfield & Rapson (1993).
12. Episode 4–3, "Breaker of Chains" (April 20, 2014).
13. Gottman & Silver (1999).
14. Gottman & Silver (1999).
15. Episode 3–8, "Second Songs" (May 19, 2013).
16. Gottman & Silver (1999).
17. Gottman & Silver (1999).
18. Episode 4–1, "Two Swords" (April 6, 2014).
19. Gottman & Silver (1999).
20. Episode 1–1, "Winter is Coming" (April 17, 2011).
21. Gottman & Silver (1999).
22. Gottman & Silver (1999).
23. Gottman & Silver (1999).
24. Gottman & Silver (1999).
25. Gottman & Silver (1999).
26. Gottman & Silver (1999).
27. Gottman & Silver (1999).
28. Episode 1–1, "Winter is Coming" (April 17, 2011).
29. Episode 2–7, "A Man without Honor" (May 13, 2012).

The ways in which we pursue freedom or security, like the ways in which we make relationships succeed or fail, all appear distinctly tied to the ways in which we were raised. Parenting styles in the Seven Kingdoms reflect the parenting styles researchers have identified among families in our own world as well.

CHAPTER NINE

Parenting Styles of the Direwolf, Falcon, Lion, and Stag

STEPHEN HUPP

"The house that puts family first will always defeat the house that puts the whims and wishes of its sons and daughters first."
—Tywin Lannister[1]

"The main source of good discipline is growing up in a loving family—being loved and learning to love in return."
—pediatrician Benjamin Spock[2]

Like so many families in the contemporary world, parents in Westeros struggle to find the best way to raise their children. When Stannis Baratheon's wife, Selyse, suggests that their daughter needs discipline for her stubbornness and, more specifically, "she needs the rod,"[3] Stannis's response is, "She's my daughter; you will not strike her." These days, parents also struggle with decisions about discipline and other controversial issues. They wonder if they should use spanking or a time-out, if they should give their children more freedom or more supervision, and if they give too much praise or too little.

If *Game of Thrones* is a reflection of contemporary society, there are many different parenting styles to reflect. Terms such as *helicopter parenting, free-range parenting,* and *tiger parenting* are common fodder for the media.[4] These parenting styles are largely creations of pop psychology with scant research behind them, and although these fad terms may help sell books, researchers only recently have started to investigate them as defined constructs.[5] However, psychologists do classify certain other parenting styles that have relatively clear operational definitions and a broad research base. Specifically, the developmental psychologist Diana Baumrind's classification approach is widely regarded as the most influential typology of parenting.[6] This typology is based on two parenting dimensions: responsiveness and demandingness.

Responsiveness refers to the extent to which parents provide "emotional support, warmth, and actions that intentionally foster individuality and are acquiescent to children's needs and demands."[7] *Demandingness* involves "the claims that parents make on children to become integrated into the family and community by their maturity expectations, supervision, disciplinary efforts, and willingness to confront a disputative child."[8] On the basis of possible variations of these two dimensions, researchers categorize parents as having at least four different styles of parenting: authoritative, permissive, authoritarian, and disengaged.[9]

In *Game of Thrones,* similar variations of these four different parenting styles contribute substantially to many of the story lines. Because Westeros contains several unique societies, each of these parenting styles comes with an additional dimension that helps it fit into the harsh demands of the Seven Kingdoms.

Direwolf Parenting: Authoritative with a Wisp of Winterfell

The *authoritative* parenting style is found in parents who demonstrate high degrees of responsiveness and high amounts of demandingness. This parenting style is represented in House Stark, which has the direwolf as a sigil; therefore, I call it direwolf parenting.

Responsiveness—high levels exhibited by the parent. In Ned Stark's short time in the series, he displays several instances of responsive parenting. When Ned watches his son Bran struggle with his bow, causing others to chuckle, he responds by gently encouraging Bran to keep trying.[10] With his daughter Arya, he demonstrates warmth by kissing her on the forehead.[11] Other parental figures in the Stark household use praise, such as Septa Mordane and Jon Snow with the younger Stark children.[12] A parent's use of negotiation is consistent with the responsive nature of the authoritative parenting style. Even though Ned starts off believing that girls should not learn to use swords, once he realizes that Arya is passionate about fighting, he provides a "dance instructor" to teach her how to use a sword,[13] showing her that he supports her psychological *autonomy* (doing things on one's own), which is also a characteristic of authoritative parenting.[14]

Demandingness—high. When parents implement disciplinary consequences, they are displaying instances of demanding parenting. Both Ned and Catelyn send Arya to her room when her behavior displeases them.[15] However, the demandingness in the authoritative parenting style allows some room for children to disagree. When Ned's girls protest about his decision to send them away from King's Landing, he explains the reasons for his decision while still holding firm.[16] Moreover, Ned broadly uses *moral reasoning* with his children, and this parenting practice has been shown to be predictive of children's moral development.[17]

Additional dimension. In addition to these two dimensions of authoritative parenting, the direwolf parenting exhibited by the Starks is uniquely tailored to the harsh realities of their home in the North. Another aspect of Ned's parenting is revealed when he requires Bran to watch him behead a deserter.[18] This action would not be included in Baumrind's description of authoritative parenting, but it is an important part of direwolf parenting. Forcing Bran to watch the beheading is not an easy decision, as even Catelyn expresses concern about her ten-year-old seeing such violence. However, because Bran may need to be Lord of Winterfell one day and display his own direwolf parenting, Ned explains, "He won't be a boy forever, and winter is coming."

Falcon Parenting: Permissive with an Eyrie Twist

The *permissive* parenting style is characterized by parents who demonstrate high amounts of responsiveness but low amounts of demandingness. This parenting style is represented in House Arryn, which includes the falcon in its sigil; therefore, I call it falcon parenting.

Responsiveness—high. Research suggests that parents are more likely to be overprotective with firstborn children and children they perceive to have medical problems; this results in an overly responsive parenting style.[19] Fearing her son's death as a result of his sickliness and the dangerous times, Lysa Arryn becomes very protective of him while he serves as the young Lord of the Eyrie. Robin rarely appears without his mother at his side, typically sharing a seat with her, and even when he is six years old, she still refers to him as a "baby" and calls him "sweet one."[20] Highly responsive to Robin's needs, she appears to take responsiveness a bit too far, as is indicated by Littlefinger when he says that she "loved her son so much she became overprotective."[21] Considering all these factors and the harsh times and culture, Lysa's overly responsive manner is somewhat predictable and in accordance with research.[22]

Demandingness—low. Lysa's parenting includes very low amounts of demandingness, as her sister refers to Robin as being "utterly without discipline" and fears he will stay that way unless he spends some time without his mother.[23] When Littlefinger gives him the gift of a crystal falcon, within minutes he throws the gift through the Moon Door, and his disregard for another person's feelings and lack of appreciation do not seem to concern his mother at all.[24] When Sansa deals with Robin's spoiled behavior by slapping him in the face, even the questionably moral Littlefinger tells her that the boy's mother should have disciplined him long ago.[25] In research, parental laxness like that demonstrated by Lysa is commonly associated with behavior problems in children.[26]

Additional dimension. Lysa breast-feeds Robin far beyond the time that is typical in Westeros, continuing to do so when he is ten years old,[27] and she often uses breast-feeding to calm his nerves.[28] This aspect of falcon parenting is a reflection of a trend that is occurring in some parenting circles today. That is, *extended breast-feeding* is encouraged by proponents of "attachment parenting" such as the pediatrician William Sears[29] and the actress/neuroscientist Mayim Bialik.[30] Some proponents of this extreme form of child-led weaning recommend it for four, five, six, or even seven years.[31] Although breast-feeding is a

Folklore Guide for Predicting the Sex of Newborns

Similar to many ancient societies and times, in the Seven Kingdoms the sex of a newborn has important implications for the legacy of a family. When speaking about his pregnant young bride, Roose Bolton says, "From the way she's carrying, Maester Wolkan says it should be a boy," and this revelation has important implications for Roose's adult son, Ramsay, whose claim to lordship in the North is already questionable.[32] How might one make this prediction? The predictive signs in the following chart are used even by some in contemporary society.[33]

BOY SIGNS	GIRL SIGNS
Carrying the fetus high	Carrying the fetus low
Carrying the fetus toward the front	Carrying the fetus toward the back
Belly shaped like a large ball	Belly shaped like a watermelon
Waistline that is trim	Waistline that has considerable bulge
Less hind weight	More weight has been gained on hind end

How valid is this method for predicting the sex of a newborn? Research shows that all the signs in this guide are successfully predictive about 50 percent of the time.[34] Put another way, the use of these signs *is no more accurate than simply flipping a coin.*

great option for most babies for one or two years, there is little to no research showing benefits from breastfeeding beyond this period.[35]

Lion Parenting: Authoritarian with a Chip off Casterly Rock

The *authoritarian* parenting style is characterized by parents who demonstrate low amounts of responsiveness but high amounts of demandingness. This parenting style is represented in House Lannister, which has the lion as a sigil; therefore, I call it lion parenting.

Responsiveness—low. Tywin Lannister shows little support for the emotional needs of his children. When Cersei at age four is praying for mercy from the gods because of the death of her mother, Tywin says, "The gods have no mercy. That's why they're gods."[36] Thus, he provides little emotional support to Cersei in her time of need. Additionally, he harshly calls his son Jaime a reckless fool filled with vanity[37] and describes his other son Tyrion as "an ill-made spiteful little creature, full of envy, lust, and low cunning."[38] In short, the lion parenting style provides little warmth to younger or older children and does not appear to value the individual needs of the children, which seem to be secondary to the needs of the parents.

Demandingness—high. Tywin Lannister is highly demanding, often requiring the unquestioning compliance of his children. This is in stark contrast to the demandingness in direwolf parenting, which does allow some room for discussion. When Cersei refuses to marry a man of Tywin's choosing, Tywin responds harshly by saying, "You will do as I command. . . ."[39] Similarly, Tywin demands that Tyrion impregnate Sansa even though she does not consent to this idea. Parental harshness like that demonstrated by Tywin has been shown to be associated with behavior problems in children.[40]

Additional dimension. Sigmund Freud shared many ideas with untestable extrapolations.[41] One such idea, the *Oedipus complex*, has received a lot of attention and involves the story of a king. According to Freud, "King Oedipus, who slew his father Laius and wedded his mother Jocasta, is nothing more or less than a wish-fulfillment of the wish of our childhood."[42] Freud suggests that a boy's first violent impulse is directed toward his father. In the case of Tyrion Lannister, Freud may appear to have been correct because Tyrion confesses that he has wished his father dead[43] and eventually kills his father with a crossbow for stealing his lover.[44] Thus, although Freud's theory about the Oedipus complex is untestable, it has become part of popular culture[45] and seems to be fitting for and exemplified by this family.

Stag Parenting: Disengaged with a Splash of Storm's End

The *disengaged* parenting style is characterized by parents who demonstrate low amounts of responsiveness and low amounts of demandingness. This parenting style is represented in House Baratheon, which has the stag as a sigil; therefore, I call it stag parenting.

Responsiveness—low. As a sign of low responsiveness in the Baratheon family, on his deathbed Robert Baratheon says to his son Joffrey, "I should have spent more time with you, shown you how to be a man."[46] He adds, "I was never meant to be a father." Robert is rarely seen with any of his children because he spends most of his free time accompanying scantily clad women, drinking alcohol, and hunting game.[47] Similarly,

Robert's brother, Stannis, spends so little time with his daughter that she asks if he's ashamed of her.[48]

Demandingness—low. Robert's low level of demandingness becomes evident when he quickly gives up trying to discover the truth about a disagreement between his son Joffrey and Ned's daughter Ayra.[49] Because Robert does not pursue the truth, both a Stark direwolf and Arya's friend the butcher's boy pay with their lives. Joffrey's smile indicates that whatever consequence he is to receive pales in comparison to Arya's consequences. Similarly, Stannis rejects his wife's ideas about how to discipline his daughter without suggesting an alternative.[50]

Additional dimension. The disengaged parenting style includes behaviors that are neglecting or rejecting of children.[51] Robert and Stannis both seem to neglect their children quite a lot of the time. It is Stannis, though, who exemplifies the stag version of disengagement when he decides to sacrifice his daughter in the pursuit of his own goals and glory; he is a parent whose own needs and wants matter more than those of his children.[52]

Effects of These Westerosi Parenting Styles

As is the case in most societies, offspring play a critical role throughout Westeros. Conflict in *Game of Thrones* centers on who is the rightful heir to the throne, and many parents in Westeros strive to have the strongest possible legacy. Tywin Lannister provides a definition of a legacy when he describes it as "what you pass down to your children and your children's children."[53] With children so central to legacy, parenting takes on special meaning in Westeros.

But which parenting style is the most likely to lead to a strong legacy? Outcomes associated with Baumrind's parenting typology have been studied across many variables, with the authoritative parenting style (i.e., high in both responsiveness and demand-ingness) being reliably associated with better outcomes in areas such as academic performance and emotional adjustment.[54] The benefits of the authoritative parenting style are also fairly robust across many different ethnicities and societies.[55]

Is the Westeros version of the authoritative parenting style, direwolf parenting, also associated with the best outcomes? Ned Stark's children seem to be fairly well adjusted considering the challenging world in which they are surviving. Robb is greatly respected in the North at the time of his death. Similarly, Jon Snow becomes Lord Commander of the Night's Watch. Ned's other children survive while they are all facing different chal-lenges and seem to be growing into respectable young adults, perhaps even heroes.

What about the other parenting styles in Westeros? Lysa's falcon parenting appears to have affected Robin negatively. He demonstrates selfish behavior and receives little respect from anyone other than his mother. Tywin's lion parenting seems to have contributed to problematic outcomes for all three of his children. Specifically, Cersei and Jaime engage in quite a few villainous behaviors, and Tyrion has an alcohol use disor-der and aggressive tendencies. Robert's stag parenting proba-bly contributes to Joffrey's horrible behavior, and Stannis's stag parenting directly leads to the death of his only daughter.

Some optimism is warranted, however, when it comes to some of the children raised under all of these parenting styles. That is, one major limitation of Baumrind's parenting typology is that it cannot easily be studied experimentally. Research-ers cannot easily assign parents into different parenting style groups and then study the outcomes with a true experimental design, making it difficult fully to understand the influence of parenting style on children's behavior. Moreover, parenting is just one of several variables that shape children into who they become. A child raised in accordance with the falcon parenting style could still grow up to do honor. A child raised in accordance with the lion parenting style could still grow into an endearing adult. Even a child raised in accordance with the stag parenting style could still become a great leader.

References

Arnold, D. S., O'Leary, S. G., Wolff, L. S., & Acker, M. M. (1993). The Parenting Scale: A measure of dysfunctional parenting in discipline situations. *Psychological Assessment, 5*(2), 137–144.

Baumrind, D. (1991). The influence of parenting style on adolescent competence and substance use. *Journal of Early Adolescence, 11*(1), 56–95.

Baumrind, D. (1996). The discipline controversy revisited. *Family Relations, 45*(4), 405–414.

Baumrind, D. (2013). Authoritative parenting revisited: History and current status. In R. E. Larzelere, A. S. Morris, & A. W. Harrist (Eds.), *Authoritative parenting: Synthesizing nurturance and discipline for optimal child development* (pp. 11–34). Washington, DC: American Psychological Association.

Baumrind, D., Larzelere, R. E., & Owens, E. B. (2010). Effects of preschool parents' power assertive patterns and practices on adolescent development. *Parenting: Science and Practice, 10*(3), 157–201.

Bialik, M. (2012). *Beyond the sling: A real-life guide to raising confident loving children the attachment parenting way.* New York, NY: Simon & Schuster.

Ciabattari, J. (2014, April). Does Sigmund Freud still matter? BBC: www.bbc.com.

Cioffi, F. (1998). *Freud and the question of pseudoscience.* Chicago, IL: Open Court.

Criss, M. M., & Larzelere, R. E. (2013). Introduction. In R. E. Larzelere, A. S. Morris, & A. W. Harrist (Eds.), *Authoritative parenting: Synthesizing nurturance and discipline for optimal child development* (pp. 3–8). Washington, DC: American Psychological Association.

Freud, S., & Brill, A. A. (1938). *The basic writings of Sigmund Freud.* New York, NY: Modern Library.

Granju, K. A., & Kennedy, B. (1999). *Attachment parenting: Instinctive care for your baby and young child.* New York, NY: Pocket.

Gray, M. R., & Steinberg, L. (1999). Unpacking authoritative parenting: Reassessing a multidimensional construct. *Journal of Marriage and the Family, 61*(3), 574–587.

Hoffman, D. M. (2013). Raising the awesome child. *The Hedgehog Review, 15*(3), 30–41.

Hupp, S., & Jewell, J. (2015). *Great myths of child development.* Malden, MA: Wiley-Blackwell.

Juang, L. P., Qin, D. B., & Park, I. J. (2013). Deconstructing the myth of the "tiger mother": An introduction to the special issue on tiger parenting, Asian-heritage families, and child/adolescent well-being. *Asian American Journal of Psychology, 4*(1), 1–6.

Lavigne, S. (1992). *Boy or girl? 50 fun ways to find out.* New York, NY: Dell.

Martin, G. R. R. (1996). *A game of thrones.* New York, NY: Bantam Spectra.

Martin, G. R. R. (2005). *A feast for crows.* New York, NY: Bantam Spectra.

Perry, D. F., DiPietro, J., & Costigan, K. (1999). Are women carrying "basketballs" really having boys? Testing pregnancy folklore. *Birth, 26*(3), 172–177.

Sears, W., Sears, M., Sears, R., & Sears, J. M. (2013). *The baby book: Everything you need to know about your baby from birth to age two.* New York, NY: Little, Brown.

Somers, P., & Settle, J. (2010). The helicopter parent: Research toward a typology. *College and University, 86*(1), 18.

Sorkhabi, N., & Mandara, J. (2013). Are the effects of Baumrind's parenting styles culturally specific or culturally equivalent? In R. E. Larzelere, A. S. Morris, & A. W. Harrist (Eds.), *Authoritative parenting: Synthesizing nurturance and discipline for optimal child development* (pp. 11–34). Washington, DC: American Psychological Association.

Spock, B., & Needlman, R. (2012). *Dr. Spock's baby and child care* (9th ed.). New York, NY: Gallery.

Stormshak, E. A., Bierman, K. L., McMahon, R. J., & Lengua, L. J. (2000). Parenting practices and child disruptive behavior problems in early elementary school. *Journal of Clinical Child Psychology, 29*(1), 17–29.

Thomasgard, M., & Metz, W. P. (1997). Parental overprotection and its relation to perceived child vulnerability. *American Journal of Orthopsychiatry, 67*(2), 330–335.

Walker, L. J., & Hennig, K. H. (1999). Parenting style and the development of moral reasoning. *Journal of Moral Education, 28*(3), 359–374.

Notes

1. Episode 3–10, "Mhysa" (June 9, 2013).
2. Spock & Needlman (2011), p. 679.
3. Episode 4–2, "The Lion and the Rose" (April 13, 2014).
4. Hoffman (2013).
5. Juang et al. (2013); Somers & Settle (2010).
6. Criss & Larzelere (2013).
7. Baumrind et al. (2010), p. 161.
8. Baumrind (1996), p. 411.
9. Baumrind (2013).
10. Episode 1–1, "Winter Is Coming" (April 17, 2011).
11. Episode 1–4, "Cripples, Bastards, and Broken Things" (May 8, 2011).
12. Episode 1–1, "Winter Is Coming" (April 17, 2011).
13. Episode 1–3, "Lord Snow" (May 1, 2011).
14. Gray & Steinberg (1999).
15. Episode 1–1, "Winter Is Coming" (April 17, 2011); episode 1–3, "Lord Snow" (May 1, 2011).
16. Episode 1–6, "A Golden Crown" (May 22, 2011).
17. Walker & Henning (1999).
18. Episode 1–1, "Winter Is Coming" (April 17, 2011).
19. Thomasgard & Metz (1997).
20. Martin (1996), p. 376.
21. Episode 4–8, "The Mountain and the Viper" (June 1, 2014).
22. Thomasgard & Metz (1997).
23. Martin (1996), p. 436.
24. Episode 4–5, "First of His Name" (May 4, 2014).
25. Episode 4–7, "Mockingbird" (May 18, 2014).
26. Arnold et al. (1993).
27. Episode 4–8, "The Mountain and the Viper" (June 1, 2014).

28. Martin (2005), p. 474.

29. Sears et al. (2013).

30. Bialik (2012).

31. Granju & Kennedy (1999).

32. Episode 5–5, "Kill the Boy" (May 10, 2015).

33. Lavigne (1992).

34. Perry et al. (1999).

35. Hupp & Jewell (2015).

36. Episode 2–9, "Blackwater" (May 29, 2011).

37. Episode 1–7, "You Win or You Die" (May 29, 2011).

38. Episode 3–1, "Valar Dohaeris" (March 31, 2013).

39. Episode 3–5, "Kissed by Fire" (April 28, 2013).

40. Stormshak et al. (2000).

41. Cioffi (1998).

42. Freud & Brill (1938), p. 276.

43. Martin (1996), p. 420.

44. Episode 4–10, "The Children" (June 15, 2014).

45. Ciabattari (2014).

46. Episode 1–7, "You Win or You Die" (May 29, 2011).

47. Episode 1–2, "The Kingsroad" (April 24, 2011).

48. Episode 5–4, "Sons of Harpy" (May 3, 2015).

49. Episode 1–2, "The Kingsroad" (April 24, 2011).

50. Episode 4–2, "The Lion and the Rose" (April 13, 2014).

51. Baumrind (1991).

52. Episode 5–9, "The Dance of Dragons" (June 7, 2015).

53. Episode 2–7, "A Man Without Honor" (May 13, 2012).

54. Baumrind et al. (2010).

55. Sorkhabi & Mandara (2013).

One theory that has become well known (while difficult to test) proposes that deep in the inherited part of our unconscious lie archetypes, universal themes that shape our stories, dreams, and expectations. Among the most primal is the concept of mother, and *Game of Thrones* offers examples of two of the most extreme.

CHAPTER TEN

The Loving and the Terrible Mother: Daenerys and Cersei as Two Models of Jung's Great Mother Archetype

LAURA VECCHIOLLA

"Thus the Great Mother is uroboric: terrible and devouring, beneficent and creative; a helper, but also alluring and destructive; a maddening enchantress, yet a bringer of wisdom; bestial and divine, voluptuous harlot and inviolable virgin, immemorially old and eternally young."
—psychologist Erich Neumann[1]

Mother—a single word that can arouse an almost instinctual response of emotionally laden memories, images, and sensations. One may naturally think first of his or her personal mother, but the concept of *mother* can evoke thoughts of any female relationship—grandmother, caretaker, queen, or khaleesi. It is no wonder that the subject of mothers has long been a prominent theme in psychological exploration. The adage often attributed to Freud, "tell me about your mother," has become ubiquitous in the public's understanding of psychotherapy—and for good reason. The individual's experience of *mother* plays an undoubtedly fundamental role in molding development. Carl Jung, the Swiss psychiatrist and founder of analytical psychology, believed that humankind is shaped not only by the biographical, personal mother but also by an archetypal and immemorial mother concept that he referred to as the *Great Mother*.[2] In the books and television series, Daenerys Targaryen and Cersei Lannister provide exemplary illustrations of the Great Mother and her opposing forces.

What is an Archetype?

Jung described *archetypes* as universal expressions of particular patterns of behavior, thinking, and feeling at work within the human psyche—patterns that supposedly have been recurrent in the human experience since the beginning of time.[3] Phenomena such as mother, father, life, and death are all archetypal and reside within the collective unconscious, according to Jung. Although the boundless array of archetypes can never be made fully conscious, they often emerge in our consciousness as images, signs, or symbols that bind us, guide us, and influence us.

Important components of an archetype include its dynamics and its symbolism.[4] The *dynamics* (effects) of the archetype refer to the internal responses an individual may have when encountering the archetype—positive and negative emotions, fantasies, and projections are all part of the archetype's dynamic force. Jung said that the dynamic aspect of an archetype can be experienced in either the unconscious or the conscious mind. However the dynamic response is experienced, an image must be attached to it for it to be processed by the conscious mind. The manifestation of an archetype in an image constitutes the archetype's *symbolic* component. In this way, the Great Mother can be seen as an image or symbol that we have attached to the otherwise indescribable internal evocation of the archetype.

Though the people of Westeros never use the term *archetype*, they seem quite familiar with its basic meaning. The leading religion throughout the Seven Kingdoms is the Faith of the Seven, which holds that there is one god with seven faces or aspects. These seven faces are all archetypal expressions of human experience—the Father, the Mother, the Maiden, the Crone, the Warrior, the Smith, and the Stranger. Like the faithful of South Westeros, Jung agreed that such a collection of symbolic figures can serve as a powerful means of expressing and understanding the depth, complexity, and mystery of the human experience.

The Great Mother

Jung's fascination with the Great Mother, which he explored in several of his written works,[5] can be attributed in part to how deeply the human experience seems rooted in this archetype. Indeed, humankind's experience of mother and mothering is interminable. Jung reasoned that the Great Mother archetype embodies all that can be understood of motherhood and appears in "almost an infinite variety of aspects" throughout history.[6] The first known images depicted by primitive humans portray the Great Mother as the divine influence of nature through symbols such as trees, fruit, and fertile soil.[7] Images of the Great Mother progressed alongside the evolution of human consciousness, eventually taking the more familiar form of the divine goddess. Although the symbolic representation of the Great Mother varies across time and cultures, her dynamic and opposing forces remain fixed and ever present.

The most notable aspect of the Great Mother, and perhaps the reason for her eternal sway over humankind, is her dual nature. She is composed of opposing forces that exist together in unison—the good and the bad. The mystery of the Great Mother lies in her duality: She is a loving and nurturing mother who also devours and destroys. This duality inspired Jung to refer to the archetype as "the loving and the terrible mother."[8] The two most prominent mothers battling over the Iron Throne—the loving Daenerys Targaryen and the terrible Cersei Lannister— best exemplify the polarity within the Great Mother.

The Loving Mother

In many ways, Daenerys Targaryen represents all that a good and loving mother embodies. Jung said that the favorable and positive aspects of the Great Mother are associated with qualities of "maternal solicitude and sympathy, the magic authority of the female, the wisdom and spiritual exaltation that transcends reason . . . all that cherishes and sustains, that fosters growth and fertility."[9]

Daenerys first seems to be more of a maiden than a mother. At the beginning of the series, she appears as a young and pure-hearted woman vulnerable to her brother's abuse and manipulation. Inexperienced and weak-willed, she enters into an arranged marriage with Khal Drogo. Not until she realizes her sexual power does her evolution toward motherhood begin. She soon becomes pregnant, and her status as a mother is established.[10]

Jung's notion of the spiritual and intuitive wisdom of the feminine that he termed "magic authority" is evident in the Dothraki pregnancy ceremony. Surrounded by the elite widowed mothers who serve as the tribe's seers, the khaleesi consumes the raw heart of a stallion and is granted her magic authority. With sacred blood running down her face and a child in her womb, Daenerys becomes the loving mother side of the Great Mother archetype.

The Great Mother archetype also represents the cycle of birth, death, and rebirth. Upon the deaths of both Khal Drogo and their unborn son, Daenerys walks through the flames of her husband's pyre.[11] Fire itself often is viewed as a symbol of spiritual transformation.[12] Emerging from the flames transformed and reborn as the true exemplification of the good and loving mother, Daenerys is no longer a mother to a Khal prince but instead the mother to three dragons and to the people. She is the divine mother.

The loving mother, according to Jungian psychology, holds and protects her young by attending to and nourishing their needs.[13] These qualities are manifested in Daenerys. With unconditional love and patience, she teaches her unruly dragons how to control their fire breathing to cook meat.[14] Her loyalty to and protection of them is fierce and unwavering. When her dragons are stolen, she insists on rescuing her winged children despite the warnings of others.

Daenerys soon becomes the divine mother, the mother to the people. This aspect of the archetype involves nurturing and protecting the people, especially when they are treated poorly by those in power. Appalled by the cruel and inhumane acts she witnesses, Daenerys frees the Unsullied, who then swear their allegiance to her authority; nurtures those who are near death, offering a dying slave a drink of water; and honors the life of each crucified slave child by properly burying each body.[15] The crowds begin to chant to her, "Mhysa," meaning mother.[16]

The Terrible Mother

In Jungian psychology, light cannot exist without dark just as pleasure cannot exist without pain.[17] Similarly, good mothers can be better understood in comparison to evil mothers. In many ways, Cersei Lannister represents all that the evil and terrible mother embodies. Jung describes the negative aspects of the Great Mother as being associated with qualities of all that is "secret, hidden, dark, and dead."[18] She devours, seduces, or poisons all life that she encounters, like some "inescapable fate."[19] Psychologist Erich Neumann describes the terrible mother as "the hungry earth, which devours its own children and fattens on their corpses."[20] Cersei's evil is apparent from the very beginning of her life, even before she becomes a mother. Tyrion recalls that at nine years old, Cersei had a servant girl brutally beaten for stealing a necklace—a pitiless act that sets the stage for future viciousness.

The incestual relationship between Jaime and Cersei is another dimension of the terrible mother embodied by Cersei—the secret and the hidden. Her relationship with Jaime is so cloaked in darkness that she cannot risk having others know her terrible secret. Although it is Jaime who pushes Bran out the window, he does so at Cersei's urging.[21] The terrible mother bears power so prevailing that those under it face nothing but death, dismemberment, or sickness,[22] and her supremacy for destruction surpasses all. When Arya's direwolf mars Cersei's son Joffrey, Cersei demands that the wolf be killed. When Arya's wolf cannot be found, Cersei calls for the life of Sansa's innocent wolf instead, indifferent to which wolf actually bit her son,[23] destruction and death being her ultimate goal. To spite her brother Tyrion, Cersei abducts his lover, Shae, and has her brutally beaten.[24]

For the terrible mother, love implies weakness. Cersei admits feeling disgusted by her experience of love. She warns Sansa,

"The more people you love, the weaker you are. You'll do things for them that you know you shouldn't do. You'll act the fool to make them happy, to keep them safe. Love no one but your children. On that front a mother has no choice."[25] For the terrible mother, love is no blessing; rather, it is a nuisance that stands in the way of ultimate power.

A Union of Opposites

Jung concluded that the route to psychological health requires a wholeness in which no aspect of oneself is left out. Inner conflict arises when aspects of an archetype are ignored or repressed. The solution, Jung argues, is the union of opposites. To achieve wholeness, the light must be accepted by the dark and the dark by the light. Each woman demonstrates glimpses of her opposite, or what might be considered the denied aspect of the Great Mother. However, neither Daenerys nor Cersei fully demonstrates a "united duality" that Jung views as a prerequisite for psychological health.[26] Like the yin-yang symbol, each woman possesses a fraction of the opposing aspect within her.

Cersei briefly demonstrates the compassion of the good mother when she visits Catelyn Stark to offer her condolences for Bran's injuries. With tears in her eyes, perhaps from grief, perhaps from remorse, she shares the story of the death of her firstborn.[27] The loving mother's unconditional devotion and loyalty to family bond is seen in Cersei's relationship with her young daughter, Myrcella,[28] especially when she is heartbroken over Myrcella's arranged marriage. Despite these occurrences, Cersei's tenderness is fleeting. She fails to integrate aspects of the good mother into her identity and therefore falls short of achieving wholeness.

Daenerys shows intimations of terribleness as well. She is not above death and revenge, especially against those who harm her loved ones. She commands that the woman who performed the blood magic against Drogo and her son be tied to Drogo's funeral pyre and with sullen satisfaction watches the woman scream in pain as she is burned alive.[29] This action demonstrates the darkness and destruction that Jung associates with the terrible mother. Unlike Cersei, Daenerys is prepared to accept her opposing side and understand it as part of her identity. Such acceptance of a few terrible mother tendencies by a loving mother is what Jung would argue is part of the pursuit of psychological wholeness and united duality.

A Song of Love and Death

The human experience of mothers and mothering is eternally complex. Humankind is shaped not only by the private, personal experience of mother but also by the universal and deeply rooted force of Jung's Great Mother archetype. The dual nature of the Great Mother can always comfort and terrify humans the world over. She appears to us in our personal dreams, fantasies, and nightmares, as well as in our collective myths, stories, and legends—one of which is the story of two women battling for the Iron Throne. Their endless opposition can serve as a powerful reminder of the dual nature within each of us and the path of unification that leads to psychological wholeness.

References

Jung, C. (1921/1976). *Psychological types*. Princeton, NJ: Princeton University Press.
Jung, C. (1953). *Two essays on analytical psychology*. Princeton, NJ: Princeton University Press.
Jung, C. (1956). *Symbols of transformation* (2nd ed.). Princeton, NJ: Princeton University Press.
Jung, C. (1959/1973). *Four archetypes: Mother, rebirth, spirit, trickster*. Princeton, NJ: Princeton University Press.
Jung, C. (1963). *Mysterium coniunctionis*. Princeton, NJ: Princeton University Press.
Neumann, E. (1954/2014). *The origins and history of consciousness*. Princeton, NJ: Princeton University Press.

Neumann, E. (1955/1972). *The Great Mother: An analysis of the archetype* (2nd ed.). Princeton, NJ: Princeton University Press.

Woodman, M., & Dickson, E. (1996). *Dancing in the flames: The dark goddess in the transformation of consciousness.* Boston, MA: Shambhala.

Notes

1. Neumann (1954/2014), p. 322.
2. Jung (1956).
3. Jung (1959/1973).
4. Neumann (1955/1972).
5. e.g., Jung (1921/1976, 1953, 1956, 1959/1973, 1963).
6. Jung (1959/1973), p. 15.
7. Woodman & Dickson (1996).
8. Jung (1956).
9. Jung (1959/1973), p. 16.
10. Episode 1–2, "The Kingsroad" (April 24, 2011).
11. Episode 1–10, "Fire and Blood" (June 19, 2011).
12. Neumann (1955/1972), p. 219.
13. Neumann (1955/1972).
14. Episode 2–4, "Garden of Bones" (April 22, 2012).
15. Episode 3–3, "Walk of Punishment" (April 21, 2013).
16. Episode 3–10, "Mhysa" (June 9, 2013).
17. Jung (1963).
18. Jung (1959/1973), p. 16.
19. Jung (1959/1973), p. 16.
20. Neumann (1955/1972), p. 149.
21. Episode 1–1, "Winter Is Coming" (April 17, 2011).
22. Neumann (1955/1972).
23. Episode 1–2, "The Kingsroad" (April 24, 2011).
24. Episode 2–8, "The Prince of Winterfell" (May 20, 2012).
25. Episode 2–7, "A Man Without Honor" (May 13, 2012).
26. Jung (1921/1976).
27. Episode 1–2, "The Kingsroad" (April 24, 2011).
28. Episode 2–3, "What Is Dead May Never Die" (April 15, 2012).
29. Episode 1–10, "Fire and Blood" (June 19, 2011).

L ife leads inevitably to death. As we encounter losses throughout our journey, we may each experience them in different ways. One psychiatrist's well-known model of the grieving process outlines five stages which a person might go through when facing one's own demise or grieving over the loss of another. How well, though, does that model really fit the variety of ways we react?

CHAPTER ELEVEN

Loss and Mourning: A Stark Contrast in Coping with Death

PATRICK O'CONNOR

"I grew up with soldiers. I learned how to die a long time ago."
—Eddard "Ned" Stark[1]

> *"There are no mistakes, no coincidences; all events are blessings given to us to learn from."*
> —psychiatrist Elisabeth Kübler-Ross[2]

The death of a person can have a multitude of effects on the lives of those involved in that person's life. In *A Song of Ice and Fire* and *Game of Thrones*, the same death shocks some characters and inspires other characters to celebrate.[3] The reactions of the surviving characters undoubtedly parallel those of viewers who experience the passing of people in their own lives. How might facing his own demise affect Eddard "Ned" Stark and then his remaining family members as well as others in Westeros after his death? How starkly do people differ in the ways they process death both before a person passes and afterward?

Death and Dying

Processing loss can be challenging, disheartening, and sometimes even surprising. People can experience any number of emotions as memories of the deceased flood their minds. Elisabeth Kübler-Ross, a Swiss-born psychiatrist, recognized the lack of formal education in medical school on how to handle the dying process.[4] During her time working in hospitals and later teaching at the University of Chicago, she discovered that many physicians, surgeons, nurses, and medical students who would be working with the terminally ill had no understanding of how to care for those patients and their families. While she was working with the patients, a common group of stages emerged when patients and their loved ones were confronted with the inevitable. Not everybody experiences all five stages, and Kübler-Ross did not mean that they must be sequential; rather, these are five stages of death processing that the terminally ill and their loved ones commonly experience before, during, and after an individual's passing.[5] These five stages are illustrated by both the dying and their survivors, although as Kübler-Ross explains, "The one thing that usually persists through all these stages is hope."[6] Hope among the dying as well as among the surviving is the only common thread for all who experience this life event.

Whether the deaths are caused by illness or execution, the characters in *Game of Thrones* work through the same stages. Their friends, family members, allies, and enemies express their own versions of those stages as well; the awareness of a person's demise is not limited to people who are moments away from it. It also serves as a reminder to each character that he or she will face it one day, and this brings about a myriad of emotions. If we focus specifically on the Starks and those immediately surrounding them, the five stages of denial, anger, bargaining, depression, and acceptance reveal themselves easily.

Denial

"No, that can't be right!" "Not me!" Responding to imminent death with denial protects an individual from such a harsh reality.[7] So much of our existence is spent maintaining life that to be given the news that those actions will soon be futile seems to go against the reality we have maintained throughout our lives. Feeding our bodies with food, sustaining our bodies with water, cleaning ourselves to keep away illness, and even the pursuit of joyous moments all serve to strengthen life and keep our spirits high.

Sigmund Freud asserted that our sense of self is fragile and any significant threat to that sense will be met with defense.[8] A false accusation, failure in a project, and death itself all threaten a person's self-concept as a well-functioning individual. Our active search for evidence that we are healthy, happy individuals is carried out simultaneously with defenses that protect us from the opposite; these behaviors are known as *defense mechanisms*.[9] For example, Arya closes her eyes when she realizes she is about to witness her father's execution. This is an expression of the defense mechanism called *denial* in the physical sense; not directly witnessing the death of her father makes the reality a bit less real to Arya. This insulates a person against experiencing the full horror that would be felt by someone who is a direct witness, such as Sansa when she does not look away as her father is beheaded.

Anger

Once reality begins to set in, a person may respond to this attack on his or her understanding of self and life with anger.[10] This can be directed outward against the dying individual, caretakers, a higher being, or the illness or reason for death or inward against the person processing the loss. Both of Ned's adult sons react to the news of their father's execution with anger.[11]

In cases in which death processing follows the murder of a loved one, the survivor may feel a need to enact revenge on the perpetrator.[12] Anger, like denial, also can serve as a protective factor. By keeping away a foreign threat that resulted in the death of another person, one can feel that he or she has prevented the same thing from happening to himself or herself. That is, lashing out in anger can feel like it protects the survivor from harm while also making it possible to get even with that which seemingly caused the illness or death to occur. For many characters in *Game of Thrones*, anger fuels this desire for revenge and often leads to acts of violence.

Robb violently attacks a tree with his sword; tearful and angry, he shouts, "I'll kill them all, every one of them! I'll kill them!"[13] Jon Snow swears revenge on the king. He discusses his actions with Jeor Mormont, Lord Commander of the Night's Watch. Recognizing that Jon's anger will not resolve his problem, Jeor asks him, "And you can bring [Ned] back?" Jeor then turns Jon's attention back to matters of the Night's Watch, ignoring his bereavement. Jon finds bravery and brotherhood in his fellow men at the Night's Watch, realizing the futility in his anger, unlike Robb, who cannot let go of his anger and is blinded by it when he chooses to pursue revenge and vengeance against those who killed his father.

Bargaining

Feeling helpless and denying the genuine threat of death, combined with feeling vulnerable to the same illness or act that led to the passing of a loved one, can lead to a desire to gain greater control in one's life.[14] This emerges in the form of bargaining, in which a person seeks to avoid the inevitable by offering something in place of death. "Maybe if we try a second round of treatment" and "Have you tried this alternative?" can be well-intentioned sentiments, but when all reliable signs point to an end, these attempts to buy time are ultimately futile. In the eighth episode of the first season of the television series, Sansa begs Joffrey for mercy for her father. She agrees that he must be punished for his alleged crime of treason, but she pleads for Joffrey to spare him from death. Sansa, who has no control, attempts to regain some by bargaining to extend the life of a loved one close to death, an act that is sadly futile.

This bargain also can arrive as a plea to feel alive one last time before death. Kübler-Ross shared a story of an opera singer who asked to sing one last time before radiation treatments for cancer, as well as losing her teeth, robbed her of the ability to sing. This is still an attempt to maintain some sense of control over a situation in which a person seemingly has none. By providing a "self-imposed deadline," as Kübler-Ross puts it, the person can rediscover a glimmer of hope that things may not be as bad as he or she thinks.[15]

Depression

Kübler-Ross indicated that two different kinds of depression emerge during this stage—reactive depression and preparatory depression—and notes that both are equally important in the grieving process to move toward the final stage.[16] *Reactive depression* is a response to losses already incurred by the individual. A loss of function caused by paralysis, a loss of financial stability from mounting medical debt, and spending less time at home as a result of spending more in the hospital are all examples of loss experienced by the dying. During this time, it is best to help the dying person adjust to these losses by offering support. Taking over obligations, running errands, and further assisting in the person's day-to-day functioning can brighten spirits as he or she takes on the physical burden of an illness and/or the psychological burden of coping with dying.

The second kind of depression, *preparatory depression*, sets in as the dying individual considers the losses that have not happened yet. This includes the loss of everything and everybody the person loves as he or she rapidly becomes aware of the end of his or her time on this planet. It is during this time that Kübler-Ross advises not trying to cheer the dying person up or to encourage that person to look on the bright side of things; rather, these are real losses that cannot be ignored, and so any attempt to impose ignorance on this person will be met with appropriate resistance. Over the course of several visits from Varys, Ned Stark encounters preparatory depression as he learns of the developments outside his prison cell.[17] From his son Robb preparing for war, to his daughter Arya going missing, to his daughter Sansa siding with King Joffrey, Ned learns that he is helpless to influence the extreme measures being taken by his family in response to his imprisonment and sentencing. At this point, it appears that Ned is becoming rapidly aware of how the world will go on without him, and he lashes out at Varys when he hears the news.

Cheering up the dying and their loved ones may help the person doing the cheering, moving him or her back to denial

Why Do We Connect So Deeply With Characters' Grief?

We connect with fictional characters because we see elements in them that remind us of our own experiences. In psychology, there is a type of figure known as a *Gestalt figure*, which is an incomplete figure that our minds automatically attempt to complete.[18] When we put three angles close to one another, the human brain wants to close the gaps and form a single figure—a triangle—because the brain is constantly looking for predictable, reliable patterns. However, this closed figure does not really exist—it exists only in the mind because it is the mind that has closed it. A fictional character such as Ned Stark is similar in that we catch only a glimpse of his personality and brief moments of his life. We learn that he is brave and honest and struggles with people who deceive him. We see people lie to him, we see him think quietly to himself, and we see him act from nobility. However, these are only the briefest moments in this character's day, considering that a fifty-minute episode may contain only ten minutes of a character with whom we connect. Yet we understand the continuity of this character's story over hours, days, weeks, and even longer. Who fills in these gaps of time? We do. When we are brought along on a fictional character's journey, we project ourselves into the moments we do not see, guided by the moments we do see, to form a mutual creation of the character's life as told by his or her creator and internalized by us. Just as the brain attempts to fill in the gaps of this incomplete figure to understand it as a triangle, it also fills in the gaps of an incomplete story to understand a character.

as the sunny side of things keeps away the sadder reality.[19] However, as was mentioned earlier, this is not something that can be kept away simply with kind words. Kübler-Ross indicated that depression serves a purpose in preparing a person for acceptance, the final stage. It is through depression that the dying and their loved ones fully grasp the gravity of the inevitable and can see it for what it truly is—an end.

Acceptance

The final stage in processing the death of oneself or another person is acceptance.[20] This is not a joyful stage in which a person is meant to feel pleased with things; rather, "it is almost void of feelings."[21] When it is expressed by the dying, that person seems to have diminished interest in life's possibilities. He or she spends more time asleep than usual, seems more disconnected from day-to-day events, and is less conversational. This can be viewed as finding inner peace—a peace so strong that even major concerns in another person's life are no longer meaningful for the dying individual. This is a time when the dying may wish to have fewer visitors and desire only silence from their visitors, symbolizing support until the end.

Ned Stark illustrates this when he is with Robert Baratheon on Robert's deathbed. Robert knows he is about to die and tells those around him that he wants the town to "feast on the boar that got [him]."[22] He then asks Cersei and the others to leave the room so that he can meet privately with Ned, the only person he has ever trusted as much as he could. He shares a few touching sentiments with his best friend, who sits quietly and listens to him expressing his final wishes. As Robert accepts his end, weak and exhausted, he asks Ned to leave to let him die, and in that moment the one dying and the survivor have accepted the passing.

Kübler-Ross noted that friends, family members, and medical personnel may encourage a person to "fight the good fight" until the end, to remain hopeful, to persist through adversity. Although this may seem noble to an outsider, Kübler-Ross said it may represent a reluctance to leave the denial, anger, or bargaining stage. This ultimately prevents a person from dying with peace and dignity, as he or she never achieves acceptance of fate.

Many beg Ned to accept the plea his daughter has placed before King Joffrey, believing that it will extend his life,[23] but Ned is reluctant, having accepted his mortality during his life as a soldier. To the end, the survivors are still bargaining, failing to accept the upcoming death. This illustrates further research conducted on Kübler-Ross's stages of grief model: People may enter and leave the acceptance stage at any time when grief-related distress is not present.[24] Ned appears to be in acceptance but reverses and moves to a previous stage by accepting the bargain. Acceptance may not be an end point in death processing, as several variables can affect one's reluctance to enter the stage.[25] Nonviolent/violent means of death is one such variable; a person may take longer than three months to enter acceptance after a violent death, as opposed to a shorter span of time after a death from natural causes.

A Stark Contrast

The death of Ned Stark affects his family, friends, and enemies in a variety of ways. In just a few episodes, viewers are able to observe characters going through Kübler-Ross's five stages of death processing. Whether denying the possibility, responding to it with intense anger and a desire for revenge, begging for a bargain, feeling overcome by depression, or accepting the inevitable, there is no one correct way to respond to death. According to Kübler-Ross, we will all encounter these stages at some point in our lives, whether it is in response to our own impending end or to the passing of someone else. Death is troubling to many people, but working through these emotional stages can remind us that we are human as we become increasingly aware of the finite nature of our time in our bodies.

References

Holland, J. M., & Neimeyer, R. A. (2010). An examination of stage theory of grief among individuals bereaved by natural and violent causes: A meaning-oriented contribution. *OMEGA: Journal of Death and Drying, 61*(2), 103–120.

Huffman, K., & Dowdell, K. (2015). *Psychology in action* (11th ed.). Hoboken, NJ: Wiley.

Kronisch, L. (1976, Nov.–Dec.). Elisabeth Kübler-Ross: Messenger of love. *Yoga Journal*, (11), 18–20.

Kübler-Ross, E. (1969). *On death and dying.* New York, NY: Macmillan.

Kübler-Ross, E. (1974). *Questions and answers on death and dying.* New York, NY: Collier.

Kübler-Ross, E. (1991). *On life after death.* New York, NY: Celestial Arts.

Newman, L. (2004). Elisabeth Kübler-Ross. *British Medical Journal, 329*(7466), 627.

Notes

1. Episode 1–9, "Baelor" (June 12, 2011).
2. Kronisch (1976).
3. Episode 1–9, "Baelor" (June 12, 2011).
4. Newman (2004).
5. Kübler-Ross (1974).
6. Kübler-Ross (1991), p. 138.
7. Kübler-Ross (1969).
8. Kübler-Ross (1969).
9. Huffman & Dowdell (2015).
10. Kübler-Ross (1969).
11. Episode 1–10, "Fire and Blood" (June 19, 2011).
12. Kübler-Ross (1969).
13. Episode 1–10, "Fire and Blood" (June 19, 2011).
14. Kübler-Ross (1969).
15. Kübler-Ross (1969), p. 95.
16. Kübler-Ross (1969).
17. Episode 1–8 "The Pointy End" (June 5, 2011); episode 1–9 "Baelor" (June 12, 2011).
18. Huffman & Dowdell (2015).
19. Kübler-Ross (1969).
20. Kübler-Ross (1969).
21. Kübler-Ross (1969), p. 124.
22. Episode 1–7, "You Win or You Die" (May 29, 2011).
23. Episode 1–9, "Baelor" (June 12, 2011).
24. Holland & Neimeyer (2010).
25. Holland & Neimeyer (2010).

Love and Belonging

TRAVIS LANGLEY

> "*Wind and words. We are only human, and the gods have fashioned us for love. That is our great glory, and our great tragedy.*"
> —Maester Aemon[1]

> "*All that we love deeply becomes part of us.*"
> —author Helen Keller[2]

People need people. At birth, we immediately depend on others to provide sustenance, shelter, and the other physical needs psychologist Abraham Maslow placed at the bottom of his pyramid as the strongest, most urgent needs in the hierarchy he hypothesized. The inclination to want others may come not only out of necessity but also out of instinct. Babies are born ready, for example, to prefer human faces over other types of stimuli.[3] Though a newborn's eyes are not yet fully developed, they are ready to see people.

Maslow saw *belongingness* (the need to belong) as a deficiency-based motive, meaning that lacking affiliation motivates people more than having it does.[4] Rejected, Tyrion might never feel accepted and may therefore think of this often. Fully accepted, his older siblings might never worry about fitting in. Loneliness and separation might also increase the yearning to be with others. Psychologist David McClelland saw *need for affiliation* as one of the three most dominant needs that drive and direct human behavior, noting that it motivated people most when they ached from lack of social interaction.[5] After her father dies and she remains at the capitol without family or friends, Sansa grows increasingly desperate and feels isolated, so much so that she risks trusting her fate to the nefarious Littlefinger. The need to connect with others is healthiest in moderation. People extremely high in the ingrained personality factor called *agreeableness*, the ones who are most persistently motivated by the need to connect and get along with others, might follow too eagerly and may make poor leaders.[6] They lead better in situations that call for *transformational leadership* skills (those requiring boldness) than *transactional leadership* skills (requiring management ability).[7] Desperation for approval can prompt bad decisions, as when Theon betrays the Starks to prove himself worthy of the Greyjoy name. He boldly leads an attack but then promptly proves himself weak when it comes to running things.

The desire for *intimacy* (closeness in relationships) is, compared to mere affiliation, less motivated by deficits. Some people share too much, to be sure, but most do not rush to divulge their innermost thoughts, feelings, or secrets. When a person opens up to another person and receives a positive response, that bit of intimacy can prime the person to want more.[8] Though Arya distrusts the Hound and names him on the list of people she wants to kill, the two reveal more to each other increasingly and reciprocally while they cross the country together in an attempt to ransom her. When ransom seems unlikely, the dangerous man does not abandon or eliminate her. Some bond has been forged.

Scholars and poets provide over a thousand definitions of love without ever pinning it down, disagreeing over what it is while agreeing that people find it important. It involves some kind of connection, but not always an intimate one. Some people love freely while others love not at all. Cersei, stingy with her love, advises her potential daughter-in-law Sansa, "Love no one but your children," because she believes love makes a person weak.[9]

Neo-Freudian Karen Horney, like so many early personality theorists, outlined a theory of personality development that reflected her own life—in her case, her quest for security and love.[10] She did shift the dialogue away from Freud's broad sexualization of personality formation.[11] Out of the many researchers who have theorized about how love develops and simply tried to decide what it is, Robert Sternberg proposed one of the most popularly cited perspectives in his *triarchic theory of love*, also known as his *triarchic* or *triangular theory of love* because of how he described and diagrammed the relationship between its three components: intimacy, commitment, and passion.[12]

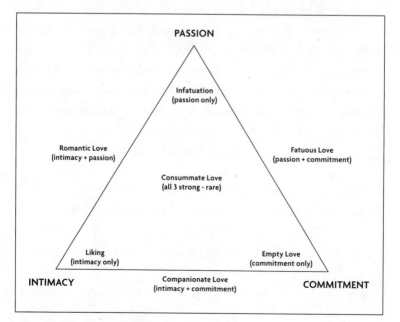

A love triangle of a theoretical kind.[13]

Intimacy, in Sternberg's terminology, refers to how closely connected people feel to one another and how much they like each other. Tyrion feels most closely connected to his brother Jaime, then to spymaster Varys. He trusts and likes them above all others. Love does not have to be romantic. It can be brotherly, motherly, or many otherly things. Tyrion's brother is also the person to whom he feels the greatest *commitment*. In addition to trusting Jaime and Varys, he misses them when they are not around. *Passion* dominates Tyrion's relationship with Shae. Over time, as they seem to be sharing and he grows to like and fall in love with her, intimacy joins the passion (*romantic love*). Jaime truly feels commitment to and passion for Cersei (*fatuous love*) without especially liking her. Ned and Catelyn Stark, who like each other and feel committed (*companionate love*), do not exhibit such passion. Lasting relationships likely see passion lessen, intimacy stabilize, and commitment build, with satisfaction based less on ardor than on companionship, common values, and shared experiences. Companionate love can be a pretty good thing. Across cultures, it predicts greater life satisfaction than passion alone.[14]

Throughout *Game of Thrones*, relationships abound in which love triangles are incomplete, where one or more components are missing. Maybe *consummate love*, which combines all three components, is even harder to achieve in such a harsh world where survival is difficult and treachery abounds.

References

Acevedo, B. P., & Aron, A. (2009). Does long-term relationship kill romantic love? *Review of General Psychology, 13*(1), 59–65.

Cassia, V. M., Valenza, E., Simion, F., & Leo, I. (2008). Congruency as a nonspecific perceptual property contributing to newborns' face preference. *Child Development, 79*(4), 807–820.

Easterbrook, M. A., Kisilevsky, B. S., Muir, D. W., & Laplante, D. P. (1999). Newborns discriminate schematic faces from scrambled faces. *Canadian Journal of Experimental Psychology, 53*(3), 231–241.

Freud, S. (1940). An outline of psycho-analysis. *International Journal of Psychoanalysis,* *21*(1), 27-84.

Horney, K. (1937). *The neurotic personality of our time.* New York, NY: Norton.

Judge, T. A., & Bono, J. E. (2000). Five-factor model of personality and transformational leadership. *Journal of Applied Psychology, 85*(5), 751–765.

Keller, H. (1957). *The open door.* Garden City, NY: Doubleday.

Kim, J., & Hatfield, E. (2004). Love types and subjective well-being: A cross-cultural study. *Social Behavior and Personality, 32*(2), 173–182.

Lim, B., & Ployhart, R. E. (2004). Transformational leadership: Relations to the five-factor model and team performance in typical and maximum contexts. *Journal of Applied Psychology, 89*(4), 610–621.

Martin, G. R. R. (1996). *A game of thrones.* New York, NY: Bantam.

Maslow, A. H. (1970). *The farther reaches of human nature.* New York, NY: Viking.

McAdams, D. P. (1980). A thematic coding system for the intimacy motive. *Journal of Research in Personality, 14*(4), 413–432.

McClelland, D. C. (1985). *Human motivation.* San Francisco, CA: Scott, Foresman.

Monzani, L., Ripoll, P., & Reiró, J. M. (2014). Followers' agreeableness and extraversion and their loyalty towards authentic leadership. *Psichothema, 26*(1), 69–75.

Rhodes, G. K., Stanley, S. M., & Markman, H. J. (2010). Should I stay or should I go? Predicting dating relationship stability from four aspects of commitment. *Journal of Family Psychology, 24*(5), 543–550.

Sayers, J. (1991). *Mothers of psychoanalysis: Helen Deutsch, Karen Horney, Anna Freud, Melanie Klein.* New York, NY: Norton.

Sternberg, R. (1986). A triangular theory of love. *Psychological Review, 93*(2), 119–135.

Sternberg, R. (1988). *The triangle of love: Intimacy, passion, commitment.* New York, NY: Basic.

Sternberg, R. (1997). Construct validation of a triangular love scale. *European Journal of Social Psychology, 27*(3), 313–335.

Notes

1. Martin (1996), p. 662.
2. Keller (1957), p. 131.
3. Cassia et al. (2008); Easterbrook et al. (1999).
4. Maslow (1970).
5. McClelland (1985).
6. Monzani et al. (2014).
7. Judge & Bono (2000); Lim & Ployhart (2004).
8. McAdams (1980).
9. Episode 2–7, "A Man without Honor" (May 13, 2012).
10. Horney (1937); Sayers (1991).
11. Freud (1940).
12. Rhodes et al. (2010); Sternberg (1986, 1997).
13. Sternberg (1986, 1997).
14. Acevedo & Aron (2009); Kim & Hatfield (2004); Sternberg (1988).

Part Four
Fires

Fire preserves life against the cold. It brings death to those caught inside. People's inner fires, their emotions and drives, help and hurt. The extremes of summer and winter, hot and cold, require balance. Even the best of intents and purposes can be dangerous if left unchecked to run away like wildfire.

Fire melts metal and tempers steel. After many instances of abuse and trauma, different processes can help people work through their experiences rather than be overcome by them. We revisit posttraumatic growth to see who might do more than grow. Who will break chains and conquer?

CHAPTER TWELVE

Enduring and Surviving: Leaders Forged in Dragon Fire

LARA TAYLOR KESTER

"The frightened child who sheltered in my manse died on the Dothraki Sea, and was reborn in blood and fire. This dragon queen who wears her name is a true Targaryen."
—Illyrio Mopatis[1]

"Life ultimately means taking the responsibility to find the right answer to its problems and to fulfill the tasks which it constantly sets for each individual."
—psychiatrist Viktor Frankl[2]

How did Daenerys become arguably the most powerful woman in the world? What makes her so different from the other leaders of Westeros and the lands across the Narrow

Sea? Why do so many men and women pledge themselves to her and her cause? Many of these questions can be answered by looking at the psychological concepts of resilience and post-traumatic growth because both are processes that can defend a person against or prevent the negative effects of trauma.

Enduring the Flames: Resilience

Resilience is part of what helps individuals work through negative stress reactions, which are in great supply in the world of Westeros. It is the ability to bounce back after difficult experiences.[3] Often resilience is attributed to personality traits such as optimism, hope, self-confidence, and an internal locus of control.[4] Three main kinds of resilience are survival, recovery, and thriving.[5]

The *survival* category involves never regaining the level of functioning from before the traumatic event. Individuals in this category are merely trying to make it through their daily lives by going through the motions. This does not mean that they have given up or are weak. To continue living in the face of adversity and trauma in and of itself can be a form of strength. Arya Stark's response after watching soldiers parade around with her brother's desecrated body attached to his wolf's head fits into this category.[6] She shows obvious signs of distress, such as her blank stare, but still shows a desire to live and avenge her fallen family members.

Recovery involves returning back to the level of functioning an individual had before a traumatic event. As a result of Daenerys's repeated trauma growing up with Viserys, it is difficult to identify a baseline level of functioning. However, when she first sees Khal Drogo and is able to stand up for herself with Viserys by telling him she does not want to marry the khal,[7] it implies some degree of self-worth and confidence. She is able to stand up for herself and her servants time and time again. She finds a sense of belonging when she marries into the Dothraki and tries to become accustomed to their way of life. She also starts to form a family regardless of the way her marriage came about. These are all signs of recovery from the abuse she suffered from Viserys.

The third type of resilience, *thriving*, entails more than learning to live with the effects of trauma or bouncing back. Individuals in this category go a step further and flourish, grow, and expand their individual development as a result of their traumatic experiences. Thriving is an important part of *posttraumatic growth:* growing as a person as a response to trauma. Jon Snow is able to create a tentative peace with the wildings, who have been his enemies for so long, after falling for and losing Ygritte.

Rising From the Ashes: Posttraumatic Growth

Posttraumatic growth is the positive psychological change that results from coping with traumatic or highly challenging circumstances.[8] Daenerys has no shortage of those experiences throughout her life; death, exile, abuse, betrayal, and struggle are just a few of the many trials and tragedies she finds herself living through. Yet she is compassionate, fair-minded, intelligent, and open to suggestion and fights strongly for what she believes in. From a very difficult past, she has grown to a point of greater cognitive and emotional development and awareness of life, a key component of posttraumatic growth.[9]

Areas of Growth

There are five identified areas in which individuals who experience posttraumatic growth show gains. Not every trauma survivor shows signs of all these areas at once. Often such people experience some types of growth and others come along later.[10]

Personal Strength. This may come in the form of a "If I made it through this, I can do anything" attitude. An example is Brienne of Tarth's insistence on completing her pledge to bring the Stark girls home even in the face of impossible odds, attempted rape, and several attempts on her life.

Exploring New Life Possibilities. Often those who experience posttraumatic growth find that there are opportunities open to them that were not available before the trauma. Before Drogo's death, Daenerys is unable to rule on her own without a man by her side. Now she is able to lead her people and make tactical decisions on her own.

Forming Meaningful Interpersonal Relationships. Close relationships are a crucial part of the human experience.[11] They allow individuals to normalize their experiences and feelings. They also allow people to feel good about themselves and provide a sense of belonging or purpose. Brienne's relationships with Renly, Catelyn, and Jaime are examples of how a person can find worth and value in caring for and being respected by others. Forming meaningful relationships also can entail developing an increased connection to those who suffer. Daenerys's affection for those who have been enslaved is expressed when she refers to the freedmen as her children.

Gaining Appreciation for Life. After a traumatic event, especially the loss of a loved one, survivors may find themselves with a greater appreciation for life and a feeling that they do not want to take it for granted.[12] In the House of the Undying, Daenerys is presented with the illusion of a life with Khal Drogo and their son Rhaego. She cries when she has to give it up, but she is able to walk away and look for her missing dragons because of her appreciation for the life she currently has as opposed to the illusion of what she dreams she could have had.[13]

Developing Spirituality. Spirituality abounds in the world of *Game of Thrones*. However, spirituality does not include only religion. It also refers to a change in belief systems or the sense of being a part of something bigger than oneself. After Viserys dies, Daenerys has a stronger identification with dragons, particularly with the idea that their bloodline comes from the blood of the dragon. She finds her strength by calling herself the "Blood of the Dragon" or the "Mother of Dragons."

An important distinction to make is that even with the positive outcomes associated with posttraumatic growth, the individual is still going through a traumatic event and still suffers. We see this when Daenerys loses Drogo, when her dragons are kidnapped by Pyat Pree, when Brienne of Tarth fails to protect Renly and is accused of murder, and when Jon reacts to Ygritte's death. Although these events may lead each character to take a meaningful action or make a positive decision, they are still painful and difficult to work through.

Posttraumatic growth has been described as both an outcome and a process.[14] The outcome refers to the changes that we can see a person has made psychologically, such as confidence and a commanding presence. The process reflects how a person can gain strength and justness and how changing can be positive in the face of adversity. This includes questioning of oneself and the choices one makes along with attempts at making meaning out of trauma and other negative events.

Meaning Making

Meaning making is one of the major pathways to posttraumatic growth.[15] It is a cognitive process that involves being able to find a way to explain the horrible things that have happened and integrate them into one's worldview. One way to attempt to make meaning is through ruminative brooding, which often looks like "What if this had happened differently?" or "What if I hadn't done that?"[16] Brooding typically keeps individuals stuck in a cycle that reinforces their negative emotions of guilt or shame. If Dany had allowed Qotho's claims that Drogo's illness and impending death were her fault for accepting the help of a Maegi to get to her,[17] she might have begun to blame herself, shut down, or become consumed with what might have been.

The other cognitive process used to make meaning of traumatic experiences—*reflective pondering*—[18] allows traumatized individuals to think about what happened and attempt to resolve the discrepancies between what they knew before the event and what they know now. This can be accomplished through assimilation or accommodation.

In *assimilation*, the individual tries to maintain a previous worldview and make the event fit it. Early on in her marriage to Drogo, Daenerys may have been going through this type of process, as she wishes she could just go back to how things were before. *Accommodation* provides a better opportunity for change to occur as it gives individuals the opportunity to change their worldview to fit what has happened to them. Dany is able to do this when she tells Viserys, "These are my people now."[19] Here she is able to accept that she has a place to belong to and is in a better place and is a better person as a result of the trauma of being sold into marriage. In this way, accommodation is the beginning of another process involved in posttraumatic growth: benefit finding.

Benefit Finding

Benefit finding—the ability to find the positive outcomes of horrific and tragic events—includes improved relationships, increased empathy and compassion for the suffering of others, decreased fearfulness, a sense of mastery over one's world, a sense that one has learned a valuable lesson, a desire to help others, changes in priorities, and an effort to avoid taking life for granted.[20] Daenerys is able to realize many of these benefits, most noticeably her increased empathy for the suffering of others. Her compassion for maltreated slaves, which is evident throughout her story, is part of what makes her so fit to be queen.

Several benefits that trauma survivors have been able to identify have been found to be catalysts for change for those individuals.[21] Realizing that one has the choice to take responsibility for and control over the direction one's life takes can be incredibly empowering. For most of their lives, Dany, Brienne, and Arya are forced to follow the rules of men (father, brother, husband), and their worth is only what the men say it is. After the deaths of Drogo, Renly, and Ned, they all become their own women in their own individual ways, and each is ready to live her life as she sees fit, no longer according to the rules of those men. Also, being listened to and being seen by another person can be a powerful validation for someone who has felt unheard or invisible. Daenerys is loved and worshipped by her people and keeps several close friends who listen to her, and Brienne connects with many on her journey, including Catelyn and Jamie. This provides both with a sense of being seen but also a sense of belonging and purpose, which is another of the benefits that bring about change.

Another of these catalysts for change is a sense of liberation and freedom. This can be anything from perceiving a sense of control, to telling a secret, to choosing to forgive. Often trauma survivors feel a loss of control during the traumatic experience, and when they are able to find a sense of control afterward, it allows them to find the internal resources to focus on growth.[22] In the same vein, a sense of mastery over one's life passions or a feeling of accomplishment or achievement also can allow for increased self-esteem and empowerment. Dany makes it her life's work to free slaves and stand up to those who would take advantage of the weak, and Brienne vows to find Arya and Sansa; this gives both something to live for.

For posttraumatic growth to happen, the individual needs to take action rather than just think about the meaning and the benefits of what happened.[23] However, it is not merely a matter of taking action but of taking action to do what is right that provides the opportunity for growth.[24] As was mentioned in the quote from Viktor Frankl at the start of this chapter, the essence of life is for an individual to take what is given to him or her and try to do what is right with it. Daenerys transforms her trauma into a reason to fight for the underdog, stand up for what she believes in, and not back down. Her people see her do it every day and love her for it. Her actions give them hope and make them feel better about themselves. Not only does she free them from their shackles, she genuinely loves them and does her best to make sure they are fed and safe. She cares for them to the extent that they call her "mother" and are inspired to go forth and do good in order to make her proud (see the sidebar).

Breaking Chains
Daenerys transitions from a child bride into a queen and leader of many, Jon from the Stark scandal to a lord commander, and Brienne from a misfit to a guardian of the defenseless. These transformations can occur because each is able to find personal strength, explore new possibilities, form close relationships, gain a greater appreciation for life, and develop a new worldview. These attributes help a person make meaning out of struggles and traumatic events and to survive and find a place in the world after them. They also enable one to find benefits

Why do We Love Survivors?

The short answer to this question is that they instill us with hope. It doesn't hurt when one of them is also a badass.

The long answer is slightly more complicated. Research has shown that individuals who spend significant amounts of time with survivors of trauma who show signs of posttraumatic growth often begin to show those signs as well.[25] This is known as *vicarious posttraumatic growth*. Improved relationship skills, increased appreciation for the resilience of others, a better self-understanding and understanding of others, and an increased appreciation for life are all possible outcomes of this phenomenon.

Viewers and readers may not be in the trenches with Dany, Jon, or Brienne (they are fictional characters, after all) but still dedicate hours of time to them and their stories. We hope for a better world with them. Their joy, strength, and successes feel like ours.

from trauma, such as an increased empathy for the suffering of others. All these things together create posttraumatic growth, which allows these individuals to thrive.

Not everyone who goes through a traumatic event will thrive or grow as an individual in the same way Dany, Brienne, and Jon do. Some may recover to a previous level of functioning. Others may find the will to go on but suffer from some of the negative effects of trauma, such as having flashbacks, shutting down emotionally, and displaying hypervigilance. There are some who may even give up on life and try to harm themselves or put themselves in danger. Trauma in and of itself is not positive or something to be sought after. However, through the lens of these characters' lives, it is possible to see how people who go through something horrible have the opportunity to grow and better themselves.

References

Barrington, A. J., & Shakespeare-Finch, J. (2012). Working with refugee survivors of torture and trauma: An opportunity for vicarious post-traumatic growth. *Counselling Psychology Quarterly, 26*(1), 89–105.

Dekel, S., Mandl, C., & Solomon, Z. (2011). Shared and unique predictors of post-traumatic growth and distress. *Journal of Clinical Psychology, 67*(3), 241–252.

Frankl, V. (1959). *Man's search for meaning.* New York, NY: Touchstone.

Hobfoll, S. E., Hall, B. J., Canetti-Nisim, D., Galea, S., Johnson, R. J., & Palmieri, P. A. (2007).

Refining our understanding of traumatic growth in the face of terrorism: Moving from meaning cognitions to doing what is meaningful. *Applied Psychology, 56*(3), 345–366.

Joseph, S., Murphy, D., & Regel, S. (2012). An affective-cognitive processing model of post-traumatic growth. *Clinical Psychology and Psychotherapy, 19*(4), 316–325.

Lichtenthal, W. G., Currier, J. M., Neimeyer, R. A., & Keesee, N. J. (2010). Sense and significance: A mixed methods examination of meaning making after the loss of one's child. *Journal of Clinical Psychology, 66*(7), 791–812.

Martin, G. R. R. (2011). *A dance with dragons.* New York, NY: Bantam Spectra.

McElheran, M., Briscoe-Smith, A., Khaylis, A., Westrup, D., Hayward, C., & Gore-Felton, C. (2012). A conceptual model of post-traumatic growth among children and adolescents in the aftermath of sexual abuse. *Counselling Psychology Quarterly, 25*(1), 73–82.

Rajandram, R. K., Jenewein, J., McGrath, C., & Zwahlen, R. A. (2011). Coping processes relevant to posttraumatic growth: An evidence-based review. *Supportive Care in Cancer, 19*(5), 583–589.

Shakespeare-Finch, J., & Barrington, A. (2012). Behavioural changes add validity to the construct of posttraumatic growth. *Journal of Traumatic Stress, 25*(2), 433–439.

Woodward, C., & Joseph, S. (2003). Positive change processes and post-traumatic growth in people who have experienced childhood abuse: Understanding vehicles of change. *Psychology and Psychotherapy, 76*(3), 267–283.

Notes

1. Martin (2011), p. 80.
2. Frankl (1959), p. 85.
3. Hobfoll et al. (2007).
4. Rajandram et al. (2011).
5. Woodward & Joseph (2003).
6. Episode 3–10, "Mhysa" (June 9, 2013).

7. Episode 1–1, "Winter Is Coming" (April 17, 2011).

8. Dekel et al. (2011).

9. Barrington & Shakespeare-Finch (2012).

10. McElheran et al. (2012).

11. McElheran et al. (2012).

12. Lichtenthal et al. (2010).

13. Episode 2–10, "Valar Morghulis" (June 3, 2012).

14. Rajandram et al. (2011).

15. Lichtenthal et al. (2010).

16. Joseph et al. (2012).

17. Episode 1–9, "Baelor" (June 12, 2011).

18. Joseph et al. (2012).

19. Episode 1-4, "Cripples, Bastards, and Broken Things" (May 8, 2011).

20. Lichtenthal et al. (2010).

21. Woodward & Joseph (2003).

22. Dekel et al. (2011).

23. Shakespeare-Finch & Barrington (2012).

24. Hobfoll et al. (2007).

25. Barrington & Shakespeare-Finch (2012).

Those who get burned may learn from it, but what message do they find in the flames? The lesson might be fear and its mark may be phobia. Those who suffer abuse can carry scars on both the outside and within. Even one who scoffs at compassion and heroism might learn a new lesson when he or she finds healing in unexpected ways.

CHAPTER THIRTEEN

The Hound, Horrors, and Heroism

JANINA SCARLET

"Heroes are those who can somehow resist the power of the situation and act out of noble motives, or behave in ways that do not demean others when they easily can."
—psychologist Philip G. Zimbardo[1]

The horrors of childhood trauma, bullying, and abuse can lead to a plethora of mental health problems including phobias and irrational fears, as well as extreme stress, hormone dysregulation, and neurochemical changes.[2] However, not every trauma survivor develops these problems. Some actually experience *posttraumatic growth*[3] (a positive change that results from making meaning of the traumatic event), and some even become heroes.[4] (For more on posttraumatic growth, see Chapter Four, "The Stark Sisters.") The Hound, Brienne of Tarth, Jon Snow, and Bran Stark all undergo severe adverse experiences in their childhood, and all are able to turn them into heroic outcomes.

Phobia Development and Treatment

A *specific phobia* is a severe and excessive fear of an object (e.g., an injection needle), an animal (e.g., mice, spiders, or bats), a situation (e.g., bridges, tunnels, or tight spaces), or natural environments (e.g., fire, water, or heights). Phobias can occur because of a traumatic interaction with a horrifying situation, as is the case with the Hound. After his brother shoves his head into a brazier (a portable heater) for stealing his wooden toy, the Hound develops a powerful aversion to fire. Not only is he extremely afraid of fire, he *generalizes* his response to fear anything related to it. His fear is so overwhelming that he is forced to desert the guard during the Battle of Blackwater when he sees the enemy ships approaching with fire.[5] He seems to exemplify a person who has developed a *specific phobia, natural environment type.*[6]

However, some phobias may not have a clear origin or cause. For most people who meet the criteria for the diagnosis of a specific phobia, the presentation of a feared object or situation is enough to trigger a panic attack or other forms of severe distress.[7]

One of the best treatments for a specific phobia is *cognitive-behavioral therapy* (CBT).[8] This is a process that involves identifying the relationship between thoughts, feelings, and behaviors and then changing the maladaptive patterns. For example, the sight of a fire may make someone like the Hound anxious because he believes that the fire inevitably will harm him. It then may cause him to escape the fear-provoking situation, as he does during the battle. A helpful CBT technique that has

been shown through research[9] to be extremely helpful in helping people reduce their phobic responses is called an *exposure.*
This refers to facing the feared object gradually and in a safe
manner. For example, if the Hound were experiencing a grad-
ual exposure during CBT sessions, his therapist might begin by
showing him pictures of fire. Once he was comfortable looking
at the pictures, Clegane might be exposed to an actual fire at a
far distance and over time be able to approach it safely, with a
reduced fear response.

Many patients who struggle with negative beliefs about their
feared objects initially may not believe themselves to be capable
of participating in an exposure. However, those who complete
the exposures tend to perform well.[10] For example, when the
Hound is forced to fight Beric, the leader of the Brotherhood
Without Banners, he comes face to face with his opponent's
flaming blade.[11] Despite his fear of fire, the Hound fights and
defeats Beric. This demonstrates that a person is able to face his
or her biggest fear if the situation is dire enough and requires it.

Bullying and Child Abuse

Other adverse childhood experiences that can be problematic
for a child's social and developmental well-being include bullying,[12] child abuse, and neglect.[13] Bullying is a deliberate and
repeated act of physical aggression or psychological humiliation
toward an individual who may not be able to defend himself
or herself.[14] According to some statistics, approximately one in
every three children may be affected by bullying,[15] which can
lead to depression, anxiety, and bullying behaviors on the part
of the survivor, as well as substance abuse disorders and other
mental health problems.[16] For example, Brienne of Tarth experiences bullying and taunting as a child and later as a young

adult. Brienne feels humiliated at a ball in her honor that her father has arranged to find a romantic match for her. At the ball, Brienne receives constant attention from the young men who are present, but her initial excitement is quickly replaced by hurt when she learns that the men have been mocking her, merely pretending to like her. Only Renly Baratheon has been genuinely kind to her, and so she pledges her life and her sword to him.[17]

Like bullying, *child abuse* can be extremely damaging to a child. *Emotional abuse* (also known as *psychological abuse*) is a form of child abuse involving emotional maltreatment. This includes trying to scare an individual, humiliating, threatening, ignoring, excessively blaming, frequently criticizing, and not providing enough encouragement and emotional support for a child. As he is growing up, Jon Snow experiences emotional abuse, especially from Catelyn Stark, who frequently berates him and blames him for being her husband's illegitimate son.[18] Long-term emotional abuse can lead to difficulties with social interactions, depression, low self-esteem, and even suicide.[19]

Traumatic Brain Injury

In addition to the emotional trauma, physical trauma, including traumatic brain injury (TBI), can have devastating effects on a trauma survivor.[20] Even minor TBI can disrupt brain functioning, causing an individual to feel dazed and confused. More severe cases of TBI have been linked with a risk of depression, posttraumatic stress disorder (PTSD), substance use disorders, chronic pain disorders, seizures, anxiety, and other mental and physical health complications.[21] TBI, particularly in association with another physical disability, puts an individual at greater risk for suicide. Some research studies estimate that

Brand New Talent

"You will never walk again, Bran, but you will fly," the three-eyed crow says to Bran.[22] Through his dreams and his connections with the crow and his spirituality, Bran is able to communicate with trees, animals, and people who are not near him. Before his fall he did not have any of these talents.

There is some evidence to suggest that TBI can lead an individual to uncover hidden talents. Although these talents ordinarily would not include the ability to talk to animals or trees, other previously unknown talents have been reported to emerge. For example, some patients discover an ability to draw or paint after a TBI or a stroke.[23] Specifically, it seems that damage to the brain's left frontal lobe can result in enhanced artistic ability. This region of the brain is responsible for the higher-order functions, such as decision making, planning, and categorizing, among other tasks.[24] How the brain's *plasticity* works is not well understood. Some researchers suggest that the injury to the frontal lobes reduces the inhibition of previously existing talents. Specifically, one of the functions of the frontal lobes is inhibition of socially undesirable behavior. It is possible that creativity occasionally may be overcontrolled by this region, and so perhaps for some individuals an injury to this area of the brain may make it easier for them to explore their creativity or, as in the case of Bran, spirituality.

approximately 31 percent of individuals with TBI are at risk for suicide.[25]

After being pushed out a window, [26] Bran Stark wakes up from his coma exhibiting *retrograde amnesia*: the inability to recall some events that took place before the injury.[27] Depending on its severity, TBI can affect an individual's cognitive abilities and working (short-term) memory.[28] The cognitive deficits are believed to be the reason TBI is one of the most disabling injuries.[29]

Heroism, Altruism, and Courageous Healing

Facing one's fears, in particular when it requires standing up for one's moral beliefs, is considered courageous[30] or heroic,[31] depending on the situation. *Heroism* refers to a virtuous act intended to assist another person despite personal ramifications. It is distinguished from similar actions such as *compassion* (offering kindness and empathy to a person who is struggling) and *altruism* (a selfless kind act not necessarily committed during another person's suffering or resulting in personal risk).[32]

Although he would have rejected the term, the Hound appears to act heroically on a number of occasions, such as when he protects Sansa.[33] The Hound appears to be acting heroically, potentially putting his life on the line because of Joffrey's whim or to protect Sansa from an unruly crowd. Brienne, too, acts heroically when she swears her loyalty to Catelyn Stark and dedicates her life to finding and protecting Catelyn's daughters, Sansa and Arya, after Catelyn's death despite the fact that she does not readily accomplish that mission. Jon Snow heroically protects Sam from Ser Alliser Thorne and at one point saves Lord Commander Mormont's life from wights, sustaining serious injury in the process.

These characters' heroic actions might actually help them recover from their childhood traumas. It seems that both heroic and altruistic behaviors are related to better mental and physical health and functioning. Some of these benefits include an improved sense of well-being, positive emotions, increased life span, reduced burnout, increased endurance, enhanced meaning (which in itself is associated with better improvements from PTSD), and increased self-efficacy, among others.[34] One of the possible explanations for this occurrence is that helping behaviors tend to improve people's mood, balance their nervous systems, and even improve their immune system function.[35]

Heroism Heals

Jon, Brienne, Bran, and the Hound all experience severe emotional or physical trauma in childhood. Nevertheless, they are able not only to recover but to become heroes by courageously facing their fears and standing up for what they believe in. Standing up to injustice, being kind to others, and connecting with one's sense of creativity or spirituality can help people improve their physical and mental health. In addition, noble heroic acts may extend the duration and possibly even improve the overall quality of a person's life.

References

American Psychiatric Association (2013). *Diagnostic and statistical manual of mental disorders* (DSM-5) (5th ed.). Washington, DC: American Psychiatric Association.

Andelic, N., Sigurdardottir, S., Schanke, A. K., Sandvik, L., Sveen, U., & Roe, C. (2010). Disability, physical health and mental health 1 year after traumatic brain injury. *Disability and Rehabilitation, 32*(13), 1122–1131.

Cantu, R. C. (2001). Posttraumatic retrograde and anterograde amnesia: Pathophysiology and implications in grading and safe return to play. *Journal of Athletic Training, 36*(3), 244.

GAME OF THRONES PSYCHOLOGY

Craig, W. M. (1998). The relationship among bullying, victimization, depression, anxiety, and aggression in elementary school children. *Personality and Individual Differences, 24*(1), 123–130.

Franco, Z. E., Blau, K., & Zimbardo, P. G. (2011). Heroism: A conceptual analysis and differentiation between heroic action and altruism. *Review of General Psychology, 15*(2), 99.

Glaser, D. (2000). Child abuse and neglect and the brain—a review. *Journal of Child Psychology and Psychiatry, 41*(1), 97–116.

Kaplan, S. J., Pelcovitz, D., & Labruna, V. (1999). Child and adolescent abuse and neglect research: A review of the past 10 years. Part I: Physical and emotional abuse and neglect. *Journal of the American Academy of Child and Adolescent Psychiatry, 38*(10), 1214–1222.

Langlois, J. A., Rutland-Brown, W., & Wald, M. M. (2006). The epidemiology and impact of traumatic brain injury: A brief overview. *Journal of Head Trauma Rehabilitation, 21*(5), 375–378.

León-Carrión, J., De Serdio-Arias, M. L., Cabezas, F. M., et al. (2001). Neurobehavioral and cognitive profile of traumatic brain injury patients at risk for depression and suicide. *Brain Injury, 15*(2), 175–181.

Lew, H. L., Vanderploeg, R. D., Moore, D. F., et al. (2008). Overlap of mild TBI and mental health conditions in returning OIF/OEF service members and veterans. *Journal of Rehabilitation Research & Development, 45*(3), xi.

Martin, G. R. R. (1996). *A game of thrones.* London, UK: Voyager.

Martin, G. R. R. (1998). *A clash of kings.* London, UK: Voyager.

Martin, G. R. R. (2000). *A storm of swords.* London, UK: Voyager.

Martin, G. R. R. (2005). *A feast of crows.* London, UK: Voyager.

Martin, G. R. R. (2011). *A dance with dragons.* London, UK: Voyager.

McAllister, T. W., Flashman, L. A., McDonald, B. C., & Saykin, A. J. (2006). Mechanisms of working memory dysfunction after mild and moderate TBI: Evidence from functional MRI and neurogenetics. *Journal of Neurotrauma, 23*(10), 1450–1467.

McGonigal, K. (2015). *The upside of stress: Why stress is good for you, and how to get good at it.* New York, NY: Penguin.

Midorikawa, A., & Kawamura, M. (2015). The emergence of artistic ability following traumatic brain injury. *Neurocase, 21*(1), 90–94.

Olatunji, B. O., Cisler, J. M., & Deacon, B. J. (2010). Efficacy of cognitive behavioral therapy for anxiety disorders: A review of meta-analytic findings. *Psychiatric Clinics of North America, 33*(3), 557–577.

Paquette, V., Lévesque, J., Mensour, B., et al. (2003). "Change the mind and you change the brain": Effects of cognitive-behavioral therapy on the neural correlates of spider phobia. *Neuroimage, 18*(2), 401–409.

Park, C. L., & Ai, A. L. (2006). Meaning making and growth: New directions for research on survivors of trauma. *Journal of Loss and Trauma, 11*(5), 389–407.

Post, S. G. (2005). Altruism, happiness, and health: It's good to be good. *International Journal of Behavioral Medicine, 12*(2), 66–77.

Schwartz, C., Meisenhelder, J. B., Ma, Y., & Reed, G. (2003). Altruistic social interest behaviors are associated with better mental health. *Psychosomatic Medicine, 65*(5), 778–785.

Sherrer, H. (Interviewer), & Zimbardo, P. (Interviewee). (2003). *Professor Philip Zimbardo: The interview* [interview transcript]: http://forejustice.org/zimbardo/p_zimbardo_interview.htm.

Smokowski, P. R., & Kopasz, K. H. (2005). Bullying in school: An overview of types, effects, family characteristics, and intervention strategies. *Children and Schools, 27*(2), 101–110.

Takahata, K., Saito, F., Muramatsu, T., et al. (2014). Emergence of realism: Enhanced visual artistry and high accuracy of visual numerosity representation after left prefrontal damage. *Neuropsychologia, 57,* 38–49.

Thorpe, S. J., & Salkovskis, P. M. (1995). Phobic beliefs: Do cognitive factors play a role in specific phobias? *Behaviour Research and Therapy, 33*(7), 805–816.

Vakil, E. (2005). The effect of moderate to severe traumatic brain injury (TBI) on different aspects of memory: A selective review. *Journal of Clinical and Experimental Neuropsychology, 27*(8), 977–1021.

Notes

1. Sherrer & Zimbardo (2003).
2. Glaser (2000).
3. Park & Ai (2006).
4. Franco et al. (2011).
5. Martin (1996).
6. American Psychiatric Association (2013).
7. American Psychiatric Association (2013).
8. Olatunji et al. (2010).
9. Olatunji et al. (2010); Paquette et al. (2003).
10. Thorpe & Salkovskis (1995).
11. Martin (2000).
12. Smokowski & Kopasz (2005).
13. Glaser (2000).
14. Craig (1998); Smokowski & Kopasz (2005).
15. Smokowski & Kopasz (2005).
16. Smokowski & Kopasz (2005).
17. Martin (2005).
18. Martin (1996).
19. Kaplan et al. (1999).
20. Andelic et al. (2010).
21. Lew et al. (2008); Langlois et al. (2006).
22. Martin (1996).
23. Midorikawa & Kawamura (2015); Takahata et al. (2014).
24. Takahata et al. (2014).
25. León-Carrión et al. (2001).
26. Martin (1996).
27. Cantu (2001).
28. McAllister et al. (2006); Vakil, (2005).
29. Langlois et al. (2006).
30. McGonigal (2015).
31. Franco et al. (2011).
32. Franco et al. (2011).
33. Martin (1998).
34. Post (2005); Schwartz et al. (2003).
35. Post (2005).

In a world where kill-or-be-killed situations are regular events and being a killer is more common than many occupations, how many lives must a person have to take—and for what reasons—to be seen as a villain? Serial and mass murderers show a wider variety of traits and motives than many might expect. How does one of the most hated sadists in the Seven Realms compare?

CHAPTER FOURTEEN

Ramsay: Portrait of a Serial Killer

COLT J. BLUNT

". . . hurry up and bring on your electric chair I want to leave here and take a nose-dive into the next world just to see if that one is as lousy as is this ball of mud and meanness. I am sorry for only two things. These two things are I am sorry that I have mistreated some few animals in my life-time and I am sorry that I am unable to murder the whole damed [sic] human race."
—American serial killer Carl Panzram[1]

"Let me state unequivocally that there is no such thing as the person who at age thirty-five suddenly changes from being perfectly normal and erupts into totally evil, disruptive, murderous behavior."
—psychological profiler Robert K. Ressler[2]

Some individuals do a lot of killing. Some people who commit multiple killings do so for *extrinsic* reasons (they are motivated to achieve other, ulterior purposes), perhaps in the name of honor or justice or under the orders of a lord. Even the Mountain, Gregor Clegane, a monster of a human being by any metric, commits his atrocities under the auspices of being a soldier. Thousands die in the Seven Kingdoms, where people often have no choice but to kill or be killed. Many die during the war for the Iron Throne, and with few exceptions, killing committed during battle is considered just and acceptable. Sometimes, though, individuals kill for their own *intrinsic* satisfaction. These are individuals who like doing it.

Modern criminology divides the killing of multiple people into three categories: mass murder, spree killing, and serial killing. *Mass murderers* kill multiple people in a relatively short period, usually at a single location. *Spree killers* kill multiple people across multiple locations without a significant break in time. *Serial killers* commit multiple murders with a temporal break between incidents. Spree killers and mass murderers often do not conceal their actions, often are identified quickly, and frequently are killed by law enforcement in a last-stand situation. Serial killers are generally more enigmatic. Their motivations often are not telegraphed yet fulfill a sort of psychological need that is beyond the reactionary anger typically seen in spree killers and mass murderers. In the world of Westeros, there may be no better example of a serial killer than Ramsay Bolton, who often kills people outside of battle and even occasionally hunts humans for sport.

Catching Killers

Serial killers are rare, though they often receive a great deal of publicity. The total number of serial killers operating in the United States is a *dark figure* (a real but unknown number) and obviously is in flux at any specific time. One tool for identifying and apprehending such offenders—*criminal investigative analysis* (more popularly known as *criminal profiling*)—utilizes aspects of a crime to construct a portrait of the possible suspect. Profilers consider known information about the crime, including the level of organization of the crime scene, the location of bodies, and available evidence, to glean psychological information about the killer. For instance, a messy crime scene with little concealment of evidence and the utilization of a weapon of opportunity (such as a kitchen knife) may suggest a *disorganized offender* motivated by anger or psychosis who failed to plan the murder, whereas a crime scene with little evidence and with the body deposited at a second location is more indicative of an *organized offender.*

The Federal Bureau of Investigation (FBI) trains its own profilers, who are stationed at the National Center for the Analysis of Violent Crime (NCAVC). Though trained in behavioral investigative techniques, profilers are not typically psychologists.

The Birth of a Serial Killer

In many ways, it is difficult to apply research regarding real-life serial killers to George R. R. Martin's world. The fictional Westeros is populated by people who have grown up in an environment vastly different from that of the modern world, where a large proportion of the research on serial killers has been conducted. Beyond this, the demographics of serial killers has shifted with time, probably as a result of changing societal norms. Whereas research traditionally indicated that such killers were likely to have been born into intact families, more recent research has suggested that serial killers are likely to experience familial schisms, including being born in single-parent homes and living through a parental divorce;[3] this is consistent with the general trend toward single-parent households in contemporary times. One thing has remained constant, though: Serial killers are likely to have experienced significant trauma and dysfunction at a young age.[4] Children who grow up to be serial killers are likely to have poor attachments with their parents and to have parents who are simultaneously permissive and authoritarian and also are likely to have experienced physical, emotional, and sexual abuse.[5]

How closely do Ramsay's childhood and development resemble those of the prototypical serial killers described in research? Little specific information is available about Ramsay's upbringing beyond the fact that he starts out life as an illegitimate child of Roose Bolton and is raised largely by a servant. Soon after his introduction, a teenage Ramsay and his men burn Winterfell to the ground. Additionally, he has trained a pack of dogs to hunt and kill humans; such training undoubtedly would involve a high degree of cruelty and neglect and demonstrates an organized pattern. In light of what is known about his character, it is unlikely that these were Ramsay's first forays into arson or cruelty to animals. It is also known that he has killed his older brother, the only surviving trueborn son of Roose, by poisoning; this possibly constitutes his first murder.[6]

Psychiatrist J. M. Macdonald[7] posited that a set of three behaviors predicts an increased likelihood of homicidal behavior in the future: fire setting, bed-wetting, and cruelty to animals. These behaviors are known collectively as the *triad of sociopathy*, the *homicidal triad*, or the *Macdonald triad*. Although subsequent research has called this triad into question, especially the idea that bed-wetting is predictive of future homicide,[8] knowledge of the triad has influenced popular perception[9] and some investigators still consider these to be important factors. Although in this case we cannot definitively check off all three components of the triad, Ramsay's known history involves incidents of arson and cruelty to animals as well as a number of other antisocial behaviors.

Researchers have noted consistently that family values, morals, and practices are transmitted from generation to generation, with children often holding beliefs that closely resemble those of their parents; antisocial behavior is no exception.[10] Ramsay has been born into a family in which cruelty, brutality, manipulation, and the exploitation of others are considered not only acceptable but a primary mode of dealing with people. The members of this family are known for their practice of flaying their enemies alive. This type of context can play an enormous role in personality development.

The Personality of a Killer

The personality traits of *narcissism* (egotism, grandiosity, and pride), *Machiavellianism* (social detachment, manipulation, and exploitation), and *psychopathy* (impulsivity, antisocial behavior, and lack of remorse)—a constellation of traits collectively referred to as the *dark triad*[11]—correlate with some of the most heinous human behavior when a single individual shows them all to a pathological extreme. Investigators look for signs of these traits in serial killers. This is not to say that all serial killers are created equal. Certainly Jeffrey Dahmer and Ted Bundy are similar in that they both killed multiple people; however, Dahmer's killings had some of their roots in mental illness,[12] whereas Bundy had a personality structure that allowed for abhorrent acts.[13]

Narcissism

From a logical perspective, it is not difficult to see how the different traits that constitute the dark triad contribute to a personality that is supportive of murder. Individuals who are narcissistic view themselves as having greater worth than those around them have. They believe they have special traits and abilities that are far beyond the reach of ordinary people and may view themselves as destined for a higher purpose. They tend to overestimate themselves and manifest that belief by putting down and taking advantage of others. They like to prove their worth but are not afraid to stack the deck in their favor.[14] Ramsay certainly believes himself to be smarter than those around him, something that is especially evident in his almost playful and teasing approach to torturing Theon at times. He also dislikes being reminded he is an illegitimate child and is known to respond violently if such references are made in his presence.[15]

Machiavellianism

Machiavellianism is named after Niccolò Machiavelli, a Renaissance-era writer, politician, and philosopher. People with a Machiavellian personality are prone to manipulate others for their own purposes and are not concerned with issues of morality, seeing their goals and motivations as trumping those of others. They can be deceitful as they are willing to do anything necessary to achieve their objectives.[16] Ramsay clearly has engaged in a number of behaviors reflective of Machiavellianism. In the book series, he has a servant pose as him, leading to the servant's execution. After assuming the servant's identity to avoid death, he similarly identifies himself as that servant to Theon and manipulates him to further his goals.[17] After Theon's confinement, Ramsay allows him to escape[18] (and even seems to assist him in the television series[19]), only to recapture him. He toys with Theon for his own pleasure and motivations and does so in as cruel and deceptive manner as possible, always letting Theon know that he is never beyond Ramsay's reach.

Psychopathy

Psychopathy is a personality construct popularized in psychiatrist Hervey Cleckley's book *The Mask of Sanity*.[20] Cleckley based his conclusions on clinical interviews with patients in secure institutions and described a personality profile involving, among other things, superficial charm, unreliability, untruthfulness, lack of remorse, antisocial behavior, lack of emotion, egocentrism, poor insight, lack of plans, and an impersonal sex life. Cleckley also specified that psychopaths are distinct from those experiencing psychosis in that psychopaths are not motivated by delusional or irrational beliefs. It is important to note, however, that psychosis and psychopathy can co-exist in the same person. The book was named after the "mask" worn by psychopaths that hides their pathology. Psychologist Robert Hare developed the Psychopathy Checklist (PCL)[21] and later the Psychopathy Checklist-Revised (PCL-R)[22] to identify the traits of psychopathy through clinical interviews, reviews of records, and contacts with collateral sources. Hare's model of psychopathy[23] is based largely on Cleckley's original framework, though Hare expanded it on the basis of his own research. In the context of Hare's refinement of Cleckley's model, Ramsay's personality manifests a number of traits of psychopathy. As was noted previously, he frequently lies and schemes to gain an advantage in situations. He appears to feel no remorse for his actions, even relishing his mistreatment and torture of others. Although he does not display a full range of emotion, he clearly has difficulty controlling his anger and will lash out violently. He is impulsive and fails to consider long-term consequences, as can be seen in his decision to torture Theon instead of ransoming him to the ironborn.[24] He has multiple sexual partners, many of them unwilling, and is seemingly at the conclusion of a second marriage in the book series.[25] All these behaviors suggest that Ramsay would score high on the PCL-R's key indicators of psychopathy.

There is clearly much overlap among the dark triad traits, largely because psychopathy includes many of the features of narcissism and Machiavellianism. It is also important to note that Machiavellianism and psychopathy, though researched constructs, are not diagnoses recognized in the *Diagnostic and Statistical Manual of Mental Disorders*.[26] Rather, the dark triad personality traits most accurately would be subsumed under diagnoses of *narcissistic personality disorder* and *antisocial personality disorder*. Additionally, not everyone with dark triad traits turns out to be a serial killer or even a criminal. For example, psychopathic traits, including traits shared by successful leaders and criminal psychopaths, can abound in the corporate world.[27] What really sets the serial killer apart from the corporate killer is motive.

The Motivations of a Killer

Why does a serial killer choose to kill rather than committing identity theft, stealing a car, or simply trolling the Internet? The answer is motive. People ultimately do different things for similar reasons. A prosocial thrill seeker may choose to skydive to get a rush, whereas an antisocial one may elect to commit an armed robbery or a "thrill kill." Either way, these individuals are motivated by the pursuit of a rush brought on by the chemical release of *endorphins* (the brain's "endogenous morphines," the chemicals that unleash euphoria[28]). Individuals with psychopathic traits can be similarly varied in their fulfillment of needs. If you derive pleasure from the manipulation of others, you may find yourself equally content in the corporate world or on a used car lot. The actions of serial killers can have widely different motivations. Some may be motivated by a symptom of *psychosis* (being severely out of touch with reality), such as harboring a delusional belief that certain people must be killed for some higher purpose. Serial killers may be motivated by hatred for a specific demographic group such as women, those with a different cultural background, or people with a different sexual orientation. Serial killers may kill a specific set of people who they feel have earned their ire. They also may be paid killers, such as Richard Kuklinski, who committed countless murders on the orders of the Mafia, though he also was noted to derive pleasure from the act of killing.[29]

Motivation can be intrinsic (doing something for its own sake, such as hitting a person for the sheer joy of hitting) or extrinsic (doing it to achieve a *secondary gain*, as in hitting a person in the process of stealing his or her money). Some serial killers commit homicide for the intrinsic reward. That is, they like the way taking a life makes them feel, as in the cases of

Ted Bundy[30] and Carl Panzram.[31] Although serial killers can be motivated by any number of things, it is the predatory nature of those who are intrinsically motivated that sets them apart. Whereas hatred can be understood, if not accepted, and psychosis can be dismissed as a defect in reason, it is those killers who are of sound mind yet choose to kill and derive pleasure from it who truly capture our attention.

Although he often hides his intentions, Ramsay largely wears his motives on his sleeve. Ramsay is a *sadist*, so named for the Marquis de Sade, a French aristocrat known for his violent sexual proclivities. Sadists derive pleasure from the suffering of others. Many antisocial acts are committed for secondary gain; that is, the commission of a crime grants an external reward, as in the case of a thief who steals money in order to buy things. Sadists, in contrast, commit crimes for the intrinsic reward as the act fulfills a psychological need. They experience pleasure, sometimes sexual in nature, from torturing, humiliating, and dehumanizing others. Throughout his appearances, Ramsay is seen repeatedly taking pleasure in the suffering of his victims, whether the torture of Theon, the duplicitous murders of multiple ironborn, the killing of women by his dogs, or the sexual assault of his unwilling wife, among many others. For the sadist, it is the fantasy of torture and rape rather than the end product that drives the behavior. Ramsay's endgame is to keep dominion over his victims, to hold their lives in his hands, and then to tear them apart piece by piece both figuratively and literally. Sadistic killers often take care not to end the lives of their victims prematurely so that they can prolong the torture and cause greater suffering. They tend to have multiple crime scenes, removing their victims to a secluded space to engage in torture, and keep mementos of their crimes. This is evidenced by Ramsay's imprisonment of Theon in a secluded cell, his prolonged torture, and the proclivity of those of House Bolton for keeping the skins of their flayed enemies. Some researchers have suggested the addition of sadism to the dark triad to create a *dark tetrad*.[32]

A Different World

"The behaviors that are precursors to murder have been present and developing in that person's life a long, long time—since childhood."
—psychological profiler Robert K. Ressler[33]

Westeros is obviously quite different from the modern, developed world. Although Ramsay's behaviors are by no means acceptable even in Westeros, there is no authority that is likely to bring him to justice. Ramsay is a Bolton, and his father is Warden of the North, affording him a high degree of protection. Unlike serial killers in the real world, Ramsay has no reason to keep his behavior secret or hide his identity. This means that he does not display many hallmark characteristics of successful serial killers, specifically sadists. Sadistic murderers often take care to avoid creating incriminating evidence and hide their identities from their victims and the authorities.[34] Without the need for concealment, a killer such as Ramsay is the proverbial kid in a candy store. Left unchecked, he will keep killing until he falls out of favor with his protectors or faces an even bigger monster than himself.

References

American Psychiatric Association (2013). *Diagnostic and statistical manual of mental disorders* (5th ed.). Washington, DC: American Psychiatric Association.

Babiak, P., & Hare, R. D. (2006). *Snakes in suits: When psychopaths go to work.* New York, NY: Harper Business.

Carlo, P. (2009). *The Ice Man: Confessions of a Mafia contract killer.* New York, NY: St. Martin's.

Chabrol, H., Van Leeuwen, N., Rodgers, R., & Sejourne, N. (2009). Contributions of psychopathic, narcissistic, Machiavellian, and sadistic personality traits to juvenile delinquency. *Personality and Individual Differences, 47*(7), 734–739.

Cleckley, H. M. (1941/1976). *The mask of sanity: An attempt to clarify some issues about the so-called psychopathic personality.* Maryland Heights, MO: Mosby.

Douglas, J. E., Burgess, A. W., Burgess, A. G., & Ressler, R. K. (2006). *Crime classification manual* (2nd ed.). San Francisco, CA: Jossey-Bass.

Elbert, T., Weierstall, R., & Schauer, M. (2010). Fascination violence: On mind and brain of man hunters. *European Archives of Psychiatry and Clinical Neuroscience, 260*(Supp. 2), S100–S105.

Gaddis, T. E., & Long, J. O. (1970/2002). *Panzram: A journal of murder.* Los Angeles, CA: Amok.

Geis, F. L., & Moon, T. H. (1981). Machiavellianism and deception. *Journal of Personality and Deception, 41*(4), 766–775.

Hare, R. D. (1993/1999). *Without conscience: The disturbing world of the psychopaths among us.* New York, NY: Guilford.

King, B. (1996). *Lustmord: The writings and artifacts of murderers.* Burbank, CA: Bloat.

Macdonald, J. M. (1963). The threat to kill. *American Journal of Psychiatry, 120*(2), 125–130.

Martin, G. R. R. (1999). *A clash of kings.* London, UK: Voyager.

Martin, G. R. R. (2011). *A dance with dragons.* London, UK: Voyager.

Nichols, D. S. (2006). Tell me a story: MMPI responses and personal biography in the case of a serial killer. *Journal of Personality Assessment, 48*(3), 242–262.

Patterson, G. R., DeBaryshe, B., & Ramsey, E. (1990). A developmental perspective on antisocial behavior. *American Psychologist, 44*(2), 329–225.

Paulhus, D. L., & Williams, K .M. (2002). The dark triad of personality. *Journal of Research in Personality, 36*, 556–563.

Pemment, J. (2012, December 10). *Brain of the intellect vs. brain of the serial killer.* Psychology Today: https://www.psychologytoday.com/blog/blame-the-amygdala/201212/brain-the-intellect-vs-brain-the-serial-killer.

Prince, R. (1982). The endorphins: A review for psychological anthropologists. *Ethos, 10*(4), 303–316.

Ressler, R. K., Burgess, A. W., & Douglas, J. E. (1992/1995). *Sexual homicide: Patterns and motives.* New York, NY: Free Press.

Ressler, R. K., & Schachtman, T. (1992). *Whoever fights monsters.* New York, NY: St. Martin's.

Rule, A. (2008). *The stranger beside me.* New York, NY: Pocket.

Seaman, D., & Wilson, C. (1990). *The serial killers: A study in the psychology of violence.* London, UK: Virgin.

Skrapec, C., & Ryan, K. (2010, November). *The Macdonald triad: Persistence of an urban legend.* Paper presented at the annual meeting of the American Society of Criminology, San Francisco, CA.

Weatherby, G. A., Buller, D. M., & McGinnis, K. (2009). The Buller-McGinnis model of serial-homicidal behavior: An integrated approach. *Journal of Criminology and Criminal Justice Research and Education, 3*(1). Scientific Journals: http://www.scientificjournals.org/journals2009/articles/1441.pdf.

Notes

1. King (1997).
2. Ressler & Schachtman (1992), p. 83.
3. Seaman & Wilson (1990).
4. Ressler et al. (1992/1995).
5. Ressler et al. (1992/1995).
6. Martin (2011).
7. Macdonald (1963).
8. Weatherby et al. (2009).
9. Skrapec & Ryan (2010).
10. Patterson et al. (1990).
11. Paulhus & Williams (2002).
12. Nichols (2006).
13. Pemment (2012).
14. American Psychiatric Association (2013).
15. Martin (1999).
16. Geis & Moon (1981).
17. Martin (1999).
18. Martin (2011).
19. Episode 3–4, "And Now His Watch Has Ended" (April 21, 2013).
20. Cleckley (1941/1976).
21. Hare (1980).
22. Hare (2003).
23. Hare (1993/1999).
24. Martin (2011).
25. Martin (2011).
26. American Psychiatric Association (2013).
27. Babiak & Hare (2006).
28. Elbert et al. (2010); Prince (1982).
29. Carlo (2009).
30. Rule (2008).
31. Gaddis & Long (1970/2002).
32. Chabrol et al. (2009).
33. Ressler & Schachtman (1992), p. 83.
34. Douglas et al. (2006).

Sexism exists. Telling truth via fiction can sometimes require depictions of sexist behavior, and fantastic fiction can provide a lens through which we might gain a different perspective on sexism in real life. In depictions of women as heroes and victims, when do the stories appropriately present sexism, when are the stories sexist, and how might any of it impact us all?

CHAPTER FIFTEEN

Women of Westeros: Fighting Benevolent and Hostile Sexism

WIND GOODFRIEND

"Frequent exposure to media images that sexualize girls and women may affect how girls conceptualize femininity and sexuality, leading them to accept more constrained and stereotypical notions about gender and gender roles."
—American Psychological Association[1]

"I'm not going to stop the wheel. I'm going to break the wheel."
—Daenerys Targaryen[2]

One of the ubiquitous forms of prejudice in both fictional and nonfictional realms is the subjugation of women. *Game of Thrones* depicts a harsh world with antiquated notions of gender in which women can be considered chattel and treated as inferior to men. This treatment is understandably abhorrent to modern mores and evolved societal norms, leading to many debates among fans of the books and the television show. No *Game of Thrones* TV storyline has created more of an outcry than the controversial and brutal rape of Sansa Stark.[3] Fans quickly became divided: Some viewers declared that they were done watching a show that glorified violence against and sexual objectification of women.[4] Others praised the show for highlighting feminist characters who consistently stand up against sexism, and that episode was nominated for an Emmy.[5] How could such disparate views of the same fictional world coexist? Psychologists can provide an insightful backdrop for this debate by discussing different types of sexism and what predicts individual reactions to them; both of these factors can help explain how *Game of Thrones* inspires such spirited argument.

Sexism

Social psychologists try to understand how our social world changes who we are as individuals, and vice versa, including both the best and the worst human relationships. Thus, social psychologists study the simultaneous human instincts toward social good (including love, cooperation, and altruism) and social bad (including aggression, hatred, and prejudice). Unfortunately, the history of humankind shows the pervasive and ubiquitous danger that stereotypes, prejudice, and discrimination have posed for millennia.[6]

Sexism in general refers to biased thoughts, attitudes, or behaviors that are based on biological sex (male, female, intersex, etc.) or perceived gender (how masculine or feminine a person appears to be). On the cultural level, sexism appears to be rampant in Westeros. Men are the leaders of the family, region, or country. Women, in contrast, generally serve in the traditional roles of wives, servants, and prostitutes. Rich women wear tight dresses and spend time creating elaborate hairstyles; poor women clean and try to keep their babies alive.

In addition to noting sexism on the cultural level, psychologists focus on studying sexism on an individual level, including the ways people react to sexism in their everyday lives. For example, a landmark study[7] on how women respond to sexism identified which *types* of women respond to sexism actively and directly versus simply ignoring it. Understanding this study can provide insight into and analysis of the characters in *Game of Thrones* and how they react or stay silent. In this research, young women thought they were engaged in a study of decision making. They were put in a group with three other students and asked to determine which people from a list would be best suited to start a new civilization on a remote desert island. Unknown to the real participants, who actually were tested one at a time, everyone else in the group was a *confederate*, someone who was pretending to be a participant but was really a scripted member of the experimental team. During the group discussion, a male confederate made several sexist remarks, such as that the islanders didn't need a professional cook because some of the women could do it but that they did need an athletic trainer to make sure the women on the island stayed "in shape."

The results showed that only 16 percent of the women in the study directly confronted the sexist comments. Most either responded indirectly through things such as sarcasm and grumbling or didn't respond at all. Who did respond? There were three criteria that made women more likely to say something. First, women confronted the sexism when they had reported antisexist beliefs in a survey done several weeks earlier. Second, women were more likely to confront the confederate when they identified themselves as active feminists (although they didn't actually use the word *feminist*). Third, a woman was more likely to say something when she was the *only woman in the group*. At first, this finding might be surprising: Shouldn't women be more likely to confront sexism when there are other women present who might show support and provide validation? On the contrary, women who were around other women were less likely to speak up. This occurred because the presence of others creates a *diffusion of responsibility*: the idea that we don't have to act because others might do it instead. When we're alone—or at least when we perceive we're alone—we take all the personal responsibility of action on our own shoulders and are more likely to act. With the large amount of sexism that exists in *Game of Thrones*, do the characters stand up for themselves and for women in general?

Fighting Benevolent Sexism

"Women should be treated like princesses." "Women and girls should be seen but not heard." "Girls are virginal angels who dream of being mothers, cooing over cherubic infants while planning how to welcome their husbands home from a hard day's work." . . .

These sentiments are examples of the basic tenets of what social psychologists call *benevolent sexism*. Benevolent sexism is made up of three primary components:

1. *Protective paternalism* is the ideology that "because of their greater authority, power, and physical strength, men should serve as protectors and providers for women."[8] The implication, of course, is that women cannot protect and provide for themselves.

Sexism Against Men?

What about bias in favor of women but against men? The same psychologists who studied hostile and benevolent sexism against women also created a parallel scale for sexism against men.[9] Benevolent sexism for men includes propositions such as the belief that men are braver and more selfless than women and that women can never be truly happy unless they have a husband to provide for them. Hostile sexism against men focuses on propositions such as the belief that men are sexually immoral and immature and hope to dominate women whenever and wherever possible.

Are there examples of sexism against men in *Game of Thrones*? The expectation that only men should serve in the Night's Watch or as soldiers is certainly benevolent sexism, as it assumes that all men will both be good at these roles and *want* to perform them. Any men who do not fulfill these expectations are branded as cowards. For hostile sexism, characters such as Cersei and Melisandre frequently act in ways that indicate their disdain for men and their belief that men should hold power only when they are chosen and ultimately controlled by a woman.

2. Benevolent sexism idealizes women as pretty, fragile ladies, undermining feminist progress by ensuring that women are kept in this passive and superficial role.
3. Benevolent sexism assumes that all women are heterosexual and seek husbands and children as their main goal in life. In essence, benevolent sexism traps women in a gilded cage of feminine expectation and limitation.

The *Ambivalent Sexism Inventory*[10] has been developed specifically to measure benevolent sexism. The inventory works when people honestly rate how much they agree with beliefs such as "Women should be cherished and protected by men" and "Women, as compared to men, tend to have a more refined sense of culture and good taste."

From birth, Arya Stark has battled the effects of benevolent sexism, and she frequently displays the first characteristic found in the study discussed above: *antisexist beliefs*. She cringes when she is compared with her beautiful and gentle sister Sansa, and she knows that being the wild and less attractive sister is not winning her social acceptance as it is not considered feminine. Benevolent sexism affects her childhood as she is taught to do needlework and other traditional female activities while being denied the right to learn to fight, both of which are attempts to mold her into a "proper" northern lady.[11]

Arya rejects all these messages and embraces the second characteristic found in the research study: active feminism. For example, she names her wolf cub Nymeria after a legendary female warrior.[12] When her half-brother Jon gives her a sword, they name it Needle, brazenly mocking the sewing needles she loathes. She frequently protests the injustice of the powerful doing what they like to the powerless. Arya continues to fight benevolent sexism by living as masculine a life as possible, rejecting her assigned feminine role and living as a boy.[13] She tries to embrace the words of her first sword master when he tells her, "Boy, girl. You are a sword. That is all."[14] Gender and its sexist lessons are meaningless to Arya.

She also lives her life according to this feminist code. Perhaps as a result of her parents' attempts to force her to conform to cultural norms for females, she treats everyone equally regardless of family name or economic status, choosing friends and enemies on the basis of whether they treat *her* with respect and dignity. She identifies the inequality between boys and girls, between men and women, early in her life when she speaks to her father.

> **Arya:** Can I be lord of a holdfast?
> **Ned:** *[laughs]* You will marry a high lord and rule his castle. And your sons shall be knights and princes and lords.
> **Arya:** No. That's not me.[15]

This lifestyle continues to challenge benevolent sexism on a higher level, because her actions represent an attempt to bring a sense of fairness to everyone she meets. Arya's escape from the gilded cage of what she is "supposed" to do and be is a strong example of a feminist character specifically rejecting social expectations of what it means to be a lady as a waste of time and intelligence. Remember that the study found that the last characteristic in women who stood up to sexism was the perception that one is alone in the responsibility to do something about it when sexism appears. Arya fits the first two criteria, but does she perceive herself to be alone? Throughout much of the story, Arya is alone as her family and friends continue to die. Arya does not have the safety net of a diffusion of responsibility; she must do things herself.

Does psychology teach that to fight for the feminist ideals of fairness and equality, women must cut their hair, take self-defense lessons, and live as men? A second character, Daenerys, provides a contrast and serves as a transition to explain the second form of sexism suggested by social psychology.

Fighting Hostile Sexism

Hostile sexism focuses on women who supposedly need to be reminded of their rightful and natural place, which is subjugated to men.[16] Hostile sexists believe that women should promise to obey their husbands and enjoy sexuality only because it leads to motherhood. Most relevant, this form of sexism includes the idea that women who seek individual power or sexual gratification are evil and unreasonable; strong, powerful women are a threat. Whereas benevolent sexism offers protective paternalism, hostile sexism offers *dominative paternalism*: the idea that women should be dominated by men.[17]

The scientific survey mentioned above, the Ambivalent Sexism Inventory, also includes items measuring degrees of hostile sexism in its respondents. This time, statements include beliefs such as that women are offended too frequently and too easily and that women in relationships enjoy controlling their husbands cruelly.[18] Who fights hostile sexism in *Game of Thrones*? Perhaps the most powerful woman in the entire realm is Daenerys Stormborn, Queen of the Andals and the First Men, Khaleesi of the Great Grass Sea, Breaker of Chains, and Mother of Dragons.[19] Unlike Arya, Daenerys does not seem overly concerned with benevolent sexism; for example, her outward appearance is extremely feminine. Daenerys's battle is focused on hostile sexism and the idea that women do not deserve power.

Daenerys often displays the first two characteristics that were found to predict standing up to sexism (antisexist beliefs and active feminism). For example, throughout her childhood she was subjugated by her brother.[20] After gaining confidence in her position as khaleesi, she finally stands up to him. When he hits her and insults her, she strikes him back and tells him, "The next time you raise a hand to me will be the last time you have hands."[21] She no longer tolerates being a victim; this culminates in her eventually becoming complicit in his murder.[22] His years of sexist abuse end in poetic justice.

Daenerys also accepts her role as a mother (again, aligning with benevolent sexist expectations). But for her, motherhood does not end her fight against hostile sexism, making her some kind of sheltered and stereotyped maternal figure; instead, she uses her dragons as tools to gain even more political power. Even the name she is given by her subjects and former slaves, "Mother,"[23] emphasizes her acceptance of feminine roles while defining what it truly means to be feminine.

Daenerys fights against the subjugation of the poor and abolishes slavery wherever she can,[24] living as an example of a strong woman who is a national dictator but uses her power to provide equality and opportunity. She also has the third characteristic that predicts opposition to sexism: She feels a personal responsibility to do something. Several times she reflects on the fact that she appears to be the last Targaryen, the last dragon; she may be the only one powerful enough to stop systematic oppression.

Feminist Fantasy or Misogynistic Dystopia?

This brings us back to the original question: Is *Game of Thrones* a misogynistic playground in which women are consistently victimized, subjugated, and oppressed, with no end in sight? Or does it spotlight strong women who rise against the machine and serve as feminist heroines, inspiring women and men to battle all forms of sexism? At least two characters consistently stand up against sexism, serving as feminist heroines. Just as a phoenix or a dragon cannot be born without fire, feminism and rebellion cannot be born without sexist oppression. Westeros contains sexism, but it may be the feminist fantasy needed to inspire fans to stand up against the oppression they see in the real world.

References

American Psychological Association (2010). *Report of the APA Task Force on the Sexualization of Girls*. Washington, DC: American Psychological Association.

Glick, P., & Fiske, S. T. (1997). Hostile and benevolent sexism: Measuring ambivalent sexist attitudes toward women. *Psychology of Women Quarterly, 21*(1), 119–135.

Glick, P., & Fiske, S. T. (1999). The ambivalence toward men inventory: Differentiating hostile and benevolent beliefs about men. *Psychology of Women Quarterly, 23*(3), 519–536.

Glick, P., & Fiske, S. T. (2001). An ambivalent alliance: Hostile and benevolent sexism as complementary justifications for gender inequality. *American Psychologist, 56*(2), 109–118.

Martin, G. R. R. (1996). *A game of thrones.* New York, NY: Bantam Spectra.

Pantozzi, J. (2015, May 18). *We will no longer be promoting HBO's Game of Thrones.* The Mary Sue: http://www.themarysue.com/we-will-no-longer-be-promoting-hbos-game-of -thrones.

Swim, J. K., & Hyers, L. L. (1999). Excuse me—what did you say?!: Women's public and private responses to sexist remarks. *Journal of Experimental Social Psychology, 35*(1), 68–88.

Whitley, B. E., & Kite, M. E. (2006). *Psychology of prejudice and discrimination.* Boston, MA: Cengage.

Zuel, B. (2015, July 17). *Game of Thrones' controversial Sansa rape episode nominated for Emmy Award.* Sydney Morning Herald: http://www.smh.com.au/entertainment /tv-and-radio/game-of-thrones-controversial-sansa-rape-episode-nominated-for -emmy-award-20150717-giehk2.html.

Notes

1. Amerian Psychological Association (2010), p. 26.
2. Episode 5–8, "Hardhome" (May 31, 2015).
3. Episode 5–6, "Unbowed, Unbent, Unbroken" (May 17, 2015).
4. See, for example, Pantozzi (2015).
5. Zuel (2015).

6. Whitley & Kite (2006).
7. Swim & Hyers (1999).
8. Glick & Fiske (1997), p. 122.
9. Glick & Fiske (1999).
10. Glick & Fiske (1997; 2001).
11. Episode 1–1, "Winter Is Coming" (April 17, 2011).
12. Martin (1996), p. 71.
13. Episode 1–10, "Fire and Blood" (June 19, 2011).
14. Episode 1–2, "The Kingsroad" (April 24, 2011).
15. Episode 1–4, "Cripples, Bastards, and Broken Things" (May 8, 2011).
16. Glick & Fiske (1997, 2001).
17. Glick & Fiske (1997, 2001).
18. Glick & Fiske (1997, 2001).
19. Episode 3–7, "The Bear and the Maiden Fair" (May 12, 2013).
20. Episode 1–1, "Winter Is Coming" (April 17, 2011).
21. Episode 1–4, "Cripples, Bastards, and Broken Things" (May 8, 2011).
22. Episode 1–6, "A Golden Crown" (May 22, 2011).
23. Episode 3–10, "Mhysa" (June 9, 2013).
24. Episode 1–10, "Fire and Blood" (June 19, 2011); episode 3–4, "And Now His Watch Has Ended" (April 21, 2013).

Self-Esteem

JANINA SCARLET

*"Never forget what you are, for surely the world will not.
Make it your strength. Then it can never be your weakness.
Armor yourself in it, and it will never be used to hurt you."*
—Tyrion Lannister[1]

*"If you want to be proud of yourself, then do
things in which you can take pride."*
—psychoanalyst Karen Horney[2]

For a long time, psychologists considered *self-esteem* (the person's evaluation of his or her own self-worth) to be a measure of an individual's well-being.[3] Low self-esteem was believed to indicate poor mental health, while high self-esteem was associated with better mental health and positive emotions.[4]

Recently, though, scientists are finding that high self-esteem might not always be desirable. In some instances, the desire to raise one's self-esteem can actually lead to aggression and violence. One of the reasons for this is that people who are sensitive to self-esteem changes—for example, narcissists like Joffrey Baratheon—may be likely to get angry when their self-esteem is threatened.[5] In fact, Joffrey turns especially violent toward Sansa whenever her brother Robb's army defeats Lannister forces in a battle.[6] It seems that when Joffrey hears of Robb's success, he may question his own self-worth and, as a result, become aggressive toward Sansa by association.

People who are especially invested in pursuing and proving their self-worth might become more sensitive to potential rejection. This means that even if a specific event is not directly relevant to the individual's self-worth, the very interpretation of the meaning behind that event can lead to personal insult and might sometimes lead to violence.[7] When Daenerys gives her brother new clothes, he becomes enraged and stabs her,[8] apparently feeling insulted after having been called a "Beggar King" in the past.

Why do people strive for self-esteem in the first place? According to the *terror management theory*, people naturally feel anxious when they think about their own deaths. Increasing self-esteem tends to reduce death-related anxiety. At the same time, reminding someone of mortality might make the person want to raise self-esteem or feel more defensive regarding threats to self-esteem.[9] After Tyrion kills their father, Cersei becomes invested in trying to prove herself as an even better ruler than her father. She frequently compares herself to him in her mind while also regretting that she was not born a boy.[10]

Relying on self-esteem as a measure of personal self-worth can be potentially problematic when the individual encounters adversity or setbacks. In such situations, even an unintentional slight might be interpreted as a terrible offense, potentially leading to violence or other maladaptive behavior. When Robb Stark does not marry Walder Frey's daughter, the Freys take this rejection as a personal attack. The Freys reinforce their own sense of self-worth by forcing Robb to apologize to them in front of wedding guests and then slaughtering them all.[11] A more adaptive method of ensuring one's well-being, particularly during painful situations, is *self-compassion* (offering kindness to oneself at a time of need). Research on self-compassion suggests it predicts psychological well-being more reliably than self-esteem does.[12]

References

Baumeister, R. F., Bushman, B. J., & Campbell, W. K. (2000). Self-esteem, narcissism, and aggression: Does violence result from low self-esteem or from threatened egotism? *Current Directions in Psychological Science, 9*(1), 26–29.

Crocker, J., & Park, L. E. (2004). The costly pursuit of self-esteem. *Psychological Bulletin, 130*(3), 392–414.

Donnellan, M. B., Trzesniewski, K. H., Robins, R. W., Moffitt, T. E., & Caspi, A. (2005). Low self-esteem is related to aggression, antisocial behavior, and delinquency. *Psychological Science, 16*(4), 328–335.

Horney, K. (1950). *Neurosis and human growth: The struggle towards self-realization.* Abingdon, UK: Routledge.

Martin, G. R. R. (1996). *A game of thrones.* London, UK: Voyager.

Martin, G. R. R. (1998). *A clash of kings.* London, UK: Voyager.

Martin, G. R. R. (2000). *A storm of swords.* London, UK: Voyager.

Martin, G. R. R. (2005). *A feast of crows.* London, UK: Voyager.

Neff, K. D., & Vonk, R. (2009). Self-compassion versus global self-esteem: Two different ways of relating to oneself. *Journal of Personality, 77*(1), 23–50.

Pyszczynski, T., Greenberg, J., Solomon, S., Arndt, J., & Schimel, J. (2004). Why do people need self-esteem? A theoretical and empirical review. *Psychological Bulletin, 130*(3), 435.

Rosenberg, M., Schooler, C., Schoenbach, C., & Rosenberg, F. (1995). Global self-esteem and specific self-esteem: Different concepts, different outcomes. *American Sociological Review, 60*(1), 141–156.

Notes

1. Martin (1996), p. 57.
2. Horney (1950), p. 89.
3. Rosenberg et al. (1995).
4. Rosenberg et al. (1995).
5. Baumeister et al. (2000).
6. Martin (1998).
7. Crocker & Park (2004); Donnellan et al. (2005).
8. Martin (1996).
9. Pyszczynski et al. (2004).
10. Martin (2005).
11. Martin (2000).
12. Neff & Vonk (2009).

Part Five

Crowns

The crown is an item upon the ruler's head representing imperial power for whoever wields it at the time. The crown is a beauty and a burden made of metal and stone. The crown is a responsibility, one that not every wearer understands. The crown is a legacy shaped by all who wear it. The crown is a target for those who would knock it down. The crown is a prize that some might wish to win.

The crown is a thing, but it represents so much more.

In the struggle to reach our goals, some of us follow more logical strategies than others. Effective problem solving requires planning, implementation, and evaluation, and not everyone is up to those tasks.

CHAPTER SIXTEEN

All Poor Problem Solvers Must Die: A Model of Winning and Losing

WILLIAM BLAKE ERICKSON AND DAWN R. WEATHERFORD

"Different roads sometimes lead to the same castle."
—Jon Snow[1]

"I suppose it is tempting, if the only tool you have is a hammer, to treat everything as if it were a nail."
—psychologist Abraham Maslow[2]

Despite their bad reputation, problems are not always negative experiences. A problem occurs any time when your *current state* (where you are) differs from your *goal state* (where you want to be).[3] Some may consider this a problem while others may not: You want to cosplay as a White Walker for an upcoming fantasy convention, but do not know precisely how to accomplish this. You do know that you can search online for costuming tips to transform yourself into the greatest ghoul at the con. Determining which method best suits your abilities and needs and then acting on this information is the act of *problem solving*. Problem solving requires effective *executive functioning*, which is a component of information processing that guides attention, planning, and decision making in novel situations.[4] With effective executive functioning, a person can notice a problem, weigh possible solutions, and implement one.

Most of the characters from Westeros to Essos strive toward the same goal: to acquire and maintain power, whether over others or simply over their own fates. Each character utilizes the best of his or her cognitive skills to move toward this goal state by addressing constraints and obstacles along the way. Each individual's best does not always meet an optimal end, and some are doomed to peril while others triumph. In this way, Martin's universe provides excellent cases of problem solving in action as characters play the game of thrones.

Detecting Problems

To solve a problem, a person has to notice it. Although this may sound obvious enough, failures to reach solutions often stem from the inability to detect a problem arising in the first place. A person must also be able to detect whether the solution is obvious or not. Finally, a problem solver must recognize constraints and tools to devise an effective solution. Each of these requires keen attention paid not only to the problem but also to its features so that the solver can plan solutions.

Navigating a Problem Space

Considering a problem within a framework called a *problem space* makes it simpler to tackle.[5] A problem space has the current state on one side, the goal state on the other, and in between are all of the subgoals that must also be met in order to best reach the goal state. If you need to pick your friend up from the doctor's office, the initial state is your friend at the doctor's office, and the goal is him seated in your car. A subgoal here would be obeying traffic laws on the way, because breaking them may hinder your ability to pick him up. Being cognizant of appropriate subgoals signifies effective use of executive functioning, because attention is not only paid to the goal but also to avoiding other problems. During the War of the Five Kings, Robb Stark focuses too much on making the most powerful alliances but not enough on the subgoals of keeping them, soon breaking his pledge to marry Roslin Frey. This act gives Walder Frey justification to side with the Lannisters, treacherously murder Robb and his mother, and decimate the Stark army.[6]

Problem Clarity

Some problems are more concrete, or easy to solve, than others. The simplest are as easy to solve as following a road map from one location to the next with no obstacles in between, and may not seem much like "problems" at all. Does Robert Baratheon want to travel from King's Landing to name Eddard Stark Hand of the King? He gathers his party and takes the Kingsroad to Winterfell.[7] In Robert's case here, taking a direct route to Winterfell is a *well-defined* problem. Perceiving it requires little effort, and the solution is clear.[8] Not all problems are like this, however. *Ill-defined* problems may be difficult to notice and have elusive solutions. Robert Baratheon is aware of the general threat to his life as king, but he never considers that his greatest threat is his allies, the Lannisters.[9] The vagueness of the problem he might call "People want to kill me" makes devising a solution nebulous, whereas a more explicit problem, called "My wife's family wants to kill me," would present a more obvious solution. Robert doesn't help himself by impairing his own executive functioning with frequent drunkenness and patronage of prostitutes, blinding him to the problems in his own house.

Functional Fixedness

Sometimes, a person encounters a problem with a concrete goal state, but constraints within the problem space make reaching that goal less than obvious. Called *functional fixedness*, this arises when a person must use a tool in an atypical way.[10] In problem-solving research, tools at your disposal are called *operators*, and a good solver understands which operators to use in a given situation and constraints imposed by the operator.[11] The classic example of functional fixedness is the candle box problem.[12] Given a matchbook, a box of tacks, and a candle, a person must affix the candle to the wall using the tacks before lighting it. Many people at first don't realize that they can tack the box itself to the wall and place the candle within it. Excellent fighters likewise know that anything can be a weapon, as the Hound discovers when Brienne of Tarth uses her teeth rather than her sword to slice off his ear during combat.[13]

Implementing Solutions

Detecting a problem, discerning its nature, and determining available operators is only the beginning. The next major step is to devise and implement solutions. Some problems have many possible solutions and some have only a few. Moreover, there are many possible techniques at the solver's disposal, each technique is appropriate for different situations, and the right technique must be selected.

Brute Force

The simplest problem-solving technique is the least efficient. Called *brute force*, it has the solver trying every possible solution until the correct one is found.[14] *Brute force* in this case does not refer to "raw physical strength," the way most people use the phrase, but instead refers to a relentless, unguided search for the solution. Early research by learning theorist E. L. Thorndike revealed brute force's effectiveness in a learning setting.[15] He placed cats in boxes from which they could see a bowl of food. The only way to escape was to manipulate the inside of the box in some way (like pressing a lever). Cats initially pushed and prodded at random, trying as many possible means to escape as they could. In so doing, they eventually found the solution. Gregor Clegane, the enormous knight known as the "Mountain that Rides," follows this approach when suggesting how to recruit scouts: "A man who sees nothing has no use for his eyes, cut them out and give them to your next outrider. Tell him you hope that four eyes might see better than two."[16] He adopts brute force elsewhere to serve the Lannisters. Is his horse not behaving well? Behead it and get another.[17] This exhaustive approach may lack nuance, but it is effective for simple problems.

Hill Climbing

Still another method for reaching a goal state produces an initial solution and then tries to improve upon it piecemeal. A final, optimal solution is then reached when no further improvements are possible. This technique is referred to as *hill climbing*: The solver is like a climber trying to get as high as possible, and from each pinnacle can see a still taller hill he or she then climbs.[18] Margaery Tyrell uses this technique so that she may end up in the position of ultimate power, charming every promising Baratheon on her way to the Iron Throne. This distinctive take on hill climbing might be referred to as "bed-climbing," for which she eventually develops a reputation. Ultimately, Cersei Lannister exacts revenge on "that smirking whore from Highgarden,"[19] by turning her over to the Faith Militant for moral crimes. This demonstrates that utilizing a single technique for all problems may work to a point, but it is not always effective if your enemies can predict your moves.

Working Backwards

Occasionally, an example problem appears worked out, and the solver must determine what operators were utilized and how in order to solve similar problems. This approach is *working backwards*, and can be seen in mathematics textbooks as an effective means of instructing students on solving complex problems.[20] Similarly, a precious few in Westeros may be granted power, and they must work backwards based on models of good rulers to project the spirit of nobility and justice befitting the realm. Ned Stark fails at working backwards to his and his family's peril. Although he may be a war hero and therefore well-respected among the great Houses, he does not anticipate the conspiracy and treachery that permeates King's Landing. Ned fails to understand that the seat of power in Westeros does not operate on principles of honor and respect, as in Winterfell. In other words, being named Hand of the King is not enough to gain allegiance from the others on the High Council. Cunning and ruthlessness are the path toward respect there, and he fails to adapt before investigating Jon Arryn's death. For this, he ultimately loses his head.[21]

Ninety-Nine Problems, But Stannis Can't Solve One

A great problem solver has an almost inhuman ability to perceive all the moving parts of a problem, prioritize them, and finally devise a successful solution. Called a *problem representation,* it requires knowing not just the initial state and the goal state, but the appropriate route to get there. Stannis Baratheon is aware of his initial state (out of power) and knows his desired goal state (becoming king). Unfortunately, he perceives the problem space as being more well-defined than it is, leading to a poor problem representation. This is partially because of Melisandre's influence, for she presents the subgoals as simpler than they are. This makes him employ simple solutions—perform some esoteric ritual here, ally with the most bitter enemies of the crown there—to the greater problem that is much more complex: No one else believes him legitimate, his armies have never fought against equals, and the Red Woman is clearly using his movement to achieve her own end. So he continues, leading to his eventual total loss to Ramsay Bolton.[22] All this, because he cannot properly represent the problem in his mind.

Making the Mind a Weapon: A Means-Ends Analysis
Simple solutions like those discussed may not always be optimal. The best problem solver uses not an individual technique, but instead examines a problem space, determines available operators, and uses them to maximum benefit. This is referred to as a *means-end analysis*, and requires the solver to recognize differences between the goal state and the current state and exploit operators related to those differences.[23] Expert chess players use this technique when they herd their opponents to checkmate. Tyrion Lannister is arguably the series' best user of this flexible technique, made clear by his longevity in the face of enormous odds. Whether he hill-climbs to earn freedom from Lady Lysa Tully,[24] uses brute force to ferret out Cersei's spy on the small council who informs on him,[25] or works backwards to prove himself a worthy Hand of the King,[26] he is not bound by any particular strategy, but uses the best means to resolve subgoals to meet his larger goal of personal security and influence.

Evaluating Results

A person either solves a problem or fails. If a failure occurs, the solver may be able to try a different solution (assuming he or she survived). However, even in success the solver must be aware of what aspect of the solution worked and why: Was I smart enough to find the solution? Did I have help? Was I just lucky? Learning the answers to these questions helps a person become an expert problem solver.

Creating and Changing Schemas
Successful problem solvers apply executive control to reflect upon the results. Reflection helps problem solvers understand

the problem within larger conceptual structures called *schemas*. Schemas are mental representations that categorize and organize information so that learners can make predictions for future actions.[27] For example, a hammer schema would include its appearance, how to use it, where it is typically found, and how it is related to other tools. If failure occurs, the schema must accommodate this new information so that the solver can more extensively explore the problem space to develop a new plan. If success occurs, the updated schema can transfer to new problems. In this way, evaluation transforms formerly ill-defined problems into well-defined problems.

Successful training begins with practice problems that must grow in difficulty with the learner's ability.[28] If problems are too easy, learners with too many successes may experience illusions of knowing without realizing that their understanding is incomplete.[29] If problems are too difficult, learners simply cannot solve them. Arya Stark's evaluative skills are vital to her survival. For example, Arya learns to wield a wooden sword before using a real blade. In addition, her practice varies by incorporating seemingly unrelated activities, like chasing cats and balancing on stairs. Practice should also include feedback clearly identifying both areas of mastery and gaps in knowledge.[30] When Arya makes mistakes, her fencing instructor identifies her failures and allows her to correct her actions as she develops mental and motor control. As she builds her schema, he transitions to indirect assistance by letting Arya plan (and possibly fail) to solve new problems on her own, and Arya herself remarks that "every hurt is a lesson, and every lesson makes you better."[31]

Positive Transfer

One way of using information learned from previous problem-solving experiences involves *positive transfer*, or reflecting upon relevant learned information and effectively implementing similar solutions to new problems.[32] These similarities are not always on the surface. Rather, the best problem solvers recognize deeper structural similarity between two problems.[33] Across her tumultuous problem space, Arya captures the true essence of the Water Dance philosophy by using elements like balance, strength, stealth, and speed to assume a multitude of varied aliases and get closer to her enemies. Likewise, the most effective problem solvers must reflect upon results under many varied situations to mentally represent structural similarities among experiences that connect otherwise independent schemas.

Negative Transfer

Success without evaluation may lead to ineffective planning in new situations in a process called *negative transfer*.[34] If a schema is not well-developed, learners develop illusions of knowing and fail to identify gaps in knowledge. For example, young Daenerys may have rarely evaluated the loyalty of her faithful servants in Dragonstone as operators in her problem space. After Khal Drogo is injured, Daenerys transfers this incomplete knowledge and urges him to allow Mirri Maz Duur to treat his chest wound.[35] Daenerys's gap in knowledge is exposed only after it is too late to evaluate the results and generate a new plan. Unfortunately, this negative transfer eventually leads to Drogo's death.

Mental Sets

Another consequence of good evaluation is the creation of new *mental sets*, combinations of strategies for solving particular classes of problems.[36] They can develop when a failure forces the solver to come up with a new solution, or when a novel situation demands a new type of solution. Those who fail to develop new mental sets face potential peril for not adapting to new situations. Daenerys treats the death of Drogo as a transferable experience to a newfound skepticism of outsiders and once-trusted advisors like Jorah Mormont. She also updates her schemas, adopts a new approach to planning, restructures problem spaces, and applies different operators to new problems. Unlike other powers in Essos, she allows the Unsullied to freely join her, thereby commanding fierce loyalty from the former slaves.[37] Daenerys lives to fight another day because she doesn't fall prey to the hazards of a fixed mental set.

Life Is Full of Possibilities

Problems are complex phenomena requiring every facet of the solver's cognitive abilities to work in concert to resolve. The players in *A Song of Ice and Fire* and *Game of Thrones* each navigate their own problem spaces, restricted to their own subgoals and aptitudes, to attain covert influence over the powerful, power over the Seven Kingdoms, conquest of the whole of the known world, or merely control over the player's own destiny. In everyday life, of course, the goals and consequences are rarely so extreme. However, if people wish to succeed, they must understand where they want to go and how to manipulate opportunities to get there.

References

Adamson, R. E. (1952). Functional fixedness as related to problem solving: A repetition of three experiments. *Journal of Experimental Psychology, 44*(4), 288–291.

Baddeley, A. D. (1998). Recent developments in working memory. *Current Opinion in Neurobiology, 8*(2), 234–238.

Bjork, R.A. (1994). Memory and metamemory considerations in the training of human beings. In J. Metcalfe & A. Shimamura (Eds.), *Metacognition: Knowing about knowing* (pp. 185–205). Cambridge, MA: MIT Press.

Bjork, R. A., Dunlosky, J., & Kornell, N. (2013). Self-regulated learning: Beliefs, techniques, and illusions. *Annual Review of Psychology, 64*, 417–444.

Chen, Z., & Daehler, M. W. (1989). Positive and negative transfer in analogical problem solving by 6-year-old children. *Cognitive Development, 4*(4), 327–344.

Duncker, K. (1945). On problem-solving. *Psychological Monographs, 58*(5), i–113.

Engel, A. (1998). *Problem-solving strategies.* New York, NY: Springer.

Fikes, R. E., & Nilsson, N. J. (1972). STRIPS: A new approach to the application of theorem proving to problem solving. *Artificial Intelligence, 2*(3), 189–208.

Holyoak, K. J., & Koh, K. (1987). Surface and structural similarity in analogical transfer. *Memory & Cognition, 15*(4), 332–340.

Larkin, J., McDermott, J., Simon, D. P., & Simon, H. A. (1980). Expert and novice performance in solving physics problems. *Science, 208*(4450), 1335–1342.

Martin, G. R. R. (1996). *A game of thrones.* New York, NY: Bantam.

Maslow, A. (1966). *The psychology of science: A reconnaissance.* Chicago, IL: Henry Regnery.

McBride, D. M., & Cutting, J. C. (2015). *Cognitive psychology: Theory, process, and methodology.* Thousand Oaks, CA: Sage.

Newell, A., & Simon, H. A. (1972). *Human problem solving.* Englewood Cliffs, NJ: Prentice-Hall.

Roediger III, H. L., & Butler, A. C. (2011). The critical role of retrieval practice in long-term retention. *Trends in Cognitive Science, 15*(1), 20–27.

Simon, H. A., & Newell, A. (1971). Human problem solving: The state of the theory in 1970. *American Psychologist, 26*(2), 145–159.

Singer, J. E. (1968). Consistency as a stimulus process mechanism. In R. P. Abelson, E. Aronson, W. McGuire, T. Newcomb, M. Rosenberg, & P. Tannenbaum (Eds.), *Theories of cognitive consistency: A sourcebook* (pp. 47–73). Chicago, IL: Rand McNally.

Spector, A. & Biederman, I. (1976). Mental set and mental shift revisited. *The American Journal of Psychology, 89*(4), 669–679.

Thorndike, E. L. (1898). Animal intelligence: An experimental study of the associative processes in animals. *The Psychological Review: Monograph Supplements, 2*(4, Whole No. 8), 1–109.

Notes

1. Martin (1996).
2. Maslow (1966).
3. Duncker (1945).
4. Baddeley (1998).
5. Newell & Simon (1972).
6. Episode 3–9, "The Rains of Castamere" (June 2, 2013).
7. Episode 1–1, "Winter is Coming" (April 17, 2011).
8. McBride & Cutting (2015).
9. Episode 1–7, "You Win or You Die" (May 29, 2011).
10. Adamson (1952).
11. Fikes & Nilsson (1972).
12. Duncker (1945).
13. Episode 4–10, "The Children" (June 15, 2014).
14. Engel (1998).
15. Thorndike (1898).
16. Martin (1996), pp. 638–639.
17. Episode 1–5, "The Wolf and the Lion" (May 15, 2011).
18. Simon & Newell (1971).

19. Episode 5–2, "The House of Black and White" (April 19, 2015).
20. Larkin et al. (1980).
21. Episode 1–9, "Baelor" (June 12, 2011).
22. Episode 5–10, "Mother's Mercy" (June 14, 2015).
23. Simon & Newell (1971).
24. Episode 1–6, "A Golden Crown" (May 22, 2011).
25. Episode 2–3, "What is Dead May Never Die" (April 15, 2012).
26. Episode 1–10, "Fire and Blood" (June 19, 2011).
27. Singer (1968).
28. Bjork (1994).
29. Bjork et al. (2013).
30. Roediger & Butler (2011).
31. Episode 1–4, "Cripples, Bastards, and Broken Things" (May 8, 2012).
32. e.g., Chen & Daehler (1989).
33. Holyoak & Koh (1987).
34. e.g., Chen & Daehler (1989).
35. Episode 1–9, "Baelor" (June 12, 2011).
36. Spector & Biederman (1976).
37. Episode 3–4, "And Now His Watch is Ended" (April 21, 2013).

The most influential areas within psychology each offer ideas on how self-control develops, the influence it has in our lives, and the consequences of having too little. Self-control might be the key to winning the most important games of all.

CHAPTER SEVENTEEN

Self-Control and the Secret to Winning the Game of Thrones

MARK CALDWELL JONES
AND WIND GOODFRIEND

"Even the truest knight cannot protect a king against himself."
—Eddard "Ned" Stark[1]

> *"It is difficult to identify any major personal problems that do not have some element of self-control failure."*
> —psychologist Roy Baumeister[2]

*S*elf-control is the ability to focus on long-term goals rather than immediate gratification, manage one's inner emotions, and exhibit behaviors that are thoughtful and purposeful. Some psychologists suggest that self-control, which also is called *willpower* or *self-regulation*, is crucial for healthy personal development. It may be even more important than self-esteem for life satisfaction, happiness, and social success.[3]

The fictional people living in the Seven Kingdoms appear to do well when they maintain control over their decisions and behavior. Self-control—or the absence of it—influences the fate of almost every notable character. In Westeros, we learn, recklessness can be deadly. Every decision is like a chess move, requiring tact, savvy, and prudence. The characters need a lot of self-control to steer the world in their favor amid the ubiquitous manipulations and conspiracies. In fact, self-control may be more useful than a sword if one wants to survive—and win—the Game of Thrones.

Psychological Theories about Self-Control

Every prominent theory in psychology offers suggestions regarding the cause, importance, and durability of self-control. Some back their ideas up with more empirical evidence than others. Some fit certain characters better than others.

Psychodynamic View

One of the first psychological researchers to consider the nature of self-control was Sigmund Freud, the founder of *psychoanalysis* or the *psychodynamic approach*, who believed that unconscious drives and conflicts direct much of people's behavior and personality development.[4] He suggested that the *id*, the childish and immature aspect of the self, is guided by the *pleasure principle*. According to Freud, the id is fueled by the desire to seek immediate pleasure and avoid pain. In contrast, the *ego* develops later and serves as a mediator between the unrealistic demands of the id and the norms and expectations of society. Guided by the *reality principle*, the ego supposedly attempts to regulate emotions and behavior into socially acceptable patterns, allowing people to achieve long-term goals instead of immediate gratification. Freud thus believed that maturity is marked by good self-control.

We can see how maturity and self-control go hand in hand as Arya Stark develops from a child to a young woman. Initially unruly, selfish, and impatient, Arya experiences a childhood marked by exuberance and a desire to break free from social expectations. Discipline comes later only in the form of sword fighting, which gives her a sense of purpose and calm in an unpredictable and dangerous world. She continues to struggle with self-control and the balance between id and ego as she reaches adolescence and decides to join the Faceless Men of Braavos. Still instinctively looking for *immediate gratification*, she feels unhappy when assigned menial tasks such as sweeping the floor and washing corpses. In her slow and mysterious training to become an assassin, she must overcome her id and focus on patience. Perhaps even more important, she must reject selfish and vengeful desires and focus on the greater good before she can serve the Many-Faced God. Arya's struggle with self-control is salient and represents a central theme in her character arc.

Behavioral View

The proponents of *behavioral psychology*[5] rejected the effect of unseen psychological forces and suggested that all behaviors are influenced by environmental rewards and punishments. In this viewpoint, the desire for immediate gratification can be nullified by social punishment and self-control can be encouraged by social demands. In other words, an environment that rewards disciplined behaviors and punishes hedonistic ones promotes self-control.

The High Sparrow is effectively a behaviorist. Unlike religious leaders who focus on the emotional benefits of spirituality, he teaches his followers that self-control results from adopting an ascetic lifestyle and rejecting environments that encourage sensuality. We see his view most clearly when the High Sparrow and his religious followers imprison Cersei.[6] Upon confession and release, she is subjected to a horrifying ritual, the "walk of atonement," which behaviorists would call a kind of *positive punishment,* which means adding an aversive consequence. This punishment is supposed to teach her that pursuing selfish pleasures will result in harsh social judgment, thus encouraging self-control through external consequences. However, Cersei's look of simmering rage shows that this experiment will end badly for the High Sparrow and his followers. Extreme punishment does not guarantee that a person's lack of self-control or lust for revenge will change.

Cognitive View

Cognitive psychology stresses the importance of thoughts and beliefs for behavior. Psychologists such as Aaron Beck and Albert Ellis believed that our emotions and behavior are a result of our thoughts and beliefs. Ellis proposed the ABC model of behavior: A real-world event (A) *activates* a set of (B) *beliefs,* and that results in certain (C) *consequences.*[7] This suggests that negative beliefs ultimately lead to poor behavioral choices and a weaker state of self-control.

This theory may explain many behavior choices. Tyrion Lannister's alcoholism and penchant for prostitutes could be a consequence of his belief that the world does not accept him and that he will never fit into his family. Arya Stark's unwavering desire for revenge may be a cognitive consequence of her perception that the world is unfair and that she has a responsibility to avenge the violent deaths of her loved ones. Finally, Cersei summarizes the Lannister family's cogni-

tive perspective on the larger world when she teaches her son
Joffrey, "Everyone who isn't us is an enemy!"[8] People with a
persistent belief that they are under threat will show signs of
constant vigilance, pessimism, and a desire to use violence to
protect themselves, all of which can complicate their ability to
maintain self-control.

Self-Control Disorders

Understanding the origins of self-control is helpful, but it
does not explain the consequences and severity of problems
of self-regulation. To make sense of those, problems related to
self-control now are diagnosed the same way as other medical illnesses. Many psychiatric disorders include some form
of self-control failure, especially impulsivity, in their criteria. Many self-control problems stand out, and the American
Psychiatric Association has created a special classification for
these conditions: *impulse control disorders*.[9] Three specific forms
of this type of disorder are intermittent explosive disorder,
conduct disorder, and antisocial personality disorder.

Explosive Emotions

Among the most dangerous mental health problems is *intermittent explosive disorder*, a condition that causes people to have
disproportionate rage that results in harm to people or property through violent, destructive behavior. By definition,
the behavior cannot be explained by another diagnosis such
as antisocial personality disorder or dementia. A person with
intermittent explosive disorder may have dozens of episodes of
rage and lack of self-control over time, leading to injuries that
require medical attention or causing thousands of dollars in
property damage.

Aerys Targaryen II, the Mad King, is someone who could have been diagnosed with intermittent explosive disorder. A ruler infamous for fits of uncontrollable rage, he demands undeserved executions and on a whim orders the burning of King's Landing. His son, Viserys Targaryen, seems to have the same problem. Viserys's intermittent explosions usually are directed toward his sister, Daenerys, whom he perceives as being weaker than he. Certainly, people with this disorder may target victims who are less powerful to avoid retaliation.

Misconduct

Conduct disorder is another impulse control disorder, but it is diagnosed in children. It is marked by a consistent pattern of breaking rules, laws, or societal norms. The questionable conduct includes loss of self-control through behaviors such as bullying, physical fights, assault with a weapon, physical cruelty to humans or animals, robbery, sexual assault, arson, destruction of property, home invasion, theft, and disregard for rules. The hallmarks of conduct disorder are socially inappropriate emotions, lack of remorse or guilt, callousness with lack of empathy, lack of concern about performance (in school or work), and lack of genuine emotional expression.

A child psychologist in Westeros might diagnose Joffrey Baratheon with conduct disorder. He enjoys torturing and hurting others, shows no concern about his performance as king, has disdain for his subjects, and displays a pattern of growing sadistic tendencies throughout his rule. He typifies what happens when someone with little to no personal self-control is given ultimate political and legal power: That person becomes a dangerous dictator and ultimately a monster.

Four Roots of Evil

When can lack of self-control lead to violence? Roy Baumeister's book *Evil: Inside Human Violence and Cruelty* proposes four root causes of human evil.[10]

- **Instrumental violence:** People commit evil acts as a means to an end; for instance, terrorists insist they have no political power and resort to horrific acts of mass murder to promote their cause.
- **Threatened egotism:** There is a popular theory that people with low self-esteem commit the most violence, but Baumeister asserts that his research indicates that this is a myth. He believes that narcissists commit the most violence; they become aggressive when their self-image is threatened by criticism. Violence functions as a way to preserve superiority and forces others to maintain respect.
- **Sadism:** Some people simply enjoy inflicting violence on others. Pathological individuals with little or no feeling of guilt may be disgusted by their first act of violence, but repeated acts of cruelty eventually produce pleasurable feelings. Because there is no shame or guilt blocking this progression, these individuals lose all empathetic identification with their victims. Over time, violence, torture, and murder become easier, making sadistic acts addictive or even fun for the perpetrator.
- **Idealism:** This is perhaps the most insidious root cause of evil. History is full of examples of political and religious "idealists" who have committed horrific violence. Followers of the Islamic State (ISIS), the Nazis, the post-Civil War Ku Klux Klan, and Communist China committed unprecedented murderous acts, all in the name of changing the world for the better.

Antisocial Personality

Antisocial personality disorder, which is classified as both a person-ality disorder and an impulse control disorder, is a long-term pattern of manipulating, exploiting, or violating the rights of others, often at a criminal level.[11] Colloquially, people with this disorder have been called psychopaths or sociopaths. Some professionals use the terms *psychopathy*, *sociopathy*, and *dyssocial personality disorder* interchangeably for this.[12]

In *Game of Thrones*, the most horrifying example of antiso-cial personality disorder may be Ramsay Bolton. He shows a pathological lack of empathetic identification with people and engages in sadistic behaviors that include torturing people, hunting them for sport, flaying and mutilating his victims, and raping his wife. People like this do not necessarily lack self-control; they have no innate desire to use it to stop their depraved behavior. Such a person has a complete lack of empa-thy and compassion. Many fans consider Ramsay the most evil character in the story because he displays this kind of unrelent-ing antisocial behavior.

The Significance of Self-Control

The importance of self-control can be shown through certain narrative conventions. When characters act ignobly, behave irrationally, or make a foolish emotional choice, there is a negative consequence. These subtextual rules metaphorically denounce failures of self-control. It is not okay to act like a psychopath in Martin's world. If you do, you pay for it—in a gory, dramatic way. A character may endure dishonor, torture, dismemberment, and even death.[13]

Theon Greyjoy shows a lack of self-control when he orders the killing of two innocent boys, which results in his being taken by Ramsay, who tortures and mutilates him.[14] Similarly, Jaime Lannister pushes a child out of a tower to protect his most shameful secret,[15] which starts a series of events that result in his dominant "sword hand" being cut off, leaving him disabled.[16] Poetic justice is salient. In contrast to the many examples of out-of-control behavior, characters with good self-control have outcomes that are more positive, showing the benefits that good self-control can bring.

Prolonged goals and patience benefit Jon Snow, who endures bullying in the Night's Watch and prejudice regarding his status as illegitimate until he eventually is elected to become the lord commander. Daenerys exhibits self-control when she endures abuse from her brother and then is forced into marriage and a life in which self-control is vital to staying alive; she then literally rises out of the flames to become one of the most disciplined and powerful people in the entire Seven Kingdoms. Clearly, self-control can lead to immense benefits and power.

Self-control researcher Roy Baumeister has proposed ideas that agree with the subtext of the *Game of Thrones*. He says, "Self-control is not just a puritanical virtue, it is a key psychological trait that breeds success at work and play—and in overcoming life's hardships." He continues, "The desire to control ourselves and our environment is deeply rooted in the psyche and underlies human engagement in science, politics, business and the arts. Given that most of us lack the kingly power to command others to do our bidding and that we need to enlist the cooperation of others to survive, the ability to restrain aggression, greed and sexual impulses becomes a necessity."[17]

Baumeister's research has uncovered several practical findings about self-control. Self-control functions like a muscle. It can be depleted by consistent use, making it unavailable for subsequent self-regulation tasks.[18] It can be strengthened or replenished by rest, positive emotions, and conservation strategies.[19]

If one removes unnecessary goal conflicts and uses self-control strategically, one can maximize the benefits of self-control.[20] In addition, self-control relies on limited energy resources such as blood glucose.[21] These insights point to a possible future in which people may recover from self-control failures and improve the use of self-control more easily.

Self-Control Wins the Game

Themes in this story and other literature and entertainment can teach us that control is an illusion. Control cannot help us escape our problems; it can only help us decide how to respond to them. Self-discipline, self-regulation, and self-control are growing interests in psychology, and research shows that these traits have both scientific validity and personal utility.[22]

Strategic self-control brings success and happiness, and exercising self-control like a muscle makes people stronger, ready to conquer future challenges. In the world of Westeros, loss of control leads to disappointing outcomes such as the loss of power or life. Improved self-control more often leads to improved well-being and success in life. No one is safe from danger, but self-control may allow us "to savor our time on earth and share joy with the ones you love."[23] *Game of Thrones* teaches us that to conquer our enemies, we must exhibit patience, focus on long-term goals, and develop personal discipline. Research teaches us that we need self-control to achieve our life goals and conquer problems in the real world. When all is said and done, these two realms, art and science, may say the same thing: Self-control is the secret to winning the game of life.

References

American Psychiatric Association. (2013). *Diagnostic and statistical manual of mental disorders* (5th ed.). Washington, DC: American Psychiatric Association.

Baumeister, R. F. (1997). *Evil: Inside human violence and cruelty.* New York, NY: Freeman.

Baumeister, R. F. (2015, April). Conquer yourself, conquer the world. *Scientific American, 312*(4), 60–65.

Baumeister, R. F., & Gailliot, M. T. (2007). The physiology of willpower: Linking blood glucose to self-control. *Personality and Social Psychology Review, 11*(4), 303–327.

Baumeister, R. F., & Tierney, J. (2011). *Willpower: Rediscovering the greatest human strength.* New York, NY: Penguin.

Ellis, A. (1957). Rational psychotherapy and individual psychology. *Journal of Individual Psychology, 13,* 38–44.

Freud, S. (1940). An outline of psychoanalysis. In *Standard edition of the complete works of Sigmund Freud* (vol. 23, pp. 141–207). London, UK: Hogarth.

Martin, G. R. R. (2003). *A game of thrones.* New York, NY: Random House.

Schreiber, L., Odlaug, B. L., & Grant, J. E. (2011). Impulse control disorders: Updated review of clinical characteristics and pharmacological management. *Frontiers in Psychiatry, 2*(21), 9–10.

Tice, D. M., Baumeister, R. F., Shmueli, D., & Muraven, M. (2007). Restoring the self: Positive affect helps improve self-regulation following ego depletion. *Journal of Experimental Social Psychology, 43*(1), 379–384.

U.S. National Library of Medicine (2012, November 10). *Antisocial personality disorder.* National Institutes of Health: https://www.nlm.nih.gov/medlineplus/ency/article/000921.htm.

Watson, J. B. (1924/1970). *Behaviorism.* New York, NY: Norton.

Notes

1. Martin (2003), p. 468.
2. Baumeister (2015), p. 60.
3. Baumeister & Tierney (2011).
4. Freud (1940).
5. Watson (1924/1970).
6. Episode 5–10, "Mother's Mercy" (June 14, 2015).
7. Ellis (1957).
8. Episode 1–3, "Lord Snow" (May 1, 2011).
9. American Psychiatric Association (2013).
10. Baumeister (1997).
11. U.S. National Library of Medicine (2012).
12. American Psychiatric Association (2013), p. 659.
13. Baumeister & Tierney (2011).
14. Episode 3–7, "The Bear and the Maiden Fair" (May 12, 2013).
15. Episode 1–1, "Winter Is Coming" (April 12, 2011).
16. Episode 3–3, "Walk of Punishment" (April 14, 2013).
17. Baumeister & Tierney (2011).
18. Baumeister & Tierney (2011).
19. Tice et al. (2007).
20. Baumeister & Tierney (2011).
21. Baumeister & Galliot (2007).
22. Baumeister & Tierney (2011).
23. Baumeister & Tierney (2011).

What is a hero? Why do some people stand up despite all odds and fight to do what is right, no matter what it costs them? Positive psychology offers some clues.

CHAPTER EIGHTEEN

Pure as Snow: The Character Strengths and Virtues of a Hero

DANA KLISANIN

"I shall take no wife, hold no lands, father no children. I shall wear no crowns and win no glory. . . . I pledge my life and honor to the Night's Watch, for this night and all the nights to come."
—Night's Watch Oath[1]

"Heroes, always deviant. Heroes, always doing something that most people don't. . . ."
—psychologist Philip Zimbardo[2]

What makes someone heroic? Although it might seem easy to answer that question, psychologists have conducted little research on it and debate what it is. Why do people identify one individual as heroic but not another? Many *Game of Thrones* fans see Jon Snow as one of the most heroic characters. But why? What are the major characteristics and qualities ascribed to heroes? Are they born in special circumstances? What propels them to action? Are they courageous? Selfless? Honest? Do they obey authority or disobey? What makes them stand out from the crowd?

Is Jon really "pure as snow"?

Heroism

Although *heroism* has been historically understudied in psychology, it has recently become a major topic of scientific inquiry.[3] Researchers are exploring the characteristics of a variety of heroes, from military heroes to whistle-blowers, activist heroes to celebrity heroes.[4] There are obvious differences between these heroes, such as the physical risk involved in a heroic act. Researchers Scott Allison and George Goethals suggest three important dimensions in which our perceptions of heroes vary:[5]

1. We view them as moral or competent, and possibility both at once.
2. We view them as being born with stable heroic traits or made into heroes by specific circumstances.
3. They inspire us or show great leadership.[6]

A famous soldier, a professional basketball player, and an award-winning actress will be viewed differently than a whistle-blower or an activist, but they each inspire us in some way, even as people argue over whether to call any of them heroes.

One of the most important findings in heroism research is related to *disobedience*, in that those who actively refuse to do wrong are seen as more heroic in their efforts to do what is right. In one of psychology's most famous experiments, a researcher in a white lab coat directed participants to administer potentially dangerous shocks to another person.[7] Surprisingly, many participants obeyed the authority figure, continuing to shock the subject although obvious pain and distress were apparent. However, some disobeyed. When Samwell Tarly arrives at Castle Black, Jon directly disobeys his commanding officer's order to fight the unprepared Sam because it is a cruel and unfair order.

In addition to refusing to obey orders to be cruel, heroic individuals will resist pressures to conform and to join others in their cruelty. In another of psychology's most famous experiments, participants were randomly assigned to play roles as either "prisoners" or "guards" in a mock jail at Stanford University.[8] What was surprising about this study is that a number of guards became sadistic toward prisoners in just a few days. Although the lead researcher, Philip Zimbardo, spent many years discussing how the roles brought out the worst in some of those assigned to be the guards,[9] he later began to look more at why some people resist the pressure to do wrong and instead stand up to do what is right.[10] When others in the Night's Watch set a fire to burn Mance Rayder to death, Jon Snow not only refuses to take part but instead shoots Rayder in order to spare him the agony of burning to death. This ability to disobey authority or resist conforming to actions that are contrary to one's moral values, ideals, or established code of conduct is a quality that many heroes share.[11]

Heroism is closely associated with morality,[12] but the study of morality is often fraught with difficulty, since it is closely bound to cultural norms, which vary widely. We see these cultural differences reflected in hotly debated issues such as abortion rights, with some individuals staunchly opposing a woman's right to choose and others championing that right. These differences are often aligned with religious views. For example, although Jon Snow does not approve of Melisandre's burning of sacrificial victims to the fire god, her followers understand, support, and carry out her wishes.

We often think of heroes as people who inspire, show great leadership, or have character strengths—and for good reason. Research shows that heroes are often leaders[13] and often share some combination of the following "eight great traits": smart, strong, resilient, selfless, caring, charismatic, reliable, and inspiring.[14] It's unusual for a hero to possess all eight of these characteristics, but most heroes have some of them. Many of these traits are widely studied in the field of *positive psychology*. The *Values in Action (VIA) Inventory of Strengths*[15] is a classification comprising 24 character strengths that fall within six broad virtue categories: wisdom, courage, humanity, justice, temperance, and transcendence. Character strengths are the *positive components* of our psychological landscape. Let's examine Jon's character strengths, using the *Values in Action Inventory of Strengths* as a guide, and see what we learn about him.

Wisdom
Wisdom is a form of cognitive strength made up of creativity, curiosity, judgment, love of learning, and perspective,[16] most of which Jon Snow epitomizes.

- While *creativity* is probably not the first character strength that springs to mind when we think of Jon, in fact, he consistently demonstrates it when he thinks of new ways to conceptualize and do things. He frequently imagines alternatives. When Jon has a sword made for his youngest sister,[17] when he urges his superior to close the tunnel,[18] and when he urges the men of the Night's Watch to make peace with wildlings,[19] he shows creativity. In each of these situations, Jon demonstrates a new way to do things or imagines new alternatives. By giving his sister a sword, Jon shows her more than affection—his gift actually empowers her to be who she is, rather than who society tells her to be. When he urges his superior to close the tunnel, Jon presents an option that others haven't thought of, thus showing creative thinking. And finally, when he urges the men of the Night's Watch to make peace with the wildlings, he extends his imagination to the limits of the possible—peace between enemies.

• Jon frequently uses good *judgment*, thinking things through without jumping to conclusions, when he weighs evidence and considers it fairly. Examples are abundant, particularly in all of his dealings with the wildlings. He consistently demonstrates the ability to consider the merits of either side of an argument, ignoring whatever emotional involvements he may have, as well as overcoming prejudice.

• *Perspective* is the ability to look at experiences and events critically, generally in more than one way. Jon's ability to take multiple perspectives is a major part of what led him to become Lord Commander of the Night's Watch. Lord Commander Mormont chose Jon to be his personal steward precisely because he valued Jon's perspective. He knew Jon would be a good advisor, and could become a great leader.

Courage

Courage is a form of emotional strength that involves using one's will to accomplish goals, often in the face of opposition. Some of the traits associated with courage are bravery, perseverance, honesty, and zest.[20] Jon is strong in all of these traits.

- *Bravery* means standing up to threats and being able to speak up for what is right. Though he is not a seasoned warrior, Jon readily faces every challenge of combat. Perhaps an even greater sign of bravery is Jon's willingness to stand up for his beliefs, especially in the face of his superiors at the Wall.
- *Perseverance*, what it takes to finish what we start, means persisting in a course of action despite obstacles. Jon's unfailing commitment in his oath to the Night's Watch, even when it meant leaving a woman he truly loved,[21] is evidence enough.
- *Honesty* means speaking the truth and showing integrity. A great example of integrity is Jon's refusal to accept Stannis's offer to legitimize him as a Stark and make him Lord of Winterfell.[22] We know this is nothing less than his lifelong dream and yet we see his integrity when he informs Sam that he will not accept but will remain true to his oath.
- *Zest* is about living life full throttle—with excitement and energy. We know that Jon is full of zest, having chosen a life of adventure at the Wall over a long and comfortable life as a member of a noble family.

Humanity

Humanity is a virtue that involves caring for and being a friend to others. The character strengths within this category include love, kindness, and social intelligence.[23]

- *Love* is about sharing ourselves with others in a meaningful way and showing them that we value our relationship with them. After Ygritte's death, Jon shows his love for her by burning her body in a private ceremony[24] and refusing the advances of Melisandre.[25]

- *Kindness* is when we help others in meaningful ways. We see this character strength in Jon when he arrives at Castle Black. He immediately stands up for Samwell Tarly, refusing to let others fight him—disobeying direct orders from his superior.[26]
- *Social intelligence* is being aware of the motives and feelings of other people and knowing how to behave in different social situations. When Stannis orders the execution of Mance Rayder, Jon reveals social intelligence by describing how well he was treated while he was Mance's prisoner in order to appeal to Stannis's sensibility as a military commander.[27]

Justice

Justice is a combination of teamwork, fairness, and leadership.[28] Jon excels in each of these character strengths.

- *Fairness* is about being unbiased in decision-making, rather than showing favoritism based on friendship or desire for personal gain. When Jon is nominated by Sam to be Lord Commander, he later shows fairness and impartiality by appointing Ser Alliser, a senior brother of the Watch who openly dislikes him, to be First Ranger.
- *Leadership* is the ability to take charge of a situation or group of people and encourage them to work together to accomplish tasks. It involves organizational skills and is considered intertwined with heroism.[29] This ability seems to come naturally to Jon. He exhibits leadership when he volunteers to take a group of men and go

Beyond the Wall to avenge Commander Mormont's death,[30] leads the defense of Castle Black during the wildling attack, and attempts to establish peace and security by suggesting that the Night's Watch gift the wildlings the lands south of the Wall in order to unite their forces and fight the White Walkers.

Temperance

Temperance protects us against excess. It encompasses forgiveness, humility, prudence, and self-regulation.[31] Jon is particularly strong in humility and self-regulation.

- We demonstrate *humility* when we let our accomplishments speak for themselves. Jon Snow is an exemplar of humility, so much so that he doesn't even speak for himself when he is nominated to be Lord Commander. It is Sam who speaks on behalf of Jon's merit, and we know that Jon's accomplishments speak for themselves because even without speaking he is elected Lord Commander.
- The fact that Jon does not just stay with Ygritte and the wildlings demonstrates a remarkable level of self-control. Rather than letting his emotions take over, he shows discipline and remains true to his vow.

Transcendence

Transcendence is unique to each person. It is often described as a feeling of interconnection with the universe. Character strengths associated with it include appreciation of beauty and excellence, gratitude, hope, humor, and spirituality.[32]

- *Appreciation of beauty and excellence* is self-explanatory. A great example of Jon's appreciation of excellence is

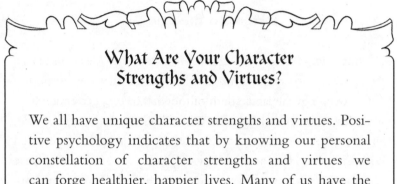

What Are Your Character Strengths and Virtues?

We all have unique character strengths and virtues. Positive psychology indicates that by knowing our personal constellation of character strengths and virtues we can forge healthier, happier lives. Many of us have the tendency to fixate on our weaknesses—complaining about the areas where we don't excel, rather than focusing on our strengths. Research in positive psychology suggests we have a better chance for health and success if we focus on our strengths.[33]

when he agrees to allow Sam to be sent to the Citadel to become a Maester. He recognizes Sam's intellectual excellence and suitability for a Maestership.

- Most of us are familiar with *hope*, the feeling or belief that something good is going to happen. Jon believes there is a future for Westeros and that the White Walkers can be defeated. Because of this, he joins forces with the wildlings.

- *Spirituality* involves a sense of higher purpose or meaning in life. Jon's character is steeped in spirituality, or adherence to moral ideals. He chooses to take his vows before the Old Gods of the North, and although it appears that Jon has broken his vows to the Night's Watch, ultimately he is actually doing what must be done to keep it. He disobeys in order to obey.

A Hero to the End . . .

Through exploring Jon's character using the *Values in Action (VIA) Inventory of Strengths*, we've found that he embodies many of the perceptions held about heroes in general. He is smart, strong, resilient, selfless, caring, charismatic, reliable, and inspiring—embodying the "eight great traits" associated with heroism. He is an inspirational leader, but his strong sense of morality and his ability to know when to disobey authority make him the most heroic character in *Game of Thrones*. To answer one of our opening questions, yes, it's safe to say that he's "pure as snow." This doesn't mean he never makes mistakes or takes the wrong action—it simply means that he is never stained with vices such as greed and cruelty. Jon's character strengths and virtues, leadership ability, compassionate nature, and creativity may make him one of his world's greatest heroes and leaders.

References

Allison, S. T., & Goethals, G. R. (2011). *Heroes: What they do and why we need them.* Oxford, UK: Oxford University Press.

Allison, S. T., & Goethals, G. R. (2013). *Heroic leadership: An influence taxonomy of 100 exceptional individuals.* New York, NY: Routledge.

Allison, S. T., Goethals, G. R., & Kramer, R. M. (Eds.) (2016). *Handbook of heroism and heroic leadership.* New York, NY: Routledge.

Blum, L. A. (1992). Altruism and the moral value of the rescue: Resisting persecution, racism, and genocide. In P. M. Oliner, S. P. Oliner, L. Baron, L. A. Blum, D. L. Krebs, & M. Z. Smolenska (Eds.), *Embracing the other: Philosophical, psychological, and historical perspectives on altruism* (pp. 30–47). New York, NY: New York University Press.

Denton, A. (2008, November 17). *Dr. Philip Zimbardo.* ABC: http://www.abc.net.au/tv/enoughrope/transcripts/s2421530.htm.

Kohn, A. (1990). *The brighter side of human nature: Altruism and empathy in everyday life.* New York, NY: Basic.

Milgram, S. (1974). *Obedience to authority: An experimental view.* New York, NY: Harper & Row.

Peterson, C., & Seligman, M. E. P. (2004). *Character strengths and virtues: A handbook and classification.* Washington, DC: American Psychological Association.

VIA Institute on Character (2015). *Home.* VIA Institute on Character: http://www.viacharacter.org

Zimbardo, P. G. (1969). The human choice: Individuation, reason, and order versus deindividuation, impulse, and chaos. In W. J. Arnold & D. Levine (Eds.), *Nebraska Symposium on Motivation* (Vol. 17). Lincoln, NE: University of Nebraska Press.

Zimbardo, P. G. (1971, October 25). *The psychological power and pathology of imprisonment.* A statement prepared for the U.S. House of Representatives Committee on the Judiciary, Subcommittee No. 3: Hearings on Prison Reform, San Francisco, CA.

Zimbardo, P. G. (2008). *The Lucifer effect: How good people turn bad.* New York, NY: Random House.

Notes

1. Episode 1–7, "You Win or You Die" (May 29, 2011).
2. Denton (2008).
3. Allison, Goethals, & Kramer (Eds.) (2016).
4. Allison & Goethals (2011).
5. Allison & Goethals (2011).
6. Allison & Goethals (2011), p. 44.
7. Milgram (1974).
8. Zimbardo (1969, 1971).
9. Zimbardo (1969, 1971).
10. Denton (2008).
11. Zimbardo (2008).
12. Allison & Goethals (2011).
13. Allison & Goethals (2013).
14. Allison & Goethals (2011).
15. Peterson & Seligman (2004).
16. Peterson & Seligman (2004).
17. Episode 1–2, "The Kingsroad" (April 24, 2011).
18. Episode 4–8, "The Mountain and the Viper" (June 1, 2014).
19. Episode 5–5, "Kill the Boy" (May 10, 2015).
20. Peterson & Seligman (2004).
21. Episode 3–10, "Mhysa" (June 9, 2013).
22. Episode 5–2, "The House of Black and White" (April 19, 2015).
23. Peterson & Seligman (2004).
24. Episode 4–10, "The Children" (June 15, 2015).
25. Episodes 1–1, "Winter Is Coming" (April 17, 2011); 1–2, "The Kingsroad" (April 24, 2011).
26. Episode 1–4, "Cripples, Bastards and Broken Things" (May 8, 2011).
27. Episode 4–10, "The Children" (June 15, 2014).
28. Peterson & Seligman (2004).
29. Allison & Goethals (2013).
30. Episode 4–3, "Breaker of Chains" (April 20, 2014).
31. Peterson & Seligman (2004).
32. Peterson & Seligman (2004).
33. VIA Institute on Character (2015).

Stories appeal to us for many different reasons. A tale rich in details, intricate in design, and grand in scope can both challenge and reward us by exercising memory, enhancing intelligence, and helping us think more efficiently. Following a complicated story might not only help you feel smarter; it might also help you *be* smarter.

CHAPTER NINETEEN

A Complex Story
Does the Brain Good

JOSUÉ CARDONA

"A mind needs books as a sword needs a whetstone,
if it is to keep its edge."
—Tyrion Lannister[1]

> *"Mental events, it is said, are not passive*
> *happenings but the acts of a subject."*
> —psychologist Hermann Ebbinghaus[2]

Some people may not see fantasy stories and television shows in general as being educational or mentally beneficial, but they may very well be, especially when their stories are intricately detailed. The complexity in stories such as *Game of Thrones* means that watching them is not just a passive exercise but a cognitively demanding one that requires effort on the part of the viewer to understand what is going on and keep track of the many threads. That hard work may benefit viewers because they are exercising parts of the brain with more intensity than they do while performing other activities, specifically other entertaining ones. As a result of the brain's *plasticity* (its ability to change in response to mental activity[3]), watching *Game of Thrones* may make a person smarter or at the very least improve key parts of the brain and influence behavior in specific ways.

Complexity

"They're only numbers—numbers on paper. Once you understand them, it's easy to make them behave."
—Petyr Baelish (Littlefinger)[4]

In the 1980s, the intelligence researcher James R. Flynn discovered that Americans were making consistent gains in intelligence despite the fact that their intelligence quotient (IQ) scores remained the same.[5] Flynn observed that Americans effectively gain about 3 IQ points each decade, which is a lot—the so-called Flynn effect[6]—even though standard IQ tests are updated and adjusted continuously to keep the average score the same. That would mean that scoring 100 on an IQ test published now would require the intelligence necessary to score 106 on a test published twenty years earlier. The rise in intelligence is attributable to many different factors, among them the increasing complexity or cognitive demands of a person's environment.[7] In light of the fact Americans over the age fifteen spend an average of 2.8 hours each day watching television, almost half of the time they devote to leisure activities, some argue that TV also has become more complex over time.[8]

Is *Game of Thrones* really that complex? With the exception of some pre–opening credits story recaps, *Game of Thrones* seems to keep exposition to a minimum. In many television shows, the characters sometimes discuss the story or action in an unnatural manner to give the viewers off-screen information or to remind them of a story that has taken place previously, resulting in unrealistic on-screen conversations. However, the characters in *Game of Thrones* rarely review information out loud for the sake of the viewer, and that alone makes the show and book series more difficult to follow than many others. For example, when Arya first sees Meryn Trant arrive in Braavos,[9] a long time has passed since she first saw him kill her fencing instructor,[10] but there is no recapping to remind the audience of who he was or what he did. Her reaction must be understood by the audience independently by remembering what happened, and any viewer who did not remember Trant by sight alone had to infer this man's importance from the look on Arya's face when she saw him and then her behavior as she followed him.

The series' complexity arises from a number of areas, including breadth of characters, scope, and the need to condense the source material, and each area requires certain cognitive skills to sort out. Once they are, the experiences not only are enjoyable but also act as exercise for the brain, improving those skills.

Memory

The audience must utilize memory constantly to keep track of the many characters, families, alliances, and locations. Because people don't necessarily read books or watch TV with a notebook, guide, or wiki open at all times (although many do—see the sidebar "Partipatory Culture and Media"), they try to remember who is on screen, where they are, what their goals are, and much more.

In the first episode,[11] viewers meet no fewer than fifteen characters essential to moving the story forward. Viewers take in all this information and then store it in *short-term memory*—a.k.a. *working memory*—temporary storage for a small amount of information before it is lost or becomes longer-lasting and is stored in *long-term memory*. Each time a specific character reappears on screen or is mentioned, the memory is strengthened. When viewers meet Daenerys, they learn only that she is one of a handful of living Targaryens. Her situation constantly changes and she is always on the move, creating new relationships that could move her in an entirely different direction. Every appearance by a character strengthens what viewers know about that character, including motivations, desires, and fears. The new information about a character and his or her journey provides more connections that expand all the information related to that character. If this is done frequently and in small bits, a character's story becomes more memorable to the audience. For instance, if a character such as Daenerys, who experiences several substantial changes, were to disappear for the better part of two years in our time (as Bran does) and disclose the events of those two years in one helping for the audience, it would be too much new information to store and too much time may have passed for viewers to remember her as vividly.

The more a person accesses a piece of information and the more it is connected to other information, the more accessible that information will be. This process is referred to as *encoding*. When a character appears onscreen, information about that character is retrieved from long-term memory and considered to be in working memory or to be actively engaged. Exercising memory can lead to improvements in recall.[12]

By jumping back and forth between its central characters, the series allows viewers to learn and recall each character regularly and build a world that is accessible despite its increasing complexity. This process is similar to the concept of *spaced repetition*, which researchers have found to be an effective way to improve the recall of information by accessing it to keep it from fading.[13]

Participatory Culture and Media

A collection of content and analyses related to *Game of Thrones* (including this book) is available thanks to a community of people who care about the source material. These are not just people who get paid for it. It turns out that people can feel driven by a need to create new things of their own choosing that they find enjoyable and fulfilling.[14] This explains why *Game of Thrones* and almost everything else has a Wikipedia article and in many cases a solely dedicated wiki, plus blogs, videos, podcasts, and even fan faction.

The term *participatory culture*[15] has been applied to cultures with low barriers to entry and high levels of acceptance that encourage the sharing of information. These cultures also tend to include a form of mentorship that allows those who know a lot about a subject to teach others and those who are curious to learn more. Interestingly, participatory cultures act as supplementary forms of education, allowing enthusiasts to gain expertise and providing exposure that can lead to other opportunities. Your *Game of Thrones*–centric YouTube channel may just get you a book deal. Maybe.

Multiple Threads

Although revisiting narrative threads can help with memory, it is important to note that jumping back and forth between multiple threads is the only effective way to pay attention to a story with so many moving parts. There are many things happening simultaneously throughout the narrative of *Game of Thrones*, and so it can be difficult to follow all those threads when too much information is shown in one episode.

The part of the brain that keeps track of multiple, simultaneous threads is the *prefrontal cortex*, the front part of the brain, which also helps with cognitive functions such as organization, prioritization, and resource management. As a series, *Game of Thrones* gives the prefrontal cortex quite a workout, but not every episode is equally demanding. This is often story-driven because in many cases visiting other story lines would lessen the impact and intensity for the audience, especially for excessive action scenes.

For example, the Battle of Castle Black[16] took up an entire episode; that episode never visited other story lines, instead focusing solely on the buildup to the battle and the characters involved in it. If it had been interrupted by scenes dealing with other events, the battle might have spanned multiple episodes or not have had the impact it did. Although it is done for entertainment on the show, focusing on one isolated thing at a time is a good way to work. According to *threaded cognition theory*,[17] the brain is more effective at focusing on one thread or task at a time than on two or more.

In everyday tasks, the notion of multitasking usually is misunderstood because the brain cannot do two similar things at once. It can do different types of things simultaneously but not the same types of things, and the most effective way to understand, learn, or complete any task is to dedicate as much brain power to it as possible.

Social and Emotional Intelligence

> *"Always keep your foes confused. If they are never certain of*
> *what you want, they can't know what you plan to do next."*
> —Petyr Baelish[18]

Who is the hero? What would winning mean? Who is the villain? These are common questions for an audience reading or watching an epic work. Viewers are witnessing human relationships, family ties and alliances, and interactions between characters and the games they are playing; becoming emotionally invested in characters; questioning behaviors and guessing what might happen next. In stories in which "the hero will win" does not apply and in fact identifying the hero is not easy or clear and in which motivations and relationships constantly change in unpredictable ways, audiences are more engaged as they need to focus and pay attention lest they miss a vital shift in the story.

In a novel, the story can be written from the perspectives of different characters, allowing readers to know how those characters see events unfolding, what they think, and how they feel about their experiences. By seeing events from someone else's perspective, readers are exercising *emotional intelligence* (EI), which commonly refers to a person's ability to perceive and express emotion.[19] Television viewers can do the same thing by observing events as an outsider and exercising their EI. Confirming what characters are thinking and feeling is possible only if those characters share that information with the audience or another character or through their behavior. The acting, the facial expressions, and the reactions of characters to one another also allow viewers to exercise their *social intelligence* (SI), which is defined as a person's ability to manage social situations and wisely behave in relationships.[20] Seeing a character interact with multiple characters enhances our understanding of that character's social network and helps us understand other social networks.

Characters such as Littlefinger, whose motivations and goals are often a mystery, provide a particularly exciting opportunity to use both emotional intelligence and social intelligence; viewers try to make sense of what he's doing in the context of what he's done, our opinion of him, and who he is with. It is not so much that we are learning about social interactions and how to read facial expressions as that we are practicing what we know in different ways and therefore becoming more invested in the story because we are reading into what is or may be happening.

People who possess high levels of both emotional intelligence and social intelligence are able to have healthier relationships and be more successful. One study[21] found both to be four times more important in determining success professionally than is IQ.

Challenge and Reward

"Most enjoyable activities are not natural; they demand an effort that initially one is reluctant to make."
—psychologist Mihaly Csíkszentmihályi[22]

Remembering all those characters, following multiple threads, and deciphering the characters' actions and intentions is hard work, so why do so many people watch the show?

The psychologist and positive psychology pioneer Mihaly Csíkszentmihályi coined the term *flow* to refer to the feeling of being "in the zone" when a person feels very productive and engaged.[23] According to Csíkszentmihályi, it is during flow that people are most happy. It turns out that a challenging

Hodor! Language and the Brain

JORDAN GAINES LEWIS

Linguistic intelligence deals with using language to understand, communicate, and solve problems.[24] While that explanation might make one particular *Game of Thrones* character seem to be very low in this kind of intelligence, it's more complicated than that. Even a person who comprehends language and uses it well within that person's own mind might not be able to express language for other reasons.

Hodor hodor. Hodor? Hodor-hodor-hodor. Hodor!

Oh, um, excuse me. Did you catch what I said?

Why does Hodor "hodor"? Why does this character use only one word, to the point that others mistake it for his name? "No one knew where 'hodor' had come from," Old Nan says when discussing her great-grandson Walder's language impairment, "but when he started saying it, they started calling him by it."[25] George R. R. Martin appears to have created a character with a neurological condition called *expressive aphasia*, an inability to express language due to brain damage.

In 1861, French physician Paul Broca reported on his work with patient Louis-Victor Leborgne, who had progressively lost the ability to produce meaningful speech, despite otherwise normal cognitive functioning. Like Hodor, he was nicknamed "Tan" because he eventually spoke only that word. After Leborgne's death, an autopsy by Dr. Broca revealed tissue damage in the brain's left frontal lobe.[26]

Hodor is a similarly extreme example of expressive aphasia. More commonly, patients have "telegraphic speech," creating sentences with just a few words—usually including at least a noun and a verb. It's caused by brain damage to what's now known as *Broca's area*, most often a result of stroke, a tumor, hemorrhage, or head trauma.[27]

If Hodor, as a stable boy for the Starks, had suffered a hoof to the head, that could account for this difficulty.

Hodor!

activity not only is engaging but produces a great sense of satisfaction and enjoyment.

In regard to television specifically, Csíkszentmihályi's research indicates that flow states while a person is watching television were not reported as often as they were for other forms of media such as video games[28] and that it was not the most efficient way to experience flow. He also described the experience of flow as being coupled with a diminished sense of one's surroundings and the feeling that time is flying by. *Game of Thrones* continuously revisits threads and characters, allowing viewers to confirm their theories and speculations or learn that they were mistaken and make adjustments. It also adds new information and refreshes old memories. It does all this and more multiple times in each episode.

Csíkszentmihályi's research into TV was done in the 1980s. Flow, in contrast, is a concept that is researched more often now thanks to the increasing complexity and feedback loops available in so many types media today. Flow is now considered an optimal mental state for enjoyment and for learning.[29]

Use It or Lose It

"It's easy to confuse what is with what ought to be,
especially when what is has worked out in your favor."
—Tyrion Lannister[30]

We may not always be able to describe why we enjoy a particular form of entertainment, but maybe now you can do that. There are many reasons why *Game of Thrones* is so popular, and "I find it challenging on a cognitive level" is not likely to be the most common. However, reading or watching complex stories will give your brain a better workout than do more simplistic television shows, and so viewers may enjoy the experience because that complexity is challenging them in ways of which they are mostly unaware.

Although some researchers argue against the idea that exercising the brain improves it,[31] others say "use it or lose it" and have demonstrated that by performing cognitive tasks, the brain gets better at those tasks.[32] Some studies have shown that cognitive exercises done just a handful of times can have positive effects that are measurable years later.[33]

Our zealous engagement makes our brains work hard, and that is a very good thing. Thus, it turns out that *Game of Thrones* is also a game of wits. It is stimulating on a psychological level beyond memory and intelligence; it also makes us think as a result of its thoroughly developed characters, relationships, and representations of real human emotions. Using our brains and thinking about why people do what they do is what psychology is all about, and *Game of Thrones* allows us to do that and have fun in the process. In addition to the many other reasons people watch *Game of Thrones*, though, some may watch because it exercises the brain and makes them smarter.

References

Bartsch, A., & Hartmann, T. (2015). The role of cognitive and affective challenge in entertainment experience. *Communication Research*.

Broca, P. (1861). Remarks on the seat of the faculty of articulated language, following an observation of aphemia (loss of speech). *Bulletin de la Société Anatomique, 6*, 330–357.

Bureau of Labor Statistics. (June 24, 2015). *American Time Use Survey—2014 Results*. U. S. Department of Labor: http://www.bls.gov/news.release/atus.nr0.htm.

Csíkszentmihályi, M. (1991). *Flow: The psychology of optimal experience*. New York, NY: Harper Perennial.

Csíkszentmihályi, M. (1997). *Finding flow: The psychology of engagement with everyday life*. New York, NY: Basic.

Ebbinghaus, H. (1913). *Memory: A contribution to experimental psychology*. New York, NY: Columbia University, Teachers College.

Eysenck, M., & Keane, M. (2015). *Cognitive psychology: A student's handbook* (7th ed.). New York, NY: Psychology Press.

Feist, G., & Barron, F. (2003). Predicting creativity from early to late adulthood: Intellect, potential, and personality. *Journal of Research in Personality, 37*(2), 62–88.

Flynn, J. R. (1984a). IQ gains and the Binet decrements. *Journal of Educational Measurement, 21*(3), 283–290.

Flynn, J. R. (1984b). The mean IQ of Americans: Massive gains 1932–1978. *Psychological Bulletin, 95*(1), 29–51.

Gardner, H. (1983). *Frames of mind: The theory of multiple intelligences.* New York, NY: Basic.

Gardner, H. (1999). *Multiple views of multiple intelligences.* New York, NY: Basic.

Green, C. S., & Bavelier, D. (2008). Exercising your brain: A review of human brain plasticity and training-induced learning. *Psychology and Aging, 23*(4), 692–701.

Home Box Office. (n.d.). *Game of Thrones viewer's guide.* HBO: http://www.gameofthrones.com.

Jenkins, H. (2009). *Confronting the challenges of participatory culture: Media education for the 21st century.* Cambridge, MA: MIT Press.

Johnson, S. (2006). *Everything bad is good for you: How today's popular culture is actually making us smarter.* New York, NY: Riverhead.

Kelly, C., & Castellanos, F. X. (2014). Strengthening connections: Functional connectivity and brain plasticity. *Neuropsychology Review, 24*(1), 63–76.

Kubey, R., & Csikszentmihalyi, M. (1990). *Television and the quality of life: How viewing shapes everyday experience.* Hillsdale, NJ: Erlbaum Associates.

Martin, G. R. R. (1996). *A game of thrones.* New York, NY: Bantam.

Mayer, J. D., Salovey, P., & Caruso, D. R. (2000). Models of emotional intelligence. In R. J. Sternberg (Ed.), *Handbook of intelligence* (2nd ed., pp. 396–420). New York, NY: Cambridge University Press.

Oakley, B. (2014). *A mind for numbers: How to excel at math and science (even if you flunked algebra).* New York, NY: Penguin.

Pedersen, P.M., Vinter, K., Olsen, T.S. (2004). Aphasia after stroke: type, severity and prognosis. The Copenhagen aphasia study. *Cerebrovascular Diseases, 17,* 35–43.

Pink, D. (2012). *Drive: The surprising truth about what motivates us.* New York, NY: Riverhead.

Salthouse, T. A. (2006). Mental exercise and mental aging. *Perspectives on Psychological Science, 1*(1), 68–87.

Schooler, C. (2007). Use it—and keep it, longer, probably: A reply to Salthouse (2006). *Perspectives on Psychological Science, 2*(1), 24–29.

Thorndike, E.L. (1920). Intelligence and its uses. *Harper's Magazine,* 140, 227–235.

Trahan, L. H., Stuebing, K. K., Fletcher, J. M., & Hiscock, M. (2014). The Flynn effect: A meta-analysis. *Psychological Bulletin, 140*(5), 1332–1360.

Willis, S. L., Tennstedt, S. L., Marsiske, M., Ball, K., Elias, J., Koepke, K. M., Morris, J. N., Rebok, G. W., Unversagt, F. W., Stoddard, A. M., & Wright, E., for the ACTIVE Study Group (2006). Long-term effects of cognitive training on everyday functional outcomes in older adults. *JAMA : The Journal of the American Medical Association, 296*(23), 2805–2814.

Notes

1. Episode 1–2, "The Kingsroad" (April 24, 2011).
2. Ebbinghaus (1913).
3. Kelly & Castellanos (2014).
4. Episode 3–3, "Walk of Punishment" (April 14, 2013).
5. Flynn (1984a); Flynn (1984b).
6. Trahan et al. (2014).

7. Schooler (2007).
8. Johnson (2006).
9. Episode 5–9, "The Dance of Dragons" (June 7, 2015).
10. Episode 1–8, "The Pointy End" (June 5, 2011).
11. Episode 1–1, "Winter Is Coming" (April 17, 2011).
12. Green & Bavelier (2008).
13. Oakley (2014).
14. Pink (2012).
15. Jenkins (2009).
16. Episode 4–9, "The Watchers on the Wall" (June 8, 2014).
17. Eysenck & Keane (2015).
18. Episode 4–4, "Oathkeeper" (April 27, 2014).
19. Mayer, Salovey, & Caruso (2000).
20. Thorndike (1920).
21. Feist & Barron (2003).
22. Csíkszentmihályi (1991).
23. Csíkszentmihályi (1991).
24. Gardner (1983, 1999).
25 Martin (1996), p. 242.
26. Broca (1861).
27. Pedersen et al. (2004).
28. Kubey & Csíkszentmihályi (1990).
29. Csíkszentmihályi (1997).
30. Episode 5–9, "The Dance of Dragons" (June 7, 2015).
31. Salthouse (2006).
32. Schooler (2007).
33. Bartsch & Hartmann (2015); Willis et al. (2006).

Self-Actualization

TRAVIS LANGLEY

"I will not tell you to stay or go. You must make that choice yourself . . ."
—Maester Aemon[1]

"What a man can be, he must be. This need we may call self-actualization."
—Abraham Maslow, founder of humanistic psychology[2]

Human beings are imperfect creatures and can never become perfect, yet we feel motivated to become more than we are. Psychiatrist Kurt Goldstein saw the master motive of a person or any organism as the pursuit of taking our possibilities and making them real, turning potentiality for who we could be into actuality—*self-actualization*.[3] The founder of individual psychology, Alfred Adler, similarly identified *striving for superiority* as the fundamental fact of life.[4] He meant superiority over the person's own current state, not necessarily over everyone else.[5] Heavily influenced by both Goldstein and Adler when he founded humanistic psychology, Abraham Maslow popularized Goldstein's term when he placed self-actualization at the top of his hierarchy of needs.[6] Although Maslow also talked about a natural motivation to progress as a person, he described self-actualization in different ways at different points in his career—not only as the motive to pursue potential[7] but later more as the state of having achieved it.[8]

Can anyone achieve self-actualization in *Game of Thrones*? Life is difficult enough on any world, much less one where everyone must worry about basic survival for themselves and everyone around them, a world where the monsters, magic, and mystical forces mingle with the mundane. In feudal society, most have neither the opportunities nor long enough lives to reach their potential. Among even those few, does anyone manage it?

Self-actualized individuals, according to Maslow, no longer feel driven to make up for deficits or to fight to keep from losing whatever they have (deficit motivation, *D-motivation*) but instead strive to enrich life and grow from within (being motivation, *B-motivation*). For example, when Jon Snow asks why Tyrion reads so much, Tyrion tells him that "a mind needs books as a sword needs a whetstone, if it is to keep its edge,"[9] indicating an appreciation for the need to grow and transcend mere survival. Unfortunately, while he shows greater self-acceptance than many others, it is often to the point of resignation and his bouts of self-loathing get in the way of developing healthier self-esteem.

Because Maslow based his ideas about self-actualization on the lives of people he admired, his views on the matter were heavily skewed by his personal preferences. He started by looking at people he simply admired (particularly anthropologist Ruth Benedict and Gestalt psychologist Max Wertheimer), trying to understand what made them different, and then identifying others who shared those qualities.[10] Although he conducted empirical research on the distribution of self-actualizing characteristics throughout the population, his original ideas had no empirical foundation; they were solely based on his unsupported preferences. Out of all the characters in *A Song of Ice and Fire* and *Game of Thrones*, the one Maslow might most easily have seen as a template for self-actualization is probably Maester Aemon.

Maester Aemon, the Targaryen heir who relinquishes all worldly claims and lives to be about a century-old scholar in the Night's Watch, demonstrates many of the qualities Maslow discerned in self-actualizers.[11]

- *Efficient perception of reality*: Though physically blind, wise Maester Aemon perceives a great deal more than most. More so than any other character, he illustrates his view on the game of thrones by staying out of it.
- *Creativity*: Open, humble Aemon exhibits flexibility, inventiveness, and originality, with a willingness to experiment.
- *Acceptance of self and others*: Aemon knows who he is while feeling neither prideful nor guilt-ridden. He makes his choices and lives with them, and he recognizes that others must grow in their own way.
- *Spontaneity, simplicity, naturalness*: Aemon expresses himself freely, for the most part, without trying to hurt others while doing so. His ideas may be unconventional. He feels comfortable enough to be himself.
- *Focus on problems outside themselves*: Aemon looks at the big picture when others avoid doing so—for example, when he counsels Jon Snow on how to help other Night's Watch members see priorities more important than petty squabbles.[12] After Aemon's passing, Jon does not fare as well.
- *Social interest*: Sympathy and empathy motivate Aemon to help others.

- *Democratic character structure*: Tolerant and accepting, Aemon listens and advises without condescension.
- *Detachment and need for privacy*: Despite interest in helping others, the self-actualized person needs solitude and can experience isolation without harmful effects. Aemon spends a great deal of time keeping to himself in places like the library, although he eventually must rely on others to read to him after he goes blind.

"No man was wiser or gentler or kinder," Samwell Tarly says when eulogizing Maester Aemon.[13] In many ways, Aemon probably best represents the self-actualized person as recognized by Abraham Maslow. Whether that set of qualities really is the peak of human potential, of course, is subject to opinion and debate.[14] Achieving individual potential as a human being might vary in more ways than Maslow assumed. Maximizing personal potential can mean something different in a culture, historical period, or world where values vary and the demands of reality make different kinds of traits optimal. The meaning of achieving true growth may differ between worlds.

References

Adler, A. (1908/1959). *Understanding human nature*. New York, NY: Fawcett.

Adler, A. (1924). *The practice and theory of individual psychology*. London, UK: K. Paul, Trench, Trubner & Company.

Adler, A. (1930). Individual psychology. In C. Murchison (Ed.), *Psychologies of 1930* (pp. 395–405). Worcester, MA: Clark University Press.

Goldstein, K. (1939/1955). *The organism: A holistic approach to biology derived from pathological data in man*. New York, NY: Zone.

Kiel, J. M. (1999). Reshaping Maslow's hierarchy of needs to reflect today's educational and managerial philosophies. *Journal of Instructional Psychology, 26*(3), 167–168.

Maslow, A. H. (1943). A theory of human motivation. *Psychological Review, 50*(4), 370–396.

Maslow, A. H. (1964). Further notes on the psychology of being. *Journal of Humanistic Psychology, 4*(1), 45–58.

Maslow, A. H. (1967). Self-actualization and beyond. In J. F. T. Bugental (Ed.), *Challenges of humanistic psychology* (pp. 279–286). New York, NY: McGraw-Hill.

Maslow, A. H. (1970). Tribute to Alfred Adler. *Journal of Individual Psychology, 26*(1), 13.

Maslow, A. H. (1971). *The farther reaches of human nature.* New York, NY: Viking.

Maslow, A. H. (1979). *The journals of A. H. Maslow.* R. J. Lowry (Ed.). Pacific Grove, CA: Brooks/Cole.

Maslow, A. H. (1987). *Motivation and personality* (3rd ed.). New York, NY: Harper & Row.

Martin, G. R. R. (1996). *A game of thrones.* London, UK: Voyager.

Notes

1. Episode 1–9, "Baelor" (June 12, 2011).
2. Maslow (1943), p. 382.
3. Goldstein (1939/1955).
4. Adler (1908/1959, 1924).
5. Adler (1930).
6. Maslow (1970).
7. Maslow (1943).
8. Maslow (1971, 1979).
9. Martin (1996), p. 124.
10. Maslow (1964).
11. Maslow (1967, 1987).
12. Martin (1996).
13. Episode 5–7, "The Gift" (May 24, 2015).
14. Kiel (1999).

Final Word:
Schemes and Plots

TRAVIS LANGLEY

"Schemes and plots are the same thing."
—Tyrion to Cersei[1]

> *"Storytelling is ultimately a creative act of pattern recognition. Through characters, plot and setting, a writer creates places where previously invisible truths become visible."*
> —author Douglas Coupland[2]

Color scheme, rhyme scheme, money scheme, life scheme, political scheme, the grand scheme of things—in one way or another, every use of the word refers to a design. Schemes are patterns. In psychology, a scheme or *schema* is a pattern of information, a mental model representing relationships between concepts, events, items, actions, or anything else we might perceive.[3] Your *self-schema* includes everything you associate with yourself.[4] Your *gender schema* includes not only your idea of what gender is but everything that even reminds you of your ideas about gender (say, the colors pink and blue).[5] Numerous characters scoff at Brienne being any kind of knight, regardless of her considerable combat skill, because in their schema only men can be knights. Everything you associate with *Game of Thrones* makes up your *Game of Thrones* schema. If another TV series reminds you of *Game of Thrones* when it opens with two full minutes of opening credits, even if it would not have that effect on anyone else, it has activated your personal *Game of Thrones* schema somewhere in your head.

The schema grows when new information gets added to it (*assimilation*), such as new characters, new actors, snacks you ate while reading one of the books, or a relative who won't shut up every time you try to watch the show. When the schema itself changes to incorporate new information (*accommodation*), that can change the way we view everything else connected through the pattern. Fans whose feelings about the series soured over one disturbing story may reinterpret everything else about it. Assimilation is easier than accommodation. Our early impressions can be powerful things. Those who like the series in the beginning often assimilate subsequent plot twists into the "interesting story" framework to make later chapters or episodes seem more interesting, resulting in persistence in reading or watching more.

The story plays with our schemas, tugging at the threads and weaving something other than the tapestries we expect to see. *A Song of Ice and Fire* books and the TV series based on them tweaks the *tropes*, the devices and conventions we have learned to expect from a story. It has few, if any, happy endings, and yet many fans keep returning for more. Heroic Ned Stark, brave and bold, the most apparent protagonist of the piece, dies with no last-minute rescue. Repeatedly, the tale subverts the tropes in defiance of expectations. The *plot*, the unfolding series of events, initially fits our existing schemas enough for its deviations to take us by surprise. Can this story's ending satisfy readers and viewers? When the deviation from convention gets woven into the scheme, would a happy ending deviate from the expected deviations?

Can the ending possibly satisfy?

Of course it can. It can't satisfy everyone, of course, but what story ever does? Some characters will triumph and some will fall. How will the story end? However its author decides—in print, that is. Television is another matter. *A Song of Ice and Fire* and *Game of Thrones* tell similar stories but not the same. Audiences get more than one opportunity to see how things turn out. The way each plot ends can not only retroactively recolor each story's schema but can also proactively prime our expectations for other storytellers as well.

Scheming and plotting can both mean that someone is contriving a plan to achieve some sinister outcome. When Tyrion says they are the same thing, is he referring to schemes and plots as Cersei means the words or as he understands them? Tyrion is a well-read man who should know of other meanings, which suggests he is making a statement about his sister's limited point of view. Her schemes involve making the plot of her life and the lives of others around her follow paths that will give her some sort of satisfaction.

"Fiction is lies. We're writing about people who never existed and events that never happened when we write fiction, whether it's science fiction or fantasy or western mystery stories or so-called literary stories. All those things are essentially untrue. But it has to have a truth at the core of it. You're still writing about people, you're writing about the human condition."

—author George R. R. Martin[6]

The plots within *A Song of Ice and Fire* and *Game of Thrones* set nonfictional stories in motion in our world as well. When Martin or the television series's creator describe how they developed these tales, their nonfictional descriptions of how they depict their fictions become elements of the big schema. The books and the series have their own patterns, both separate and shared—patterns inside the pattern, schemes within the greater schemas, constellations with overlapping stars. Fans' personal accounts of how this epic affected them, whether good or bad, join the pattern. So do the actors' professional experiences, online debates about the stories' worth, disputes over controversial story lines, podcasts and blogs analyzing it all, and even this book you hold in your hands. We are all part of the pattern that builds around this tale that George R. R. Martin began once upon a time. Every thought that any of us honestly share about this grand epic with its intricate characters is nonfiction about fiction, truth about lies.

References

Bem, S. L. (1981). Gender schema theory: A cognitive account of sex typing. *Psychological Review, 88*(4), 354–364.

Cahan, E. D. (1984). The genetic psychologies of James Mark Baldwin and Jean Piaget. *Developmental Psychology, 20*(1), 128–135.

Farley, C. J. (2011, July 8). *'Game of Thrones' author George R. R. Martin spills the secrets of 'A Dance with Dragons.'* New York Times: http://blogs.wsj.com/speakeasy/2011/07/08/game-of-thrones-author-george-r-r-martin-spills-the-secrets-of-a-dance-with-dragons/.

Markus, H. R. (1977). Self-schemata and processing information about self. *Journal of Personality and Social Psychology, 35*(1), 63–78.

Villarreal, R. (2009, November 12). *Douglas Coupland: 'Generation A' loneliness.* SFGate: http://www.sfgate.com/thingstodo/article/Douglas-Coupland-Generation-A-loneliness-3281278.php.

Notes

1. Episode 2–5, "The Ghost of Harrenhal" (April 29, 2012).
2. Cited in Villarreal (2009).
3. Cahan (1984).
4. Markus (1977).
5. Bem (1981).
6. Farley (2011).

About the Editor

Travis Langley, PhD, editor of *The Walking Dead Psychology: Psych of the Living Dead*, *Star Wars Psychology: Dark Side of the Mind*, and *Captain America vs. Iron Man: Freedom, Security, Psychology*, is a psychology professor who teaches courses on crime, media, and mental illness at Henderson State University. He received a bachelor's degree from Hendrix College and graduate degrees in psychology from Tulane University. Dr. Langley regularly speaks on media and heroism at conventions and universities. *Necessary Evil: Super-Villains of DC Comics* and other films have featured him as an expert interviewee, and the documentary *Legends of the Knight* spotlighted the way he uses fiction to teach real psychology. He authored the acclaimed book *Batman and Psychology: A Dark and Stormy Knight*. *Psychology Today* carries his blog, "Beyond Heroes and Villains." Follow him as @ Superherologist on Twitter, where he ranks among the ten most popular psychologists. Keep up with Travis and the rest of the book's contributors through **Facebook.com/ThePsychGeeks**.

He lost track of how many swords he owns.

About the Contributors

Colt J. Blunt, PsyD, LP, has worked as a forensic examiner throughout his career and serves as a guest lecturer and trainer for a number of organizations and educational institutions. His academic interests include the intersection of psychology and law, including the study of criminal behavior. He contributed to *The Walking Dead Psychology: Psych of the Living Dead* and *Star Wars Psychology: Dark Side of the Mind*.

Jenna Busch is a writer, host, and founder of Legion of Leia, a website to promote and support women in fandom. She co-hosted "Cocktails with Stan" with Spider-Man creator and comic legend Stan Lee, and has appeared in the film *She Makes Comics*. She has been a guest on *Attack of the Show!*, NPR, Al Jazeera America, and multiple episodes of *Tabletop* with Wil Wheaton. She's a comic book author, co-host of *Most Craved*, and weekly feminist columnist for Metro. Jenna co-authored a chapter in *Star Wars Psychology: Dark Side of the Mind*. Her work has appeared all over the web. She can be reached on Twitter @JennaBusch.

Josué Cardona, MS, is known for his work in mental health, education, technology, language, and culture, with an emphasis on geek culture. He is a frequent speaker at popular culture and professional conventions and was a contributing author to *The Walking Dead Psychology: Psych of the Living Dead*. He is the creator of Geek Therapy and the PsychTech podcast.

Erin Currie, PhD, is a geek for all things psychology. As a licensed psychologist and founder of MyPsychgeek, LLC, she provides professional development consulting that focuses on helping people in science, technology, and all geekdom to realize their full potential in both their personal and professional lives. Her writing, therapy, and consulting work all combine lessons and metaphors of sci-fi and fantasy, with assessments and techniques established in the field of psychology—because it's more fun that way. You can find her on Twitter @mypsychgeek.

William Blake Erickson, MA, is a doctoral candidate and researcher at the University of Arkansas. His research interests include eyewitness memory, face recognition, and the impact of stress on memory. He has published in journals such as *Applied Cognitive Psychology*, *Psychonomic Bulletin and Review*, *Psychology, Psychiatry, and Law*, and *Journal of Police and Criminal Psychology*.

Wind Goodfriend, PhD, is a professor of psychology and the director of both the gender and women's studies program and the trauma advocacy program at Buena Vista University in Storm Lake, Iowa. She earned her bachelor's degree at Buena Vista University, then earned her master's and PhD in social psychology from Purdue University. Dr. Goodfriend has won the "Faculty of the Year" award at BVU several times and won the Wythe Award for Excellence in Teaching, and she is the principal investigator for the Institute for the Prevention of Relationship Violence.

Jonathan Hetterly, MA, LPC, works with teenage and young adult males, specializing in treating substance abuse, addiction, and failure to launch struggles at Southeast Psych in Charlotte, North Carolina. He contributed to *The Walking Dead Psychology: Psych of the Living Dead* and *Star Wars Psychology: Dark Side of the Mind*. Follow him at Twitter @jhetterly or ShrinkTank.com, and hear him on the "Shrink Tank" and "Change Your Tune" podcasts.

Stephen Hupp, PhD, is a licensed clinical psychologist and a professor of clinical child and school psychology at Southern Illinois University, Edwardsville. He is the coauthor of the book *Great Myths of Child Development*, which emphasizes "what every parent needs to *not* know" by debunking myths about parenting, development, and child psychology. You can find more information at StephenHupp.com and on Twitter @StephenHupp.

Mark Caldwell Jones, MA, LPC, is the author of the fantasy novels *The Samurai and The Jabberwocky* and *Opal Summerfield and the Battle of Fallmoon Gap*, a novel that was called "a dazzling debut" by Kirkus Reviews. He's a licensed professional counselor and holds a master's degree in psychology. His nonfiction book, *The Life Calling Formula,* was the central tool he used during his fifteen years in private practice. He's now a professional writer living in Los Angeles and is currently working on his first original television show. Read more about his projects at markcaldwelljones.com and follow him @JonesMarkC on Twitter and Instagram.

Lara Taylor Kester, MA, holds a degree in counseling psychology as well as a certificate in traumatology and treatment from Holy Names University. She is a registered marriage and family therapy intern who works with at-risk and foster youth in the San Francisco Bay Area. She created TherapeuticCode.com and is a contributing editor at GeekTherapy.com.

Dana Klisanin is an award-winning psychologist. She studies the impact of interactive technologies on the personal, collective, and mythic dimensions of humanity. She has investigated how the use of digital technology is changing how we think about altruism, heroism, and what we value. Dana is CEO of Evolutionary Guidance Media R&D, Inc., and Executive Board member of the World Futures Studies Federation and c3: Center for Conscious Creativity. Her work has been cited in news outlets, including the BBC, *Time, USA Today*, and the Huffington Post. She is the author of numerous book chapters and journal articles, and is a popular blogger at *Psychology Today.*

Jordan Gaines Lewis is a neuroscience PhD student at Penn State College of Medicine, where she studies the interplay of sleep and obesity. She is also a pop-sci writer with her blog *Gaines, on Brains*, a past TED speaker, and has contributed to *Scientific American*, the *Washington Post, The Guardian*, and NBC. Follow her on Twitter @GainesOnBrains.

Martin Lloyd, PhD, LP, received his doctorate in clinical psychology from the University of Minnesota. He has worked in various prisons and high-security hospitals, including the U.S. Medical Center for Federal Prisoners and Patton State Hospital. He currently practices as a forensic psychologist in Minnesota and occasionally teaches forensic psychology at Gustavus Adolphus College. He dedicates his sections of this book to his parents, who truly hate Joffrey.

Kyle Maddock is a host of "A Podcast of Ice and Fire," the Geekie Award–winning and longest-running podcast dedicated to George R. R. Martin's *A Song of Ice and Fire*. He hosts the *Game of Thrones* aftershow at AfterBuzzTV and is a frequent guest on other YouTube shows, podcasts, and panels. Outside of his passionate geek life, Kyle is an actor who can be seen in shows such as *How I Met Your Mother* and *Happy Endings*. Follow him on Twitter @kylemaddock.

Patrick O'Connor, PsyD, is the creator of Comicspedia, an online tool that assists therapists in bringing comic books into therapy. He teaches at the Chicago School of Professional Psychology, where he debuted the course, Geek Culture in Therapy, in which students discover how geek culture plays a role in our understanding of ourselves and others and how geek culture artifacts are the vehicles through which we develop this understanding. He can be found on Twitter at @Comicspedia.

Janina Scarlet, PhD, is a licensed clinical psychologist, a scientist, and a full-time geek. She uses superhero therapy to help patients with anxiety, depression, chronic pain, and PTSD at the Center for Stress and Anxiety Management and Sharp Memorial Hospital and is also a professor at Alliant International University, San Diego. Janina authored chapters in *The Walking Dead Psychology: Psych of the Living Dead* and *Star Wars Psychology: Dark Side of the Mind*. She can be reached via her website, www.superhero-therapy.com, or on Twitter @shadowquill.

 **Jay Scarlet** holds master's degrees in psychology and in library and information science. He currently works at Chula Vista Public Library, and is a past member of the Young Adult Library Services Association (YALSA)'s Research Committee. He has also contributed to the website Legion of Leia and the book *Star Wars Psychology: Dark Side of the Mind*.

 **Laura Vecchiolla** is a doctoral student of clinical psychology at the Chicago School of Professional Psychology. Her dissertation research aims at connecting the empowering themes of myth and the hero's journey to the process of trauma recovery. As she begins her career as a psychologist, Laura plans to use her eternal love of myth and story to continue to help others in their own journey toward growth and healing.

 **Dave Verhaagen** is a nationally board-certified psychologist, bad magician, snappy dresser, and current creative director of Southeast Psych Presents, the media division of Southeast Psych. He is the author or co-author of eight books, including *Therapy with Young Men* and *Assessing and Managing Violence Risk in Juveniles*.

 **Dawn R. Weatherford**, PhD, is an assistant professor at Arkansas State University. She directs the Memory, Attention, and Perception (MAP) research laboratory, where she investigates topics in cognitive psychology, ranging from face processing to education at both the applied and basic theoretical levels.

Index

Sexism (*continued from previous page*)
  on individual level, 197–198
  against men, 199
  overview, 195–196
Sex of newborns, predicting, 122
Sexual assault, 53–54. *See also* Rape
Sexual sadism, 64
Shared meaning, creating, 113
Short-term memory, 254
Simplicity, 267
Social intelligence, 245, 257–258
Social interest, 267
Sociopathy, 234. *See also* Psychopathy
Sociopathy, triad of, 185
"Soft startups," 110
Solutions, detecting, 214
Specific phobia, natural environment type,
  172–173
Spirituality, 163, 247
Spontaneity, 267
Spree killers, 182
Sternberg, Robert, 153–154
Stockholm syndrome, 80
Stonewalling, in marriage, 106
Striving for superiority, 265
Submission, 89–90
Survival, 159–169
  overview, 159–160
  posttraumatic growth and, 161–168
  resilience for, 160–161
  vicarious posttraumatic growth and,
  167
Symbiotic relatedness, 98–99
Symbolism, of archetypes, 133

Talk therapy, 2
Television viewing, complexity of,
  252–253
Temperance, 246
Terrible mother concept, 136–137
Terror management theory, 208
Threaded cognition theory, 256–257
Threatened egotism, 233
Thriving, 160, 161
Tiger parenting, 118
Tolerance, for partner's faults, 110
Torture, 71–83
  defined, 72
  effects of, 77–79
  forensic psychology and, 73
  goals and methods of, 72–77
  overview, 71–72

Stockholm syndrome and, 80
transformation due to, 80–81
trauma of, 51–53
Transactional leadership, 152
Transcendence, 246–247
Transformational leadership, 152
Trauma, 49–59, 171–179
  bullying and child abuse, 173–174
  heroism and healing, 176–177
  phobia development and treatment,
  172–173
  posttraumatic growth, 54–56, 171–172
  posttraumatic stress disorder (PTSD),
  52
  recovery from, 56
  risk of, 49–50
  sexual assault and, 53–54
  survival and, 159–169
  torture and, 51–53
  traumatic brain injury (TBI), 174–176
  traumatic loss and bereavement, 50–51
Triad of sociopathy, 185
Triarchic (triangular) theory of love, 153
Turning-point opportunities, 33

Union of opposites, 137–138
United Nations (UN), 72

Validation, 109–110
Values in Action (VIA) Inventory of
  Strengths, 242–248
Ventromedial cortex, 21
Vicarious posttraumatic growth, 167
Violence. *See also* Serial killers
  acceptance of death and, 148
  psychopathy and, 20
  self-control and, 233
Vividness effect, 14
Vlad the Impaler, 24

War, rape and, 66
Well-defined problems, 215–216
Wertheimer, Max, 266
Whole authentic self, 92–93
Willpower, 228
Wisdom, 242–243
Withdrawal-destructiveness, 99
Working backwards, 218
Working memory, 254

Zest, 244
Zimbardo, Philip, 241